Acknowledgements

No idea can readily be said to be original – for every 'new idea' is a development of the countless ideas which have gone before. Any book is therefore merely an expression of the knowledge, experience and skill acquired during the author's lifetime of contact with other people. To all those people who have in any way been influential in my own development and learning and who have therefore contributed, often without my knowing, to the ideas expressed in this book, I owe my gratitude.

However, my special thanks are due to my ex-head of department, Gordon Bolt, to my colleagues at Bristol Polytechnic and to all my students, young and old, with whom over the years I have learned about the process of communication.

For their patient and tireless, practical and moral support I thank my husband, Mike, and my two children, Matthew and Abigail, and for her awe-inspiring speed and efficiency I thank Jackie May who helped me type the manuscript.

Pan Breakthrough Books ope   the   uccessful self-education. The series provides e   wledge using the most modern self-study techniq

Expert authors have produced cl   nate y texts on business subjects to meet the par   eeds f people at work and of those studying for rel   nt exam   tions.

A highly effective learn   patte n, enabling   aders to measure progress step   step, has been devi   d for Breakthrough Books   the National Extensi   College, Britain's leading speciali s in home study.

Nicki Stanton is Head of Business Studies at Swindon College. She was previously Senior Lecturer in Business Communication at Bristol Polytechnic for six years, where her activities included teaching at diploma and degree level, management training in the South West Regional Management Centre, and consultan y work. Before starting her teaching career she worke for Josiah Wedgwood & Sons and Berni Inns. Her inte   st in business education curriculum development has le to her appointment as a Business Education Council Moderator and member of the BEC B1 Board and Validation Committee. She is also a UK member of the American Business Communication Association.

Pan Breakthrough Books

Other books in the series

Pan Breakthrough Books

What Do You Mean, 'Communication'?

An introduction to communication
in business

Nicki Stanton

Pan Original
Pan Books, London and Sydney

10

First published 1982 by Pan Books Ltd,
Cavaye Place, London SW10 9PG
© Nicki Stanton 1982
ISBN 0 330 26541 5

Printed and bound in Great Britain by
Richard Clay (The Chaucer Press) Ltd, Bungay, Suffolk

Contents

Introduction

I can't really improve my ability to communicate with just timetabled classes in business communication. I need something in between so that I can get lots of practice and check my own progress. [Student on a BEC business studies course.]

I haven't the time to attend a course on communication, but I do recognize the importance of communication at work and would like to improve my own skills and find out more about the subject. Can you recommend a book that I can work on, on my own? [Trainee supervisor.]

I've enjoyed this course, but obviously we've only been able to touch on the tip of the iceberg. Is there a book which I could use to continue studying business communication and which would give me, above all, some practice in using the techniques you've suggested? [Manager at the end of a three-day course on business communication.]

In answer to all these queries and many others, I could recommend any one of a number of books on business communication – many of them interesting and valuable contributions to the subject, but the vast majority are either highly academic and rather awe-inspiring or else, despite being practical and down-to-earth, really dependent on the presence of a teacher to guide, correct and check the student's progress.

In writing this book, my aim has therefore been

- to provide students on BEC National and Higher level courses and professional courses and their teachers – and indeed anyone in business who is interested in improving their communication skills and their knowledge of the way in which communication works – with a self-contained book which will both stand on its own, without the aid of a teacher, and complement a taught course; this is achieved through exercises and self-assessment questions which provide feedback to the reader on his ability and progress;

- to provide practical help with the skills of communication, but in particular with the often neglected skills of effective listening and reading, and with the real problems that lie behind advice like 'plan and prepare your message carefully' and 'choose your words and construct logical sentences and paragraphs in a way which gets your message across';
- to combine in one book not only a practical guide to the techniques and skills on which effective communication depends, but also a discussion of the way in which communication operates in modern organizations, and an explanation of the complex process of communication which is at the root of what we term 'breakdowns in communication'.

Becoming an effective communicator involves:

- understanding the way in which communication takes place;
- appreciating why communication sometimes fails;
- being sensitive to the way other people think and feel;
- understanding the techniques which we can use to improve our chances of communicating what we really mean.

All this, like any skill, requires effort and practice.

My job in writing this book is to help you ask the right questions and think about the answers – before you communicate, while you are communicating and after you have communicated.

The basic principles of communication are universal and can be applied in every aspect of your life, but this book looks at these theories, principles and practice in the context of communication in business. Whether or not you are a part of business, public or private – indeed whatever organization you belong to – you are affected by business in one way or another: as a customer, as an employee, as an owner or investor, as a shareholder, as a supplier, or simply as a neighbour.

How to use the book

Early on in each chapter you will find a description of the aims of the chapter. The text of the chapter will provide you with the essential knowledge which, in conjunction with your own experience, should enable you to tackle the practical questions which appear throughout the text. These questions are of three kinds:

Self-checks These are usually fairly short questions aimed at testing your knowledge and awareness of the essential issues at that point in the text. They will help you to study actively by encouraging you to think about what you are reading and about your experience of the way people communicate. The text that follows each self-check question will provide you with some answers to these questions so that you can check how close your answers are to those that I provide. Try to discipline yourself to write down your answers to the self-check questions before you read the text that follows, since it is all too easy otherwise to convince yourself that you really know the answers and don't need to write them down. Put your confidence to the test.

Since it is also very tempting to glance ahead at the text, you might like to try using a card to cover it up, so that you can really be satisfied that you are answering the questions without the aid of any clues.

Finally don't be put off if you find that your answers don't completely match mine. Communication is a very complex process for the very reason that we all think about communication slightly differently. However, do consider the difference between your answers and mine – you will gain a great deal just from recognizing that others may not always think the same as you, and from reflecting on the reasons for and the potential results of these differences.

Reviews These are rather like self-checks in that they often consist of quite short questions or activities which you can mark for yourself, as the answers are provided immediately after the questions. However, as their name suggests, they look back and help you to assess how well you have grasped the points you have just read in the previous text. For this reason, you will usually find reviews either at the end of a chapter or at the end of major sections within a chapter.

Activities Although learning to communicate effectively does depend on being aware of the general principles and theory that lie behind the process of communicating, success largely depends on practice. Throughout the text you will therefore come across these longer exercises designed to encourage you to have a go at putting the principles into practice or observing how other people communicate. Activities are usually related to the part of the text you are reading or are about to read, so you should try to carry them out before reading on. However, because there are no 'right answers' provided in the text, you may like occasionally to treat these activities as an opportunity to break off from studying. You can then complete the activity at some convenient moment during the next few days before carrying on with the book.

Here again I know how easy it is to skip these activities and kid yourself that, since you know you could do them, there is really no need to bother. So my advice again is to be very strict with yourself, since you cannot hope to improve your expertise by merely reading about communication.

Using a tape-recorder

One of the problems of a self-study book on a subject like communication is that a book is, of course, an example of written communication and most of your answers will also be written. And yet the vast majority of the communication we take part in is spoken. In order to redress the balance somewhat, you will therefore find that some of the activities ask you to make use of a tape-recorder, so that you can assess for yourself how you sound, and how well you express yourself when speaking.

In addition, and if you have ready access to a small tape-recorder, you might like to consider using it to record some of your answers to the self-checks and review questions.

I have dealt with the various aspects of communication in the order I feel makes sense and many of the chapters will obviously assume some of the knowledge and techniques suggested in earlier chapters. However, each chapter is a self-contained unit and where there are links between chapters these are indicated in the text, so if you prefer to choose your own order of studying to fit in with your own needs, you should be able to do so without too much difficulty.

A final word

Above all, I hope that you will enjoy learning about communication and find it as rewarding and fascinating as I do. Unlike many subjects, every minute of every day provides a never-ending stream of examples of what you are studying.

Nicki Stanton   *January 1982*

Part 1
The process of communication

1 | Breakdowns in communication

Well, it was just a breakdown in communication.

Over and over again, we hear this comment as an explanation for things that go wrong both at home and at work – rows, bad feelings, inefficiency, poor service to customers, labour disputes, mistakes which take their toll in extra work, frustration, lost tempers and strained relationships. Communication is always blamed – perhaps because it is the easy way out.

But are we justified in leaving it there? Simply blaming the process of communication as if there was nothing further we could do? Could we learn from the mistakes of the past and use that knowledge to avoid committing the same mistakes again?

Let's look in this first chapter at some typical communication breakdowns to see if an analysis of what went wrong, and why, can provide a clearer understanding of the process of communication, the traps that await the unwary and some tips on how to avoid falling into them.

Case 1

The sales department of Nevabreak Glass Co. consisted of twelve salesmen and a sales manager. Andrew Giles, aged forty-three, had worked there for eight years and had watched several men younger than him get promoted to area salesmen. However, he had been assured by Mike Pembroke, the sales manager, that he was in line for the next vacancy on the road.

At last, Ben Brown aged sixty-three was about to retire and Giles thought his chance had come. It did not occur to him to remind the manager of his promise and the manager did not think to reassure Giles that he had not forgotten.

As Brown's retirement approached and nothing was said Giles

began to get more and more anxious. His anxiety increased one day when he saw Brown going into the manager's office with a young man. Eventually, all three of them emerged from the office. The manager shook hands with the young man saying: 'Well, we're really glad you've decided to join us. You'll soon learn the ropes with Mr Brown introducing you to his area.'

Giles was furious. Obviously the new man was going to take over Brown's area. Now he knew why the manager had not raised the subject. He went home that night and indignantly recounted the injustice to his wife. They both decided that if that was the way a company repaid years of faithful service, he would be better off leaving, since he obviously had no future with Nevabreak.

The next morning he delivered his resignation letter to an astonished manager, who took some time convincing Giles that the new man was, in fact, being taken on to fill the vacancy left in the office by Giles when he was promoted on Brown's retirement. The new man was only going to accompany Brown for a week or two as part of his training so that he had some idea of the business and the customers before starting in the office.

Self-check

1 Who was responsible for this 'breakdown in communication'?
2 How did Giles get the message that a new recruit was going to get Brown's job?
3 Was Giles justified in assuming that he was not going to be promoted after all?
4 What could have been done to avoid this breakdown in communication?

ANSWERS

1 In a sense everyone involved was responsible for this breakdown in communication because, even unwittingly, they all conveyed messages which together led Giles to believe that he was not going to be promoted. However, the manager should have been sensitive to Giles' need to be kept informed. He was guilty of not putting himself in Giles' shoes and realizing

the anxieties that Giles might be experiencing as the weeks went by and nothing was said.

But Giles must take a lot of the blame for his own anxiety and the consequent misunderstanding. His interpretation of the only words he heard was distorted by false assumptions, he 'listened' to the *inferences* not the *facts* of the situation. He jumped to conclusions! This was his biggest mistake, but he made a mistake earlier in the story: he didn't communicate his anxiety to his boss – he kept it to himself.

2 Giles got the message from a lot of nonverbal 'clues' – the silence of his manager, the arrival of the young man, the way the manager shook hands encouragingly with him as he left the office – and from interpreting the verbal message in the light of his own anxiety. Nothing in the words actually spoken confirmed that the young man was going to get Brown's job.

3 Putting all the 'clues' together, perhaps it was understandable that Giles thought he wasn't going to be promoted, but he should have realized, as we all must, that inferences are not the same as facts, and that he had a responsibility to communicate his thoughts and anxieties so that the other person had a chance to deny or confirm the 'facts'.

4 The manager should have realized that Giles needed the promise of promotion confirmed when Brown's retirement approached. Giles should have asked the manager to confirm that he was to get Brown's job, rather than silently worrying that he might not. If either of them had communicated earlier the 'breakdown' would never have occurred.

Case 2

From the moment that Sarah joined the department she and the supervisor, Joan, didn't really get on. Sarah was older than Joan and considered that she had had just as much experience, if not more, than Joan. She therefore resented being told what to do by a younger woman, although Joan tried extremely hard to couch her requests in a conciliatory tone of voice, to the extent that she sounded as if she was asking Sarah to do a favour which Sarah could refuse if she wanted to.

The department was frequently asked to do extra jobs which

Joan thought were more interesting than the routine jobs. She was therefore surprised and hurt to discover that when, in trying to be fair, she offered the jobs to Sarah instead of doing them herself, Sarah either refused or did them very grudgingly. In fact, gradually the story got round the office that 'poor little Sarah' was being treated very unfairly by an 'overbearing' Joan. Joan became more and more distressed by this undeserved reputation; it seemed as if she couldn't win. If she asked Sarah to do the other interesting jobs, Sarah accused Joan behind her back of overworking her; if she didn't ask her to do the jobs but did them herself, Sarah complained that Joan was keeping all the good jobs to herself.

At last, after about a year of this when Joan was seriously considering leaving because the atmosphere and the relationship between them had become so unbearable, an occasion arose when Joan was faced once again with asking Sarah whether she wanted to do a particular job or not. Joan chose her words very carefully, inviting Sarah to do the job if she wanted to, but offering to do it herself if Sarah didn't want to do it. As usual, Sarah hesitated and said she would let Joan know later. The job was urgent and a decision had to be made fairly soon. Still Sarah hesitated and finally said that she couldn't give Joan a decision and that anyway she needed to discuss things with Joan.

Feeling almost ill with apprehension at the prospect of yet another scene, Joan decided to get the interview over and done with, and so immediately invited Sarah into an empty office 'to discuss things'.

To Joan's utter amazement, Sarah announced that the reason she hadn't been able to give an answer to the question about the job was that she was going to have to leave because her husband was moving to another part of the country. Joan was so overcome with relief that the interview was not going to consist of the usual tense conversation about allocation of work, that without thinking she said, 'Oh! What a relief!' She immediately realized Sarah would inevitably interpret this exclamation as relief that she was leaving. But, it was too late – the words were out and couldn't be taken back.

Self-check

1 Why is Sarah likely to have got the wrong message from the words, 'Oh! What a relief!'?
2 What does this 'breakdown' tell us about the problems of communicating?
3 What could Joan have done to avoid being misunderstood and causing unnecessary offence?
4 What are the disadvantages of oral communication?

ANSWERS

1 Sarah must have realized that their relationship was very strained, and that Joan would probably be glad she was leaving. She is less likely to be aware of how hard Joan has been trying to avoid scenes by bending over backwards to give Sarah a choice and not put any pressure on her either to do a job or not to do it. Sarah is therefore more likely to understand from the words spoken that Joan is relieved she is leaving, rather than relieved that there won't be another strained discussion about work allocation.

2 The problem with communicating is that it is not simply a question of saying what you want to say. The message can be misunderstood because the other person will attach meanings to the words in the light of their own feelings and experiences, and in the light of the whole context of the message. In this case, the words spoken cannot be separated from all that has gone before, or from the total relationship between the two people concerned.

3 Joan could perhaps have thought quickly before she spoke. She might then have realized, as she did later, that her words might be understood differently from the way she intended. Had she thought before speaking, she might have kept her relief to herself and chosen words which related specifically to the news of Sarah's resignation.

4 Although there are many advantages in speaking rather than writing, the problem with speaking is that, in being a more immediate form of communication, it makes it more difficult to think about what you're going to say before you say it. And a related disadvantage is that, once said, the words cannot be

'unsaid', unlike written words which can be planned then revised and corrected before the message is actually transmitted.

Case 3

Stan Micton, the young newly appointed personnel manager of one of the divisions of a large engineering firm, was asked by the personnel director, David Hawson on behalf of the personnel committee (a joint union-management committee) to conduct a study, and then write a report, about how communication between management and workers might be improved. The committee agreed precise terms of reference for the study:

(i)   to report on communication practices in the company;
(ii) to collect the views of employees about the effectiveness of communication; with the aim of
(iii) improving productivity and awareness of the firm's business.

Stan Micton constructed a questionnaire, agreed it with the committee, and interviewed a representative sample of sixty people. They told him in no uncertain terms about how secretive many managers were, that the grapevine was the only real source of information, and that this had bred distrust of the management as a whole.

He then presented the results to the committee, telling them the whole truth as it had been told to him, warts and all. The committee were impressed both by the size of the problem they clearly had to tackle, and by the candour of the response from the workforce. They therefore sent the personnel manager away to write the first draft report; the report was to be hard-hitting with no punches pulled. It was to be written in a racy style.

The personnel manager, who by now had become fired with enthusiasm at the thought of contributing to a radical change for the better in the way his new firm was run, took them at their word. He burned the midnight oil and ignored his family at weekends, to produce a detailed report on everything he had been told during his study. The report when finished had eight pages of recommendations, and fifty pages of summary of all the evidence collected.

The report was circulated as planned (although it was typed and copied only just in time) to the members of the personnel committee on a Friday for them to read over the weekend ready for a meeting to discuss it on Monday. Stan treated himself to a bargain break weekend, secretly rather pleased with his efforts.

On Monday, the meeting seemed to go well enough at first. The personnel director had suggested, as committee chairman, that since the report was long and detailed, they ought to discuss the recommendations first. That took all the morning; they were amended rather more than Stan had expected, but they were agreed.

Then, in the remaining ten minutes of the meeting, it was unanimously decided that the report was rather longer than required; it need only be eight to ten pages long, including recommendations. A small sub-group of two was set up to help Stan shorten it. It was all over and settled before Stan could open his mouth; he thought the manufacturing manager said something about 'expected something concise and to the point'. And the meeting was over.

As he walked over to lunch, however, he began to get an uneasy feeling that all was not well. As soon as he got to the dining room he collared Sam Dyson, the data processing boss, who had become his 'father confessor' over the past few months.

'What did you think of the meeting, Sam?' he asked.

'That isn't really what you want to ask me, is it?' replied Sam.

'No,' said Stan, 'it's just that I've got a feeling that I did something wrong but I can't put my finger on what.'

'You wrote a lousy report,' said Stan. 'I'd have sent it straight back if it had come to me. Too long, too much irrelevance, and too many typing errors. The others were all too polite to say anything. It read like a first draft, not a report to a committee. I told David on the train coming in this morning that if I were him I'd scrub the meeting.

Having sat in stunned silence over lunch, Stan decided that he must get to the bottom of the problem. He therefore made an appointment to see David Hawson at 4.00 p.m.

It took Stan half an hour to get the truth from him: David was a gentleman of the old school, and didn't like to upset people. But in the end the whole story came out.

The committee hadn't wanted to hear *everything* that had been said during the interviews. They had been expecting a report on how to improve communications. That, after all, had been the terms of reference. And they had been embarrassed to read statements which expressed distrust of their colleagues and their supervisors. Some of them, including the union representatives, had even felt the report was inflammatory.

Stan had committed the cardinal report-writing sin. He had strayed from the terms of reference. He had been asked to write a vivid report about what needed to be done to improve communications. He had written instead a negative report about everything that was said to be wrong with the company.

It took two days to precis the report down to eight pages; in doing it, Stan had to agree that more than half the report was about gripes on everything but communication; matters like pay, car parking, too much waiting time, poor promotion prospects – the perennial problems in fact of running a business.

Self-check

1 What else was wrong with Stan's report?
2 Where does report writing begin?
3 Whose reponsibility was it to stop this kind of basic breakdown in communication happening?
4 Where did Stan's troubles start?

ANSWERS

1a It was too long. No report need be fifty pages long, unless it has a huge amount of evidence to present. Always start off by writing as short a report as you can. If your reader wants more information, he can ask for it. If you give him too much, he will not be able to digest it, and you will have failed to use your report for its primary purpose: as a medium of communication.

 b It was typed and checked in a hurry. There is no excuse for handing over a piece of writing that contains spelling, grammatical, or typing errors. Even the man who asks for a 'rough draft' does not want to be distracted and irritated by such irrelevancies. Remember:

- getting it right comes before getting it done on time;
- if you plan properly you can do both;
- check carefully and slowly – and you cannot do that if you are pushed for time;
- get someone else to read aloud the rough while you follow the fair copy.

2 Writing of any kind begins with an objective. If you lose sight of the objective you risk losing everything. Keep your eye on the ball.

3 It could be seen as David Hawson's job, as chairman of the committee, to ensure that the committee's executive agent, in this case Stan Micton, was clear about what he had to do. He could have done this by:

- stating the objective of the report at the end of the meeting at which Stan presented the initial results;
- ensuring that the minutes of the meeting reported that summary;
- asking Stan to 'feed back' on what he had to do. In other words, ask Stan to repeat in his own words his understanding of what he had to do.

As Stan's boss, he also had a responsibility to help Stan, perhaps by looking over his planned report structure, or reading the first section as soon as it had been written. But it was Stan's responsibility too. It takes two to communicate.

4 Stan's troubles started when he did not *listen* properly to the committee's specification for the report.

Case 4

David Shrewsbury, a bright young manager, had been given the responsibility of taking Zak Baumer, an American author who was writing a book on the firm, around factories to meet people. The tour included a meeting with the managing director, John

Sherwood, who was a brilliant engineer and manager, but had a bit of a reputation for irascibility. This day was a particularly bad one – he was in the middle of trying to prevent what looked like being a major strike. David knew this but he had to do his job. On the way up to the meeting David ran into the MD's personal assistant, Stella Minery. Stella told him that she thought John would want to put off the meeting with him. David therefore decided to go in and see him on his own to clear the ground.

As soon as David walked in, John said: 'We'll have to put it off. Sorry. Got this strike meeting in five minutes. I'm going to have to address the meeting myself. Sorry David.'

'Perhaps we don't have to scrub your seeing Zak,' said David. 'Zak's meant to be picking up the real atmosphere of the firm; he's seeing the unions. Why not let him sit in on the meeting? Then he'll really pick up atmosphere.'

'No. It's not on. Too risky. It's a private matter within the firm. We can't wash our dirty linen in public. You'll have to do something else with him.'

'OK, but I think you're wrong. Still, I suppose I'll just have to kill the time some other way,' said David.

John Sherwood stopped in his tracks. He looked as if he was about to blow a gasket.

'What the hell do you think you're saying? This is a major crisis. You can't talk about killing time. We're paying that man Baumer through the nose. You bloody well do something useful with him; you must be off your chump. Get out of my sight. Go on – get out!'

David got out.

|| *Self-check*

|| What went wrong?

ANSWER

At first sight, David's biggest mistake was to use the wrong words. 'To kill the time some other way' was, to say the least, rather a blunt way of putting it. It was guaranteed to remind the MD that since they were paying the American a lot of money to write the book and fly over from the United States, they could hardly afford for him to merely 'kill time'. The MD might also have understood that his interview with the author would also have been 'killing time'!

However, David was also at fault in two other ways. He failed to think about the situation properly in advance, and he missed an opportunity.

David was so immersed in his own problem, that of getting the author in to see the managing director, that he failed to think about the MD's problem. It is easy for us, looking at the situation objectively, to compare the importance of the two problems, and realize that an imminent major strike is rather more serious than an interview with an author about a book, even if the book has been commissioned by the firm: one problem could wait, the other could not. But even if David had not been aware of the impending strike, he should have realized that the MD was quite likely to have other quite weighty matters on his mind. In view of the fact that he did know about the strike, his crime was even worse: he completely underestimated how preoccupied the MD was likely to be.

Now let's look at the missed opportunity. What was David really trying to achieve in 'clearing the ground'? He wanted to persuade the MD that, despite his need to avert the strike, he also needed to make sure that the company's money was not wasted letting the author waste time when he could have been 'picking up the real atmosphere of the firm'.

Had David used the argument of the cost of the author's visit as a way of opening the subject, he would have appealed to the MD's other interest, that of not wasting company money. He might then have persuaded the MD to satisfy two interests at once, by allowing the author to sit in on the meeting with the unions (which is what David really wanted anyway).

Of course he would still have had to choose his words very carefully. But if he had tactfully suggested that the cost of the author's time would obviously be of concern to the MD, while at the same time showing the MD that he was equally aware of the seriousness of the industrial relations problem, he might (just might) have succeeded in achieving his own objective.

In this chapter we have tried to analyse typical breakdowns in communication in order to highlight some of the danger areas and mistakes it is all too easy to make when communicating. We have seen that breakdowns like these are usually not caused by one simple error, nor by only one person; that 'facts' are not always what they seem; that words can mean very different things to different people; that words are not in fact the only means of communicating. We have also seen that failure to think about what we are doing, both before we communicate and while we are communicating, can land us in trouble that is very difficult to get out of.

However, while it is comparatively easy to be wise after the event, it is not always so easy to avoid falling into the traps oneself in a real situation. To stand any chance of avoiding them we need to be constantly alert to what is going on when we are communicating.

Activity

Try to be particularly observant during the next few days to any failures in communication, both those you are involved in and those involving other people. Buses, trains, shops and canteen queues can be a fascinating source of material for communication analysis. Make a note, even if only a mental note, of what went wrong and then spend a little time reflecting on the reasons that lie behind the breakdowns.

©1966 *Daily Mirror Newspapers Ltd.* Andy Capp by *Reggie Smythe Courtesy of Field Newspaper Syndicate*
Reproduced by permission of Mirror Group Newspapers

2 | Understanding the process

I know you believe you understand what you think I said, but I am not sure whether you realize that what you heard is not what I meant. [Anon.]

How then, can we try to prevent these breakdowns occurring? If communication breaks down, how can we put things right? How can we recognize that a breakdown has occurred? In all the examples in the last chapter, the person 'communicating' thought he was communicating what he intended to communicate. He was either amazed or annoyed to discover he had not succeeded; or worse still, perhaps he never did discover that he had failed to communicate. Communication then is not just a matter of uttering words and hoping for the best – although to judge from the little attention that most of us pay to it, we do tend to behave as if communication will just happen.

Certainly, we all spend a lot of time communicating. Approximately seventy per cent of our waking time is spent in some form of communication with other people. But we must not assume that because we spend a lot of time communicating, we are doing it effectively. Perhaps the very fact that communication seems to be such a natural, common activity leads us into a false sense of security or complacency.

Much of this book will encourage you to practise various aspects of the skill of communication, but practice does not necessarily make perfect! Practising *bad* habits will not turn us into better communicators. Just as with sport, if you are anxious to improve your ability to communicate it is necessary to recognize that good practice is based on sound theory. So let's examine this process of communication to discover how it works, and what the basic principles are.

The process of communication is very complicated, so don't

be alarmed if you find some of the ideas and concepts in the next few chapters difficult to grasp – they will become clearer as you progress through the book.

You are unique

Let's start by thinking about you. You are not just a 'thing' in a world of 'things' which are static and unchanging. Even as you read this, all sorts of 'happenings' are going on inside you, in response to 'messages' which are created within you, and messages which you are receiving from the world around you. These messages are called 'stimuli'. Some of them are internal: you may have some nagging worry at the back of your mind which is causing you to concentrate on that, rather than on what you are reading. Other stimuli are external: messages received from outside your body by your five senses (hearing, sight, smell, taste and touch). Some are received at a conscious level: an ambulance passes the window, for example, with such a loud siren that you have no option but to take notice of it. Other external stimuli are received at a subconscious level: although your brain is receiving the message, you are not necessarily thinking consciously about it. For example, you may be hardly aware of the sound of a television in another room; that is, until I mentioned it. All these messages, internal and external, are constantly vying for your attention, and causing you to take part in a kind of internal communication process or 'talk to yourself', to decide whether you will react consciously to them. For example, you may be trying to decide whether you really are thirsty enough to go and get a drink, or whether to go and watch television rather than carry on reading.

Selective attention

Your brain automatically receives all the available stimuli but it attends to relatively few; it only causes you to think about some of them. Your brain acts like a kind of filter system allowing you to take notice of some stimuli and shut out others and it does this by a kind of priority ordering system. So, for example, as long as the temperature is not too uncomfortable you will not be aware of it but as soon as it becomes too extreme your brain will cause you to react by making you shiver or sweat so forcing you to take notice of it.

It is clear that if we are to receive a message properly, we must first somehow have our attention drawn to it. People attend to messages either voluntarily or involuntarily. Involuntarily attention is given to a message when the receiver feels it poses some threat to his personal wellbeing, e.g. loud noises, bright lights, sudden movements, in other words anything unexpected. Voluntary attention on the other hand is normally given to those messages which are somehow seen as being interesting to the receiver. But again, he will maintain his attentive state only as long as the message is of more interest than other activities he could be doing.

In Case 4, David Shrewsbury failed to show the MD that his message was of at least equal interest as the threatened strike.

This fluctuating and selective nature of attention is one of the primary obstacles faced in establishing and maintaining good communication. As we shall see, the responsibility for establishing and maintaining attention falls on both the person sending the message (the transmitter) and on the person receiving the message (the receiver).

Selective perception

Consciously or unconsciously you select what you want to receive or experience. You may simply change your position so that you alter the stimuli that can reach you, and as we have seen you may actually choose to receive some stimuli and reject others. But what of the stimuli you *do* choose to receive? Do you 'understand' them in the same way that someone else would? Receiving a message is not the same as understanding it, because you have to make sense of the stimuli, you have to interpret it, or decode it. You do this by using your previous experience and knowledge of things, which enables you to recognize different stimuli and fit them into various categories; so the noise of the siren had certain attributes which helped you to recognize it as the noise of some kind of emergency vehicle. You probably had to look in order to see what other attributes it had, which then enabled you to recognize it as a fire engine or a police car or an ambulance. But someone who had never seen any of these things, an Indian in the Amazon forest for example, would probably just have been frightened by the noise: he would not have been able to make sense of it because it would not have fitted into any of his categories of experience. In just the same way, if you talk about things and ideas outside the range of people's experience they have no means of understanding.

However, the process of perception is even more complicated than this. In decoding the stimulus of the siren and the ambulance, different people will give them different meanings. To a little boy the siren and the sight of the ambulance will probably cause excitement, whereas to an adult the same stimulus might cause a feeling of fear or anxiety or even sorrow if they have previously experienced ambulances in relation to an accident. In other words, the way in which people interpret or perceive the messages they receive will depend on their experience; because everyone is different and has had different experiences they will 'see' things differently, even when looking at the same thing.

Activity

Look at this picture and then write down on a piece of paper what you think it is.

Well, you may have seen a boy on a donkey, or the cliffs of Dover with grass hanging over the edge or almost anything; but most people, when they look at this picture, see a woman. Is that what you have written down? But suppose I were to go a bit further and say it is a picture of a smart young woman, would you still agree? You may do, but many of you looking at this picture will see an old crone with a pointed chin and a hooked nose looking down towards the left-hand corner of the page, rather than a smart young woman with a black velvet band round her neck looking away from you. Whichever you saw you will probably be surprised that other people are just as adamant as you in seeing something different, but if I had not pointed out that it was possible to see at least two different things in this picture, you might never have realized that there are two different points of view. So the problem here is not just that it is difficult to see the same picture from different points of view, but that you might never have realized that anyone could possibly see it differently from you unless it had been pointed out.

It is important to remember, then, that other people will not necessarily 'see' things in the same way as you. Sarah, in Case 2, didn't 'see', or rather 'hear', the words in the same way as Joan.

But there are other reasons why people may 'see' and 'hear' the same thing differently. What we choose to experience is affected by our different needs, desires and interests. In Case 1, Giles saw the arrival of the young man and 'heard' his boss's words differently from everyone else because of his personal anxiety. He perceived these innocent events as a threat to his promotion.

Like attention, our perception is selective, and the way we perceive things will be influenced by our previous experiences and the environment in which we exist, because from different experiences and environments, different sets of attitudes, beliefs, values and needs develop. Let's look a little more closely at these, since they are so influential in the way we communicate.

Attitudes and beliefs

From the environment we live in and the things we experience as
we grow up, we develop certain beliefs in or about things. For
example:

> Cars cause accidents and pollute the air.
> Passing exams makes getting a job easier.
> People who do wrong are punished.
> People who work hard will be rewarded.

or   It doesn't matter how hard you work, no one appreciates it.

These beliefs cause us to develop attitudes to things. Once we
have formed the attitude, we are conditioned to react in a certain
way. We don't have to stop and think about how we should
react; we tend to react automatically: 'I don't like people like
that,' we may say.

People may share the same attitude towards something and
yet have very different beliefs about it. You may have a positive
attitude to work or studying and so may someone else, but your
reasons may be different from theirs. In communicatng it is all
too easy to assume that other people who share our attitudes
share our beliefs and so on.

Because our beliefs and attitudes are so much a part of us, we
tend to be very unwilling to change them unless the evidence is
very strong indeed.

‖   *Activity*

‖   Look back at Case 1. Towards the end of the story Giles
‖   reveals his attitudes and beliefs. Can you list them?

He looks unfavourably on companies which do not promote
people who have given long service (attitude). He believes that
companies like that are unjust because he believes 'years of
faithful service' are usually rewarded. He also believes that he
has no future with the company.

Our beliefs result from

• our experiences;

- personal observation;
- evidence provided by other people;
- motivation.

We believe what we have personally experienced and observed, and we tend to believe what other people believe as long as we trust them, though the pressure to believe what 'everyone else' believes can be very strong. But we also believe what we *want* to believe; our attitudes and beliefs will depend on what motivates us.

Motivation

Psychologists believe that all behaviour is motivated, and that people have reasons for doing what they do and how they do it.

Goals and values

We all have certain goals which we try to reach. Some are short-term goals (to pass an exam, to finish writing a report, to get a job), and some are long-term (to run our own business, to buy a yacht, to retire to the Seychelles). We are likely to believe whatever will help us to achieve our goals.

Sometimes our beliefs are more general – for example, abstract ideals about the way people ought to behave (people should be 'ambitious', or 'considerate towards their fellow men', or 'honest', or 'independent and self-sufficient'; or about the things that are worth trying to achieve ('financial security', or 'inner contentment', or 'a world in which all men are equal'. These are the things we value highly and become part of our 'value systems'.

Activity

What 'value' did Giles indicate that he held? And what was his short-term goal?

He obviously regarded 'years of faithful service' as a 'good thing'; therefore part of his value system was the deeply felt belief that companies ought to reward long service. Since he believed the company didn't hold this value, and since his goal was reward in the form of promotion, he was furious with the company and decided to resign.

An individual's goals and value system will influence how he perceives the world around him and therefore the way in which he behaves, communicates and interprets the communication of others. His attitudes, beliefs and values, are so deeply held that he will be very resistant to changing them.

Needs

One psychologist* developed a hierarchy of needs which helps to explain how these basic human needs are ordered.

- At the lowest level we must fulfil the very basic needs associated with survival: food, water, reproduction and shelter. Everyone, regardless of his environment, has these needs.
- The next group of needs are learned from living in a particular environment and will therefore differ from one environment to another; or rather the way in which they are satisfied will differ from one environment to another. First is the need for security – to feel safe and free from threat.
- At the next level is the need to belong, to be accepted by others. That need accounts for people joining various groups and for the way they behave as part of a group. Some people need more acceptance than others.
- At the next level of need we are concerned with the way in which people regard us and the way we regard ourselves – in other words, esteem.
- Finally, the highest level of need, sometimes called 'self-actualization' or 'self-fulfilment', refers to the need to achieve things, to be satisfied with what we do and feel that we are achieving our potential, whatever that is and at whatever level.

* Abraham Maslow, *Motivation and Personality*, New York: Harper & Row, 1959.

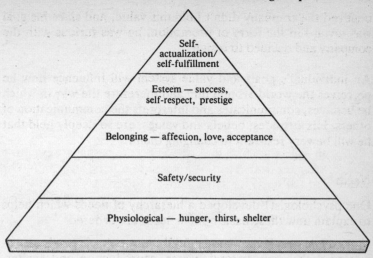

Maslow suggested that these needs form a hierarchy, as in the diagram above, because we are able to move from one level of needs to another only when we have satisfied the needs at the previous level. For instance, someone who is starving will not be too concerned about the extent to which he can achieve self-fulfilment.

While these needs may be universal and shared by all people, the means of satisfying them will differ greatly. Safety and security to a family fleeing from their home in the midst of war may mean the arrival of peacekeeping troops or a Red Cross helicopter; but in modern Western society safety and security could simply mean job security.

When communicating, it is necessary to motivate receivers to listen to your message. This can be achieved by appealing to their needs; by telling them how they can benefit by listening or doing what you request. Gaining attention through motivation, or the use of need satisfaction, is a far stronger method of gaining co-operation than through such devices as fear-arousal, coercion or exhortation, and so on. Success depends on finding out what a person's needs are and choosing the most appropriate appeal.

Another psychologist, Herzberg*, identified the following six factors or 'satisfiers' which affect people who work:

- Achievement.
- Recognition.
- Advancement.
- The work itself.
- The possibility of growth.
- Responsibility.

Although you may feel that at work you perhaps have little control over the way these factors affect others, you should be aware that the need for satisfaction in different ways will often explain other people's behaviour, and your own, and will therefore affect your communication with them.

Activity

What motivates you at work or college and in your spare-time activities? Think about the following points as you try to answer these questions:

1 If you won the football pools or inherited enough money to live comfortably without working, would you carry on studying or working? If not, what would you do with your time?
2 If you would carry on working, would it be because of your interest in the work, the sense of accomplishment it gives you or just to keep you occupied?
3 Suppose you did not work, what would you miss most:

- the people you know through work, friends, contacts?
- the feeling of doing something?
- the kind of work you do?
- the feeling of doing something important, worthwhile?
- regular routine?
- feeling of interest?
- something else? If so, what?

* Frederick Herzberg, B. Mausner and B. Synderman, *The Motivation to Work*, New York: John Wiley, 1959.

4 Now think about your spare-time activities. How do you spend your time, and why do you do those things in particular? What needs do these activities satisfy?

5 How do you rate yourself on Maslow's hierarchy of needs? How do you satisfy your needs?

6 Can you see how these different needs will affect what you communicate about and how you communicate?

To sum up then,

• the way a person perceives his world and the messages he receives, and

• the way he communicates to other people

are influenced by a complex web of interrelated factors which will differ from one person to another.

Factors which affect perception and motivation (and may therefore cause barriers to communication)

Age Leads to different experiences, interests, values, attitudes, needs, languages – 'the generation gap'.

Background Social upbringing gives different needs, values and expectations.

Education Different education gives different fundamental knowledge, and different levels give differences in range of vocabulary and concepts.

Health Affects the quality of the five senses, energy, resistance to stress, level of adjustment and also causes limitations on occupations.

Intelligence Affects mental agility, therefore influences the ease with which different types of concepts can be understood and manipulated.

Interests Preferences for intellectual, practical, social, domestic, active, passive, constructive activities will direct attention to different things.

Language Involves differences in verbal ability and use of accent, dialect and jargon.

Needs Different people have different needs and wants and the same person has different needs and wants in different circumstances.

Occupation Leads to differences in people, activities and ideas experienced.

Personality The extent to which certain personality characteristics are predominant – energetic, assertive, passive, withdrawn, sociable, tough, tender, secure, insecure, stable, aggressive, etc.

Race Racial and ethnic origins lead to problems of colour prejudice.
Religion Influences values, culture and beliefs.
Sex Affects the ease or difficulty of communicating with the opposite
  sex.
Training Affects the level of skill, occupational experiences, use of
  technical jargon.

Since these factors will be present in varying degrees and combinations, they will affect one another in such a complex way
that it is difficult to describe very precisely the influence of any
one factor, but we must always be on the lookout for their
existence and try to anticipate their effect.

Why do we communicate?

We communicate as a reaction to internal or external stimuli.
People speak and listen to satisfy personal needs, to establish
relationships, to understand the same things, to believe what is
understood, and occasionally to entertain. If we consider the
reasons why we communicate we will also gain insight into the
effects of communication.

To satisfy personal needs

When we make requests and issue commands, we are using
communication to satisfy needs. When someone says: 'Pass the
water, please', or 'Can I have a return to London?' they are
using communication to fulfil a need. Communication that focuses the spotlight totally on the speaker (measured by frequent
use of words like 'I', 'me', 'my'), however, can some become
ineffectual. Once communication becomes overwhelmingly ego-
centric and the speaker 'talks to hear himself talk' or only to
satisfy his own needs without concern for other people's needs,
his communication may be ignored. David, in Case 4, was
tending to communicate purely to satisfy his own needs, and
ignoring the needs of the managing director.

Communication is therefore concerned not only with our own
needs but also with the needs of other people. We must be aware
of the needs that lie behind other people's speaking and
listening.

To establish relationships with other people

In order to satisfy most of our needs, we have to relate to others. A significant portion of your day is probably spent establishing and maintaining rapport with other people. Even simple greetings like 'How are you?' or a nod of the head serve to recognize others and to provide a link in the relationship with others. One research study revealed that a major purpose of telephone calls from one business executive to another within the same organization was to maintain friendly links. A certain amount of rapport-building indicates a healthy relationship and this sort of communication leads to trust as well as liking between people.

To create understanding between ourselves and other people

We use communication to share with others, and gain from others, important information about people, places, things, events and personal feelings. The effects of information sharing are twofold: first, the information may serve to satisfy our need to know about our environment and, second, awareness of something is the first stage in the persuasion process, so we may wish to inform others as a basis for future persuasion.

To persuade people and create change

Many messages are intended to persuade people to change their behaviour, their beliefs and attitudes. For example, toothpaste or deodorant advertising is appealing to our need to be accepted and liked, and this motivates change. In some cases, these persuasive messages are intended to gain acceptance of one idea which will be a building block for later persuasion. However, in other cases, persuasive messages may be direct, designed to bring about immediate change.

To entertain

Although much of our communication may appear to be superficial and intended merely to entertain (e.g. joke-telling, story-telling and 'visiting' communication such as small talk, bar and coffee-break conversation), this communication can have other less obvious but very significant intentions and effects. The comedian, making satirical digs at politicians, is providing re-inforcement for those who support or deny the point of the joke, reinforcing their beliefs and attitudes about politics, the political climate or politicians; and much of the traditional story-telling which has entertained children through the centuries has had the effect of reinforcing beliefs and moral values such as 'good wins over evil'.

In one recent study it was found that the small talk which supervisors engaged in with their workers positively influenced the attitude of the workers to their job, and therefore affected worker morale and production.

W. Michael Blumenthal, formerly chairman of the Bendix Corporation and later US Secretary of the Treasury, put it like this: 'You can't operate successfully if you are cut off from people'.* As an example of his methods of keeping in touch with his employees he advised this technique for memos: deliver it yourself and have a chat. He felt the content was unimportant: sometimes it was business-related, sometimes it was concerned with personal life, but either way it gave him a better understanding of the people who worked for him.

Why do people take notice of information?

Information is most readily received if it:

- is *relevant* to the individual's needs and interests;
- *confirms* the views and attitudes he already holds.

Two significant findings illustrate this. First, party political broadcasts: people tend to watch the broadcast of the party they support and switch off the broadcasts of the other parties. Second, advertising: research into the response of readers to advertisements shows that we are more likely to read thoroughly an advertisement for something we have already bought. In both cases, we find the views expressed are comforting because they

* Herbert E. Meyer, 'How the Boss Stays in Touch with the Troops', *Fortune*, June 1975.

confirm our original beliefs and attitudes. Also of course, in the case of advertising, we are anxious to convince ourselves that we have made the right choice. We are not inclined to look for evidence which will make us start wondering whether we are really right.

Does this reflect the way you behave? Think back to the last time a party political broadcast was shown on television? What did you do? Why?

And what about advertising? Don't you find your eye being attracted to advertisements for things you already own? Of course you also look at advertisements for things you would like to own – in other words, things you need or things you are interested in.

For similar reasons, information is likely to be rejected if it:

- is *relevant* to the individual's current needs
- but *challenges* his established attitudes.

Can you think of any examples where this has been true of you?

The communicator must be guided by two very important principles. To be successful, any communication must:

- *relate* to the audience's needs and interests;
- *confirm* views and attitudes already held.

But information which either *does not relate* to the needs of his audience or *challenges* their present views, has to be presented very *forcefully* indeed if they are to take notice.

How do we communicate:

Given the complexity of human beings and the many complex factors involved, it does seem a wonder that we manage to communicate as well as we do. But by being aware of the complexity of the potential problems we can anticipate the difficulties and try to avoid them. We can think more consciously about what we are doing and make intelligent decisions about the most effective way to communicate in any given situation. The rest of this book will be concerned with the nature of those decisions; but before we go on to look at specific situations in which we need to communicate, and the techniques which help

us to communicate effectively, let's take a straightforward look at what has to happen in the process of conveying a message from one person to another.

First of all, we have to decide whether to communicate or not. If we do choose to communicate we then have to decide what we want to communicate. Next we have to translate the idea (the feelings, the opinions, etc.) in our head into a 'code' which we can transmit. I will use the word 'code' because, although we can transmit our ideas in the form of pictures, we usually use words, and words are only symbols which represent the ideas. The words themselves don't have meanings; people give meanings to words.

Depending on their attitudes, beliefs, experiences and the context of the communication, people will attach their own particular meanings to the words they utter and the words they hear. In Case 2, the words 'Oh! What a relief!' meant one thing to Sarah and quite a different thing to Joan. The words, then, are symbols: when we want to communicate an idea, we have to translate it into a code which is appropriate to the receiver. The code may be words (verbal communication) or facial expressions, gestures or pictures, and so on (nonverbal communication), or a mixture of both verbal and nonverbal. We will call this process of encoding choosing the 'medium' of communication.

We also have to choose the most appropriate 'channel' of communication to convey the message: we may decide to write, or telephone, or speak to someone face-to-face. Having selected the appropriate medium and channel to convey our idea, we transmit the message.

Now the process takes place more or less in reverse, in that the receiver has to translate the coded message back into an idea which he understands. But throughout the process things can go wrong as we have seen: the 'barriers' listed on page 39 can distort the message. The communicator translates his ideas into code as a result of his own experiences, attitudes, etc. and the receiver translates the code back in the light of *his* experiences, attitudes, etc. The resulting idea may therefore not be the same as the one the communicator wanted to convey. Just to add to the problems, other barriers may get in the way and distort the message (a crackling telephone line, poor handwriting, loud background noise). These barriers can even prevent the message being received at all. Someone who is preoccupied with something else may not even 'hear' your message.

It is therefore essential to check that the message has been received in the way it was intended. We can do this by getting the receiver to give us 'feedback'. In spoken communication this feedback can be immediate (David Shrewsbury in Case 4 understood in no uncertain terms that the MD had misunderstood his message), and face-to-face spoken communication also provides nonverbal feedback. We can often tell from a frown, a scowl or a smile whether we have been understood in the way we intended or not. We usually get the opportunity to correct any misunderstandings fairly quickly – as long as we give the receiver a chance to give us feedback and are alert to the signals that something has gone wrong; provided, too, that it is not already too late, as it was in David's case and in the case of Joan's 'Oh! What a relief!'

In written communication, however, there is no chance for feedback or, at least, any feedback will be rather a long time coming and therefore not of immediate use.

Looked at diagrammatically, then, the process of communication looks rather like this:

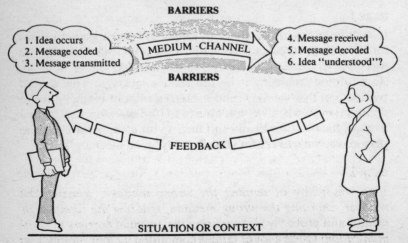

The Process of Communication

Of course, in practice, people communicating take it in turns to be the communicator and the receiver in a continuous cycle, but in future we will call the person who initiates the communication the communicator.

The traps that await us as communicators are therefore:

- failing to communicate at all;
- sending the wrong message;
- ignoring the receiver;
- choosing the wrong medium (the wrong words, etc.);
- choosing the wrong channel (a letter instead of a personal visit?);
- ignoring the potential barriers to communication;
- ignoring the feedback;
- omitting to seek feedback;
- ignoring the situation or context in which the communication takes place.

Review

Now look back at the four case studies in Chapter 1 and say which traps each of the communicators – Giles's boss, Joan, Stan and David – fell into. (Since Giles received a message, we will say that his boss is the communicator.)

CASE 1

Giles's boss was really guilty of *failing to communicate*, as was Giles himself, of course; we could also argue that Giles's boss was guilty of *ignoring the receiver* and *sending the wrong message*, since without realizing it he did send a message. This should remind you that we may send messages without realizing we're doing so, even when we don't mean to (the yawning student in a lecture; the person who doesn't turn up for an appointment; the person who fails to return your friendly 'good morning').

CASE 2

Joan was guilty of *sending the wrong message, ignoring the receiver, choosing the wrong medium, ignoring the situation or context* and probably also *ignoring the potential barriers to communication*! Quite a lot of crimes committed by four thoughtless words!

CASE 3

Stan was guilty of *sending the wrong message* (he ignored his terms of reference) and *choosing the wrong medium* and *ignoring the receivers* (the report was too long, contained too many irrelevancies and too many errors). He was probably also guilty of *omitting to seek feedback* in that he should have thought to seek some advice from his boss by letting him look at the rough draft of the report before submitting it to the committee.

CASE 4

David was first of all guilty of *sending the wrong message, ignoring the receiver, ignoring the potential barriers to communication* and *ignoring the situation and context*. Having chosen the wrong message he was also guilty of *choosing the wrong medium*. No wonder he was told to get out!

Remember . . . Don't worry if you have found some of this chapter rather complex and theoretical. You can always refer back to the ideas which we have looked at as you progress through the book; the various concepts are mentioned in relation to the practical task of communicating. The chapter will serve as a useful foundation for the rest of the book, since it is intended to explain why the techniques which are suggested to help you communicate are so necessary.

3 | Which way is best?

You have worked for your present firm for three years and have been promoted to supervisor. The firm has recently decided to introduce a 'harmonization programme'. Under this scheme, everyone in the firm, from the managing director to the odd-job man, will have similar conditions of work and fringe benefits (though not the same salary). They will all clock on and clock off work, eat in the same canteen, have the same holidays, pension scheme and so on. The unions support the scheme although obviously there are many people who are unhappy about it – mainly because they are unsure of exactly what to expect, and because they see it as a threat to their hard-won privileges.

Each supervisor has been given the responsibility of introducing the scheme and explaining the details to his own section.

Self-check

Which method of communication will you use:

- a formal meeting at which you will speak to the whole of your section (thirty people)?
- a detailed memo issued to everyone?
- a notice on the section's noticeboard?
- an informal discussion with small groups in the course of the working day?
- an informal question and answer session with everyone present?

Why have you chosen that particular method? List the factors that you would consider in making your choice of method. Which method would you feel happiest and most comfortable using? Why? (Be honest!)

Keep your answers to these questions in front of you as

we look at the advantages and disadvantages of the various forms of communication.

Whenever you have to communicate, one of your first decisions will have to concern the best and most effective method of communication. In this chapter we look at the ways in which methods of communication may be classified in order to compare their advantages and disadvantages from the point of view of both the communicator and the receiver(s). We also look at another very important aspect: the reasons why people knowingly and unknowingly often choose the least appropriate method – because, simply, they are human, with all the pressures, and anxieties and fears that human beings are prone to.

Armed with this knowledge, you will be in a better position to appreciate the reasons organizational communication is not always as effective as it might be, which will be the subject of Part 2. However, a thorough understanding of the reasons, both considered and instinctive, why people opt for particular methods of communication should enable you to analyse the reasons for your own preference.

Let's look first at the difference between written and spoken (or oral) communication, which is a fairly common way of classifying available methods.

Activity

Did you consider the advantages and disadvantages of these two broad divisions of communication when deciding which method to use in the question at the beginning of this chapter?

Compare your list of factors with mine, opposite.

One-way v. two-way communication

Communication is often divided simply into one-way communication and two-way communication. Although two-way communication is usually regarded as 'better' this need not necessarily be the case.

WRITTEN OR ORAL COMMUNICATION?

	Written	*Oral*
Advantages	• Better for facts and opinions. • Better for difficult or complicated messages. Can be reviewed. • Useful when a written record is required for reference purposes. • Can be both written and read when individuals are 'in the right mood'. • Can be carefully planned and considered before transmission. • Errors can be removed before transmission.	• Better for feelings and emotions. • More personal and individual. • Provides far greater interaction and feedback. • Can make more impact. • Generally less costly. • Allows you to correct and adjust your message in the light of feedback and nonverbal cues.
Disadvantages	• More time-consuming and costly. • Feedback is either non-existent or delayed. • Lacks nonverbal cues which help interpretation.	• More difficult to think as you speak. • Something once said cannot be erased. • Some people can't or don't like reading. • You can never be sure the message is read. • Lacks warmth and individuality.

Self-check

Can you think of four examples of one-way communication?

One-way communication

One-way communication is where there is no opportunity for feedback – at least not immediately. This category would include any face-to-face communication where there is no real opportunity for the receivers to question the communicator or clarify their understanding: for example, a lecture or meeting at which the communicator addresses the audience, usually fairly large, but there is no discussion and no question time. This category would also include practically all written communication, in that although a communication may be intended to elicit some response or feedback, this does not take place immediately. One-way communication is generally considered to be the least satisfactory method, although it does have some advantages which perhaps account for its survival.

DISADVANTAGES

Room for error Since the receiver cannot ask questions or clarify understanding, and the communicator cannot check that his message has been understood in the way he intended, the possibility of misunderstanding is much greater than with two-way communication.

Lower confidence Because of the possibility of error the receiver is likely to feel very unsure that he has understood what was intended. Ideally the communicator should not be overconfident either; he should anticipate possible misunderstandings and try to compensate for them. But as we have seen, unfortunately all too often the communicator behaves as if he is confident he is being understood – even if secretly he is aware that there is a vague possibility he is not.

Higher frustration This lack of confidence on the part of the receiver (and hopefully on the part of the communicator) can give rise to feelings of frustration. If the receiver knows he does not understand something and has no means of checking, he is left in an impossible position of feeling unable to act. Usually this frustration or irritation is directed at the communicator for failing to make himself understood.

If a worker is constantly expected to carry out instructions and do his job, with no chance to check how he is doing because his supervisor is not available and takes no interest in him, then the consequences can easily be those ailments of industry which constantly pepper the headlines of newspaper reports: industrial accidents, faulty products and service, low morale, high staff turnover and so on.

Even the communicator, if he is sensitive to the dangers, can become frustrated at having to use methods of communication which do not permit immediate feedback which would enable him to tell whether he was being understood or not. This may account for why many people dislike writing, or even speaking, when it is one-way. They are aware of the potential misunderstandings, but can do little about it.

However, although one-way communication has obvious disadvantages and should perhaps be avoided whenever possible, it does have advantages.

Self-check

Can you think of any advantages of one-way communication – either for the communicator or the receiver?

ADVANTAGES

Time Normally one-way communication takes less time than two-way. It is obviously quicker to address an audience of fifty than to talk to each person individually, and it also takes less time to convey a message if discussion and questions are not encouraged. The saving in time is probably the main reason why people commonly opt for a one-way method: time seems to be a commodity in such short supply in this hectic age. However, a word of warning: it may seem quicker to speak to a large group of people at once rather than see them all individually, and it may seem quicker to toss off a memo than take the trouble to talk face-to-face or telephone people one by one, but it is only quicker if comparatively little thought is given to the preparation of the message. The communicator who recognizes the problems inherent in issuing a one-way message will probably spend considerable time trying to overcome the potential problems and misunderstandings, and preparing the message – be it a talk or a speech, a memo or a report – in such a way that it is as appropriate as possible for as many people as possible, and is open to as little misinterpretation as possible. The consequence of this is in many cases that the good communicator will spend almost as much time preparing and presenting a one-way message as he would if he were to opt for two-way communication.

Air of efficiency Another attraction of one-way communication is that it creates an air of efficiency, even though this is often only a superficial impression. Certainly a speaker addressing a group of people who are all sitting or standing intently listening to him will appear to be more in control of the proceedings and more impressive than that same speaker in the midst of a lively discussion in which many people are speaking, if not all at once, then at least close on one another's heels. Similarly, the man who is known to sit at his desk dictating memos to all and sundry gives the impression of being more efficient, calm and business-like than his colleague whose office door is always open as people come in and out to discuss things.

However, knowing what we now know about the real effi-ciency of communication, we should not be too quick to see this 'air of efficiency' as a real advantage, even if it does seem an advantage to some communicators and explains why people have to admit they prefer one-way.

Security A related advantage as far as the communicator is concerned is that one-way communication tends to protect the communicator from the often uncomfortable experience of being questioned and challenged. It is easy to see that if you are a little unsure of your subject matter, or unwilling to face questions you cannot answer, or enter into debate about whether your opinions are valid or not, one-way communication allows you to avoid these discomforts. If you do not allow feedback you can avoid the danger of having to say, 'I don't know the answer to that.' You are in control. You can dictate how little or how much you communicate, and what you communicate about. This is a very natural wish on the part of most people. It takes courage and self-confidence to be prepared to expose yourself to what may be a threat to your self-esteem.

In fact it is perhaps true to say that the more unsure of himself someone is, the less he is prepared to allow people to know about his shortcomings. This is sad, because in fact it is probably also true that the person who is prepared to admit his ignorance, or allow that his opinions may not be right or universally held, is often the person for whom we feel the most respect.

Of course, another advantage of one-way communication associated with this very understandable need to protect oneself from open attack is that, even if secretly we may be aware that we are failing to communicate, we are not constantly reminded of it by people asking for clarification. We are able to push this anxiety away, and in effect bash on regardless kidding ourselves that we are communicating effectively.

However, this 'advantage' while perhaps being an advantage for the communicator is obviously not a real advantage of one-way communication.

So far all the advantages have turned out on closer examination not to be real advantages. Does this mean that one-way communication can never be more effective than two-way?

This is not an easy question to answer. It will depend on the reason why the communicator is communicating, what exactly he wants to achieve, the degree of understanding he needs to achieve to be effective (after all, 100 per cent understanding is not always necessary) and, above all, it will depend on the skill and ability of the communicator. If he is sensitive to the potential barriers, makes an effort to overcome them, communicates clearly and fluently and anticipates the questions people might want to ask, he may well succeed, on occasions, in making one-way communication work more effectively.

However, given man's natural tendency to opt for one-way rather than two-way, it is perhaps as well to look at the advantages of two-way.

Self-check

What is the overriding advantage of two-way communication? Can you think of any others?

Two-way communication

As has been implied, two-way communication allows for *constant feedback*. Perhaps a two-person, face-to-face conversation, where both participants are free to contribute as much as they want to, is the purest example. Each person takes it more or less in turn to be the communicator and receiver, and both therefore get instant feedback. In other words the communication loop has been closed.

ADVANTAGES

Accuracy With two-way communication, the communicator and receiver(s) are able to check that they are understanding one another as intended; therefore the message is likely to be understood more accurately.

Confidence Consequently both the receiver(s) and communicator are likely to feel more confident that the message is understood.

Less frustration The degree of frustration and irritation felt is likely to be less than with one-way. Certainly the receivers are less likely to feel irritated by the communicator since they have the chance to ask questions, ask for repetition and clarification.

However, perhaps surprisingly, there will always be some frustration, but it is usually experienced by the receivers towards *one another*. Inevitably different people will need repetition and clarification of different things, and this can cause impatience. If the communicator is interrupted too often, some people may find the interruptions and the nature of other people's questions disconcerting and confusing. Similarly, the communicator may feel impatient with the receivers at times, and conscious that his concentration on the delivery of his message is disrupted by the constant participation of the receivers.

DISADVANTAGES

Time Perhaps the major disadvantage is that two-way communication normally takes much longer: sometimes as much as two or three times as long to deliver the same message. But the time taken obviously increases in proportion to the number of receivers, since the more receivers there are, the more interruptions and misunderstandings there may be, and the more discussion and questioning there may be – although this will depend on the extent to which the receivers are prepared to take advantage of the opportunity to contribute. Often the presence of others will inhibit people from running the risk of asking questions in case they 'make a fool of themselves'.

There are other disadvantages, but these are more apparent than real.

Lack of control Two-way communication involving a group of people is inevitably going to mean a lot of interruptions which can become distracting and confusing. In order that this does not develop into complete disorderliness – and you will have experienced this on occasions in discussions or at meetings – it is necessary for the receivers to exercise a degree of self-control and for the communicator to be able to control what is going on. He may be able to do this in quite subtle ways; but however much he is actually in control, an outsider is likely to regard any two-way communication as less orderly and apparently less efficient than one-way. In view of this some communicators are uneasy in two-way situations, particularly with more than two or three people. For an unskilled communicator, this potential lack of control over what is going on can be seen as a real disadvantage; an event which starts out ostensibly as two-way can often end up one-way as the communicator takes over more and more obvious control until he is allowing no one but himself to speak.

Insecurity This temptation to exert control, by preventing others from questioning and discussing, often stems from anxiety on the part of the communicator if he feels insecure in his ability to answer questions.

Anyone who is unprepared to admit his ignorance will strive

to avoid two-way communication situations, and resort to the comparative safety of one-way.

It is not possible to state simply and categorically that two-way communication is better: in choosing between the two, the communicator must weigh up the advantages and disadvantages of the two methods in relation to his purpose, his own communication skills and of course the time he can afford. However, it is true perhaps that, wherever possible, two-way communication is more likely to overcome many of the communication barriers, provided the communicator has the confidence and willingness to cope.

Activity

Next time you are involved in a communication situation, e.g. a meeting, a discussion or merely watching a television studio debate, think about what is happening, how the communicators and receivers are behaving and whether the situation is predominantly one-way or two-way compared with what was originally intended.

Activity

If you are at college, compare the relative effectiveness of lectures and tutorials/small group discussions.
Write a list of the advantages and disadvantages of each, as you see them.

Hierarchy of communication levels

One of the problems which arise from dividing communication situations into simply two categories – one-way and two-way, or written and spoken – in order to assess their respective effectiveness, is that these categories tend to overlap in certain situations. Not all spoken communication is two-way – compare the possibility of two-way communication in a talk to five people, and in a talk to fifty-five people.

None of these methods of categorizing communication emphasizes the absence or existence of the face-to-face element, which includes that very important area of human communication – nonverbal communication.

One way of combining all these essential elements in the process is to talk in terms of a hierarchy of communication effectiveness.

LEVEL ONE

Usually the most direct and therefore the most effective communication occurs in a two-way, face-to-face situation where both verbal and nonverbal symbols and language are apparent to both parties, and where instant feedback is possible, e.g. person-to-person conversation.

LEVEL TWO

At this level, communication is two-way but not face-to-face. Even though feedback is possible, as in a telephone conversation, nonverbal signals are not apparent.

LEVEL THREE

This is the least effective level of communication. It is one-way and in business usually takes the written form. Neither feedback nor non-verbal signals are available.

Although it is important to do so at all levels, the communicator must do everything possible to prepare third-level messages that will be effective enough to reduce the impact of potential barriers. The good writer and the popular radio commentator are examples of those who have succeeded at the third level.

Because this level is the weakest and the most indirect, there is ample justification for emphasizing the need to improve our knowledge and skills in written communication, which is one of the major aims of this book.

Now look back at the answers you gave to the questions at the beginning of this chapter. How well had you considered the various factors which will influence the effectiveness of different methods of communication? Would you change your mind about which method you would use to communicate to your section about the details of the 'harmonization programme'? Were you honest about which method you would prefer to use? This method may be different from the one you know you *should* use.

However, there is no best method. Theoretically an informal question and answer session would probably be the most effective, but only if you were confident enough to handle it: able to encourage the quieter ones, tactfully suppress the noisier ones, subtly guide the discussion so that you still managed to give all the information that you had been instructed to give, and confident enough in yourself to be able to say: 'I don't know the answer to that one, but I'll find out and let you know.' This may therefore be the method to aim for, given this particular task and situation, but the best method for you at the moment may be different.

Part 2
Communication in organizations

Now for a change of direction. We need to stand back and take a wider view of the organization and its communication problems. In Part 2 we will look at organizational communication, the information needs of employees – management and labour – and the methods of communication available.

4 | The company speaks

The manager has a specific tool: information. He does not 'handle' people; he motivates, guides, organizes people to do their own work. His tool – his only tool – to do all this, is the spoken or written word. No matter whether the manager's job is engineering, accounting or selling, his effectiveness depends on his ability to listen and to read, on his ability to speak and to write. He needs skill in getting his thinking across to other people as well as skill in finding out what other people are after [Peter Drucker, *The Practice of Management*, Pan Books, 1968].

I have called this chapter 'The company speaks' because this title contains two essential ideas, both of which have significance for improving communication.

First of all, it contains the idea that a company is a single entity with a personality – an image of its own – in the eyes of all the people who ever come into contact with it. They may be employees, customers, suppliers, people who work for government agencies or other organizations, or just members of the general public who merely know of it through reading about it in newspapers and magazines or hearing about it on the radio or television; but though they may each have their own perception of the company, as we have seen, they will probably also have some agreement over its general image.

Activity

How would you describe the image of the organization to which you belong? (Just list as many words as you can think of that describe it.) What about the last organization you belonged to before that? In what ways were they different?

You might have written words like: formal/informal; successful/unsuccessful; lazy/hardworking; friendly/unfriendly; authoritarian/democratic; honest/dishonest; profitable/unprofitable; modern/old-fashioned; efficient/slipshod; getting better/getting worse.

Were the words you wrote down 'good' words or 'bad' words? What was it about the organization that prompted you to write the words you did? What caused you to see the organization like that? Do you think the chief executive/principal/headmaster would have agreed with your description? Would he have liked your description?

People say things like, 'It's a good employer', 'It's a successful company', 'It's go-ahead' or 'It's on the rocks', 'It's got no future', 'It's old fashioned.' How do they form these very powerful views about companies or organizations? How does an organization create an image in the eyes of its employees and the public and what can it do to improve its image? How, in other words, does it communicate?

Secondly, the title of this chapter contains the idea of speaking. But only people can speak – even computers that speak have to be programmed by people. So the title serves to remind us that when 'the company' speaks there must be real human beings, like you or me, behind the message. Before we look at what and how a company communicates, let's examine what this really means.

An attitude that is all too common tends to see companies or business organizations as 'things' which seem to have a life of their own quite beyond the power of any of us to influence. 'The company has decided. . .' 'In the interests of the company. . .' 'The company cannot agree to. . .' Statements like these reinforce our perception of companies and organizations as being something above and apart from ordinary human beings. And yet, companies and organizations are made up of people – ordinary human beings like you and me.

Now, it is true that there is something special which happens to a group of people; something which seems to give that group of people (be it a society, a small family firm, a large corporation or a local council) an identity of its own, a power somehow greater than the power of any of the individuals that constitute the group. It is also true that, in many cases, this special something is beneficial to the people that make up the organization; and, indeed, is something to be aimed at, by striving for agreement from its individual members on the aims and objectives of the organization and gaining cooperation from all its members in achieving these goals.

However, there also seem to be considerable disadvantages in the common view of 'the company' or 'the organization' as being some kind of *in*human being quite separate from the people of which it is made.

The major disadvantage seems to be that we the individual members, the human beings that make up the organizations, forget our individual responsibilities; forget that what we do does have an influence on the organization because we are each a part of it. Too frequently we may hear people making moving pleas that 'communication must be improved' or that 'channels of communication must be provided' as if these things were inanimate objects which have nothing to do with people, least of all them. How many people, when they are quick to complain that in their organization 'communication is non-existent' or 'no one ever tells you anything', ever stop to examine their own behaviour? Do they realize that they are part of that communication system? That they are one of the channels of communication? That they are equally responsible along with everyone else in that organization for improving communication? From the chief executive to the post-room clerk, from the commissionaire to the finance director, from the canteen manager to the salesman – everyone who works in an organization must realize that he is a part of the communication system, that he has a duty and an obligation to communicate as effectively as possible, before he can demand that everyone else should communicate more effectively.

Your responsibility

So when you hear people make statements like, 'No one ever tells you anything round here!' ask yourself whether *you* always pass on all the information you should – to your boss, to your subordinates or to your colleagues.

> *Activity*
>
> Think of a recent breakdown in communication in your own organization. What could you have done that might have helped prevent it?

Whatever job you do, whether you have a job or not, you inevitably talk and write and go to meetings of some kind or another, and so you have the same obligations to communicate effectively as the 'men at the top'. They may have slightly, or very, different responsibilities but you have *as much* responsibility to improve the quality of communication in your organization.

So, as we go on to look at company communication – why organizations communicate, what they communicate and how they communicate, try to keep asking yourself, How am I involved? How does this apply to me? How can I use this idea, or theory or principle to help me to communicate more effectively and so improve the communication system?

The organization's responsibility

Yes, of course the organization has a responsibility too. You may have been thinking while you read the last section, Well, that's all very well, but I can't do it all on my own; I'm only a very small cog in a very big machine! No one expects you to take responsibility for the efficiency of the whole communication system – unless you are the chief executive – but let's look at the system of which you are, or may become, a part.

Why organizations communicate

All organizations, regardless of size, products or services produced and geographical location, must communicate to survive. Just as we as human beings are being constantly bombarded by messages from the outside world to which we must react in order to satisfy our needs, so an organization is constantly receiving messages from its environment to which it must react if it is not to fail or die. Just as the nervous system in your body will react if the external temperature falls, causing your body temperature to fall so that you must search for some form of heat – a fire or extra clothing, so a change in the organization's environment – failure of the coffee crop in Tanzania, for example – may cause a rise in the cost of its raw materials to which it must react, perhaps by increasing the price of its finished products so that it can remain a profitable business. Just as you must constantly receive messages from the people around you to which you must react or they will soon stop communicating with you, so the organization must communicate with its immediate environment – its customers, competitors, suppliers and the general public – in the form of letters, telephone calls, receipts and bills, advertising, statistical returns and so on.

If we continue this analogy, then the people in the organization represent the nerve-endings all over the body receiving the messages from outside and passing them up to the brain – the decision-making centre of the organization (see the diagram on page 68); they are then responsible for sending messages back through the nervous system – the communication system – to the various parts of the organization, so that they will react appropriately:

> Information flow in a communication network is the lifeline of a business enterprise; it is like blood flowing through the veins and arteries of the body [Samuel Eilon].

Management needs information from outside the organization, and from within the organization, in order to make decisions and in order to influence others to then carry out those decisions – see the diagram on page 69. Let us look at each of the factors represented in this diagram in turn.

Information and communication

Anyone who has looked at a page of apparently meaningless statistics will know that there is a great difference between information and communication. The bare figures represent information, but communication has not taken place until those

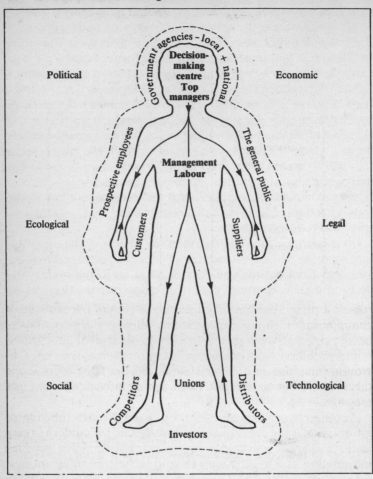

The organization communicates with its environment

figures have been interpreted; until the person looking at them has given them some meaning. As we have seen, a human being receives information but then interprets it in the light of his experience or expectations. So the business manager or decision-maker always has to base his decision on the way the information is interpreted both by him and by the person who

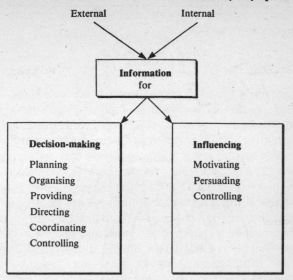

passed it on to him. This of course is the root of the problem of communication in any organization. Messages are continually being passed between people in a constant chain of information – interpretation – information – interpretation and so on. Obviously the more people there are in the chain the more scope there is for different interpretations and distortion of the original message.

Another important consideration when we are thinking of information is the sheer quantity that abounds in modern organizations. The now-everyday use of computers which produce information at a frightening rate and in frightening quantities, together with larger and larger organizations employing more and more people who all require information and produce information, has led to an information explosion. But not a communication explosion. One estimate suggests that a typical business executive can receive and absorb only one thousandth to one hundredth of the available information relevant to making decisions. It is therefore essential that the information going up the organization usually in the form of some kind of report, whether formal or informal, routine (often forms full of figures) or special investigative reports, oral or written, must be as clear and concise as possible.

Decision-making

Management's function, then, is to make decisions to solve problems. To do this, it must first of all determine what exactly it is trying to achieve: what its objectives are. It must then search for alternative solutions to the problem, compare and evaluate those alternatives, select the best alternative and carry out its decision. Throughout this process there is a constant flow of information to and from the decision-makers at every stage, and particularly at the last stage, because it is not enough to make a decision, arrange for it to be carried out and then forget all about it. There must be a system of feedback and control to check that the decision carried out has achieved the original purpose or objective. Modifications may be necessary, lessons may have been learned which will influence future decisions, creating new information which must be fed back into the system. Thus at each stage there is a constant inflow and outflow of information and the whole process (as represented in the diagram opposite) is a never-ending cycle.

Planning

In order for an organization to operate at all, its management must make plans which must be communicated in varying degrees of detail to the different levels and sections of the organization. The highest level of plans are the *objectives* which can be laid down for the organization as a whole, as well as for specific areas of operation like production, sales, marketing, industrial relations. These are the very long-term plans which state in general terms the overall philosophy. This statement of objectives must then be translated into *policies* which represent the courses of action to be followed in order to achieve the objectives. Policies are not usually so long-term and should be reasonably flexible in order to respond to influences both inside and outside the organization, but they are stated in fairly specific terms. In turn, policies are then translated into *procedures* – the

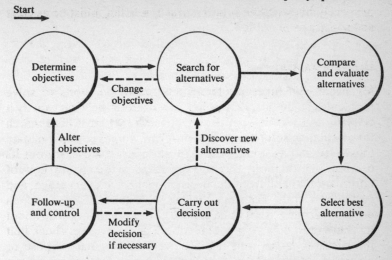

Start

Communication and the decision-making process

rules and procedures for the everyday regulation of all the activities which are necessary to achieve the overall objectives. Although they are stated in very precise terms they may be very frequently changed, almost on a day-to-day basis. Failure to communicate these objectives, policies and procedures to the right people at the right time may not only result in inefficiency in the operations of the organization, but also in low morale and dissatisfaction among the employees. Increasingly too, it is becoming advisable to *consult* more people at more levels in the organization when devising policies and establishing procedures than has traditionally been the practice of most managements.

Self-check

Let us assume that you want to travel to Glasgow from where you live (if you live in Glasgow, then you want to travel to London). Your *objective* is: to get to Glasgow (or London).

Now write down the policies which you will adopt in achieving your objective.

Now write down the procedures you will follow in order

to achieve your objective within the policy constraints you have set.

(If you can't tackle this question – don't worry, it is a difficult area to understand. Just look at the answer and use the suggestions as an example of the difference between objectives, policies and procedures.)

ANSWER

Objective: to get to Glasgow.
　Your policies might include:

- cost to be less than £55;
- journey time to be under eight hours (not including sleeping time, if you do the journey overnight);
- chances of travel sickness to be minimal;
- no limitation on luggage;
- easy transport of luggage door-to-door.

Procedures might be: Taxi to station, overnight sleeper to Glasgow, taxi to destination.

Organizing

Once the goals and policies have been established it is obviously necessary to devise a framework within which the necessary activities can take place. Although there are various approaches when designing an organization structure it is probably sufficient for our purposes to recognize that there are basically two kinds of organization: the *formal* organization and the *informal* organization.

　The *formal* organization is the one established by management with a clearly defined hierarchy of authority and areas of responsibility and is usually communicated by means of an organization chart (see opposite, top).

　From a communication point of view, it is obvious that with a tall, narrow organization structure like this, there can be very little direct communication between the chief executive and the people working at the lowest levels. Any message, whether it starts at the bottom to go up, or starts at the top to go down, is going to have to pass through so many people that it will be

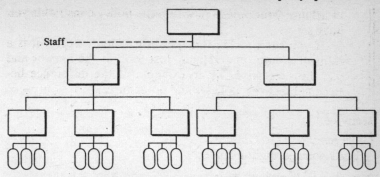

prone to numerous interpretations and distortions. Even in the chart below, where an obvious attempt has been made to reduce the number of levels in the hierarchy by producing a short and wide organization with only two levels of management, it is likely that there will be very little communication between departments across the organization.

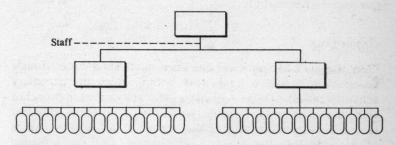

It is unlikely that one manager with thirteen different departments to oversee in this way is going to be able to communicate properly with all the people with whom he needs to keep in close contact.

It is therefore necessary to use other devices to encourage more participation, involvement and understanding by increasing upward, diagonal and horizontal communication as well as the more common downward communication. We will look at some of these devices in the next two chapters.

Activity

Could you draw an organization chart for your organization, or even your section? Try.

Is your organization chart tall and narrow, or short and wide? How many people report to each boss?

Research shows that the optimum number of people reporting to each boss is six. In some organizations there can, in practice, be any number from two to thirty. If a team of people are doing very similar jobs, in which they exercise a great deal of independent skill (e.g. skilled craftsmen, salesmen, typists), there may be as many as thirty; if there is a complicated process of management to operate there may be as few as four. The number of people any one person is directly responsible for is called the 'span of control'.

In any organization, despite the formal structure laid down by the management, there will also be an *informal* organization which will inevitably develop to cater for the social and emotional needs of employees. An organization chart will not show the pattern of informal relationships which employees automatically establish to meet the demands of particular circumstances. 'You're pally with the purchasing manager. Next time you see him at the club, have a quiet word with him and see if he can get hold of some widgets. I need them urgently and you know how long it'll take if I go through the proper channels!' is an example of behaviour which is very common in all organizations and which, if management does not take account of it, can be more powerful than the official structure and positively destructive of any systematic organization of work and decision-making.

Providing

Mechanisms also have to be set up and maintained so that the resources the organization needs to do its job – men, money and materials – are available when required.

Managers at all levels are responsible for forecasting their need for materials and, of course, staff. Even if there is a personnel department which looks after the recruitment of staff, managers at all levels should be involved in the selection process and also the training of staff in order to provide the right people with the right skills at the right time.

Directing

Closely allied to this last function is of course that of directing resources and, in particular, staff. Perhaps more than any other function, directing is the one which involves interpersonal relationships, involving as it does face-to-face interaction and the exchange of ideas, opinions, and views, as well as giving orders and directives.

Coordinating

Acquiring the right staff and materials and issuing instructions and orders is obviously only half the battle. The manager needs to be able to act as an overseer and guide, combining and integrating all the resources and activities under his control.

One writer has likened the role of the manager in these last three functions to that of the conductor of an orchestra:

> . . . endeavouring to maintain a melodious performance in which the contributions of the various instruments are coordinated and sequenced, patterned and paced, while the orchestra members are having personal difficulties, stage hands are moving music stands, alternating heat and cold are creating audience and instrument problems and the sponsor of the concert is insisting on irrational changes in the programme [Leonard Sayles, *Managerial Behaviour*, New York: Harper & Row, 1964].

Certainly directing and coordinating will put a manager's ability to communicate to the severest test – a test which despite a high level of technical knowledge and judgement, many a manager has failed.

Controlling

Just as we saw that it was necessary to follow up the result of a decision and feed back into the system lessons learned from this checking and monitoring, so the whole management process is continuous and circular in form. The function of control is the means by which the manager can measure whether objectives are being met and, if they are not, take corrective action. Control is the feedback system that informs the manager how well plans are being carried out. Feedback depends on information which may well come from a machine, requiring simply the resetting of some dials; but it may also come, as we have seen, from the organization's external environment, in the form of material shortages, competitors' lower prices, changes in legislation to do with employment law or safety regulations, for example. The control mechanism depends on management's constant readiness to receive the messages present inside and outside the organization and a readiness to respond quickly and appropriately.

Influencing

In order to carry out many of the functions we have just looked at, one of the things the manager will have to do is to influence people. By 'influence' we mean motivate, persuade or cause people to behave in a certain way. Gone are the days when a manager's word was law and he could order and direct without fear of being disobeyed. Nowadays, it is recognized that employee morale is one of the most essential ingredients in the success of any organization in achieving its objectives. Though he may still be responsible for issuing 'orders', the wise manager will realize that a more effective way of getting a job done would be to motivate a subordinate to *want* to do what is needed and to do it with the feeling that it is in his own best interests.

Activity

What is the main way in which businesses use information to influence people?

Perhaps a more obvious form of business persuasion is advertising: motivating and persuading people to buy its goods and services through television, radio, the press and posters. Nowadays, advertising has become a multimillion-pound industry. Many organizations will employ advertising agencies, skilled in the art of persuasion; but an organization can create a good or bad image in other ways than merely advertising. A manager who treats an interviewee in an offhand way, or appears unable to answer the candidate's questions about the organization or the industry in a helpful manner, is doing as much to create a bad image of the organization in the eyes of the public as the man who produces a poor product or service. The clerk who delays answering a customer's complaint, the telephone operator who deals with callers in an offhand inefficient manner, the commissionaire who is rude to a visitor – these, and there are probably countless other examples that you can think of from your own experience, can make the task of creating a good company image that much harder. Whilst the company may be spending thousands of pounds a year on advertising and public relations, there are secret forces at work in most organizations, unwittingly undermining these efforts: ordinary people like you and me, who do not regard their job as being anything to do with advertising or public relations, but who, through very typical human failings like laziness and thoughtlessness, are contributing unconsciously to the creation of a bad image:

> Visual communication (i.e. advertising using trademarks, colour, packaging, etc.) does not create a company or corporate image, but may play a large part in helping to establish and maintain it. The finest designers cannot correct or overcome poorly conceived and manufactured products, bad service, or overpricing [S. B. Rosenblatt *et al.*, *Communication in Business*, New Jersey: Prentice-Hall, 1977].

Review

1 Why should reports be as concise as possible? (You may feel that this is a difficult question to answer in relation to this chapter because there were no explicit reasons given in the text; but there were some clues, so think about it for a while before you try to answer.)
2 Why is information used in business?
3 List the main responsibilities of management for which information is needed or produced.

ANSWERS

1 Reports are probably the main method of passing information up the organization. However, if a report is unclear, incomplete or ambiguous, or if the writer has been unwilling to be honest about problems and difficulties which exist, the actions taken or the decisions made on the basis of the report may well turn out to be incorrect or costly. Nevertheless, we have also seen that the average manager is subjected to a never-ending stream of information – facts, opinions and ideas – most of which he cannot absorb. Reports should therefore be seen as a method of condensing much of this information into a form and length which the manager can cope with. But how concise? Henry Ford used to refuse to read any memo or report longer than a single page. ICI instructs its executive directors to return to the sender any communication longer than two pages. It will obviously depend on the purpose of the report, but the ability to summarize competently and write complete but concise reports are invaluable skills. (See Chapter 11, 'Acquiring and organizing your material'.)

2 An organization uses information from outside and inside

• to make the decisions necessary to keep it functioning, and in order to influence others to carry out those decisions.

3 Decision-making consists of: planning, organizing, providing, directing, coordinating and controlling.

  Influencing consists of: motivating, persuading and controlling.

Activity

Try writing a short plan (including a statement of your objective and your policies, and not more than twelve actions or procedures) for conducting a campaign to get your local council to provide a zebra crossing, or demolish a dangerous building, for instance.

5 | Why don't they tell us what's happening?

The American Telephone and Telegraph (AT&T) Company has more shareholders, more employees and more assets than any other business in the world. It is second in sales only to General Motors Corporation. It is significant that the world's largest business is in the communication field but perhaps it is not surprising that with all its technical know-how, its vast financial resources, its equipment and complicated telecommunication systems, it nevertheless recognizes that communication between people within the organization poses a problem.

In an issue of the house magazine of one of its subsidiaries, the Bell Telephone System, one article begins:

> Within the greatest communication organization in the world we are hurt and puzzled by a seeming communication failure – the problem of talking with our employees. The fact that we are perhaps no worse off than any other comparable organization (perhaps even better) is small comfort. In a corporation of more than one million population, such a gap can be destructive. We should perhaps replace the omnipresent safety plaque with one that reads, COMMUNICATE OR PERISH.

Self-check

Why is communication so important in this – or in any – organization? Jot down any reasons you can think of.

It would be easy to suggest that the reason that this organization finds internal communication a problem is because of its vast size. But there are other very significant reasons, which this chapter will explore together with the kind of information people want and need.

The attitudes and needs of employees are changing: they want to be more fully informed about company policies and plans.

Management, too, has increasing needs for effective communication: the pressures of competition are increasing, government regulations are increasing, organizations are growing more complex and society is demanding the right to control the activities of organizations. Whether a commercial, industrial or government organization is large or small, it must establish effective communication channels to ensure that those who must make decisions know what is taking place throughout the organization, and that those who must carry out those decisions know what they should be doing and, above all, why.

Self-check

In what directions is communication important in an organization?

In order to help us discuss the complex web of communication activity that is going on inside any organization, we usually classify this communication in terms of the directions in which it flows:

- upwards – for subordinates to keep their superiors informed about their work;
- downwards – so that everyone in the organization knows what is happening and why;
- sideways – so that people are aware of what their colleagues in other departments are doing.

We also often talk of 'official' or 'formal' communication – that which is supposed to be taking place – and 'unofficial' or 'informal' communication – that which is actually taking place.

Upward communication

In the last chapter we discovered why management needs information and how it uses this information. It is obvious, then, that to make the best decisions and plans for the organization, top management must encourage all employees at all levels to communicate upwards, so that they are as well informed as possible.

However, common observation suggests that in fact there is a very substantial tendency for subordinates in relationship with superiors to conceal and distort their real feelings, opinions, beliefs and problems. In ancient Greece, the bearer of bad news was killed. Nowadays, we still tend to behave as if something similar might befall us. If we have bad news or an unpopular message to convey we are very likely to tone down the seriousness of what we have to say, somehow believing that if we do not, we will in some way be directly blamed for what we are only reporting. This tendency may well explain the frequent complaint from managers, particularly senior managers, faced with imminent catastrophe like a strike or a complete machine failure, that they are never told how serious a problem is until it is virtually too late to do anything about it.

An example of concealing problems or difficulties for a different reason might be the supervisor who fears that if he admits that he has a problem to his boss, it somehow suggests that he is not as capable at his job as he should be.

As for concealing or distorting our real feelings and opinions, we must all be able to think of examples from our own experience where we have watered down our own real opinion to an extent that we have almost been guilty of lying rather than face the difficulty of disagreeing with a superior – be it a boss, a teacher or anyone we regard as being superior in status. It takes a lot of courage to say bluntly: 'I think that's a rotten idea!' or even words to that effect, tactfully.

Self-check

Can you think of any reasons which might explain why we have this fear, when common sense tells us that honesty would be more helpful both to us and to the superior?

One reason put forward to explain this concealment and distortion is that subordinates believe that if they admit their real opinions, feelings and difficulties, their superiors may penalize them in some way. The reason for this fear of being penalized is that in most organizations it is the subordinate's boss who probably has the most influence over the things that matter to the subordinates – financial rewards, promotion prospects, job satisfaction and so on. Certainly there is a great deal of evidence, from studies that have been carried out, to suggest that the greater the influence a superior has over a subordinate's pay and promotion prospects, for example, the more the subordinate will tend to hide or distort his real problems and opinions.

This tendency would therefore seem to discourage the very kind of upward communication on which good management and decision-making depends.

How can upward communication be encouraged? What can a superior do to reduce the probability that his subordinates will conceal or distort their real feelings, opinions and difficulties?

As we have seen with other communication problems, just being aware that this tendency to filter upward communication exists is a step in the right direction. Beyond this, it seems necessary for the manager to think of ways in which he might reduce his subordinates' conscious or unconscious fear of being penalized if they do try to be honest in admitting their feelings and problems. He needs to create a relationship or climate in which they feel they will not be penalized. How can he do this?

Self-check

Can you think of two things a manager might do to encourage his subordinates to be more open with him?

REMOVE THE SUPERIOR'S RESPONSIBILITY FOR PAY AND PROMOTION

Well, obviously one way would be to reduce the degree of control and influence that the superior has over the personal goals – like pay and promotion – of the subordinate. But this is really rather an unrealistic alternative, given the traditional authority structure in most modern organizations which gives the boss power to sack, block promotion and block salary increases. This, therefore, is not a very practical suggestion.

REWARD OPEN COMMUNICATION

A more practical course of action, but still very difficult, would be for the manager to start rewarding openness and honesty rather than penalizing them. He could begin by telling his subordinates that he expects them to have difficulties and to disagree with him from time to time. However, as you may guess, words will not necessarily be enough. If the subordinate accepts this invitation, but on the first occasion that he disagrees with his boss he is met with hostility, then he will quickly realize that the boss does not really mean what he says and will revert to telling the boss what he actually wants to hear rather than what he says he wants to hear. The manager must therefore back up his words with actions. When a subordinate disagrees with him or admits a difficulty, he must react in such a way that the subordinate finds the situation rewarding or at least non-threatening. This will mean that he must sometimes suppress his natural reactions because any expression of hostility or impatience will be perceived by the subordinate as a threat or a penalty which will prevent honesty in the future.

SET AN EXAMPLE

A second alternative, and one which would support the last suggestion, is for the boss to behave in the way he wants his subordinates to behave. In others words he uses himself as an example by admitting his difficulties when talking to his subordinates: taking them into his confidence by revealing his own feelings and opinions about his own problems. The more a boss discloses his own feelings and difficulties both to his subordinates and to his own superior, the more willing his subordinates will be to disclose theirs.

To sum up then:

> Managing upward communication involves building a relationship with subordinates in which disclosure is encouraged and rewarded. It must be a supportive relationship – one in which subordinates feel that the superior will not take advantage of them if they fully speak their minds. For full disclosure to occur they must know that they can express their feelings, difficulties and opinions without fear of reprisal. They must look upon the superior as a source of help rather than as all powerful judge [Gary Gemmill, 'Managing Upward Communication', *Personnel Journal*, February 1980].

Of course, you do not have to be a manager or even a prospective manager to try out these techniques. They can be just as effective and rewarding in any personal relationship. A willingness to confide or to seek help depends on trust that the disclosure will not be taken advantage of by the confidant.

Downward communication

In the last section we looked at the problem of ensuring that the decision-makers get the best possible information available to enable them to make the best decisions in terms of planning, organizing and controlling the activities of the organization.

However, top-level managers are not the only ones who require information in order to function effectively. As we saw, every level of supervision in an organization needs to encourage upward communication. But every level of the organization (except perhaps the very top level), right down to operating employees who probably have no supervisory responsibility, needs information to be passed *down* the organization. People work better when they know exactly what their superiors want from them, what their duties, responsibilities and privileges are. They need to know what is expected of them – not necessarily in minute detail (this will depend on the circumstances), but certainly in general terms. For this reason, managers and supervisors must issue instructions and directives, and statements on policy and procedures.

Self-check

What do people want to know? Can you suggest three types of information that all employees need.

Generally speaking all employees need three types of information: personal information related to their employment in the organization, such as pay and conditions; job information so that they know what they are supposed to do and how they are supposed to do it; and finally what we might call company, organization or group information, in other words information about the group of which they are a part – what its objectives and policies are, what it does and how well it does it.

Self-check

Without any more help from me, try to list under the three headings: 'personal', 'job' and 'organization' as many things as you can think of that all employees might need or want to know. To start you off I have given one example under each heading.

Personal	*Job*	*Organization*
1 Pay and rewards	**1** How it is to be performed	**1** Current, new and proposed products

Your first two lists will obviously not look exactly like those below and you may have put some things under different headings. This does not matter since in some cases the information could probably come under more than one heading.

Personal

1   Pay and rewards.
2   Pension and health benefits.
3   Holidays and sick-leave entitlements.
4   Job security.
5   Future employment prospects.
6   Opportunities for promotion.
7   Training opportunities – on-the-job and off-the-job.
8   Health, canteen and rest facilities.
9   Union and grievance procedures.
10   Hours of work and meal breaks.
11   Discipline procedure.

Job

1   How, when and where it is to be performed.
2   The rate and quality of work required.
3   Duties and responsibilities.
4   To whom he is responsible (and *for* whom he is responsible, if relevant).
5   What other people in his section and/or department do and how his job fits in.

6   Personal performance results.
7   Section/department performance results.
8   Safety regulations.

Most organizations nowadays recognize their responsibilities for communicating the information listed in these two categories and will probably use a combination of staff handbook, induction training programmes and the normal working relationship between supervisor and subordinate. It is however worth noting here that many organizations assume, simply because they have set up mechanisms for conveying this information, that effective communication is automatically taking place. Once again it is a question of monitoring systems at frequent intervals to ensure that the information is up to date, relevant and reaching the right people at the right time. For instance, many organizations discover on investigation that their induction programmes are run so infrequently that many people have never been on one; and those who have experienced it, either too soon or too late for it to have been of any real value. Job descriptions are also an effective method of laying down the procedures and responsibilities of a job, but they too can become rapidly out of date if not reviewed regularly, and are often written in such general terms as to be virtually meaningless. As one employee commented: 'not worth the paper they're written on!' Whatever mechanisms an organization provides, it will of course probably fall to the supervisor to ensure that much of the personal and job information an employee needs is effectively communicated, and he should strive to create the kind of atmosphere in which employees have no qualms about asking questions and requesting further explanations.

How much should we tell them?

It is the third type of information – often referred to as 'company communication' – which presents the real problems and is fraught with controversy. What should we tell them? How much should we tell them? Who should tell them? – these are only some of the problems which cause so much heart-searching. When it comes to controversial and sensitive issues like redundancies, layoffs, takeover bids, loss or profit made, many managements skate round the problems by saying: 'Well, they're not really interested anyway', or 'Well, they won't understand it.'

In fact, all the research that has been carried out (and there has been a great deal during the past thirty years or so) confirms that employees are vitally interested in most of the issues traditionally regarded as the prerogative of top management. They want to know the goals and objectives of the organization, what the organization's policies are on various things like sales, pricing and research, and what the financial situation of the organization is. They recognize that these things, far from being irrelevant to them, will have an inevitable effect on those matters which are closest to their heart: job security, pay and promotion prospects and so on.

One study showed that employees could put to best use these three types of information:

- anything which gave them better insight into their work, and its relation to the work of others in the firm;
- anything which gave them a sense of belonging to the firm;
- any information which improved their sense of status and importance as individuals in the firm.

Bearing these things in mind, our list of topics to be included under 'organization' might include these:

Organization
1 Current, new and proposed products (and, most important, how and where these are used, particularly in the case of a company which makes parts or components which are installed into other products by other organizations).
2 History and development of the organization.
3 Position in the industry – compared with other firms in terms of sales, productivity, profit, rate of return on capital employed.
4 Organization structure.
5 Names and some information about executives.
6 Changes in management personnel – comings and goings, but more important, changes in responsibility.
7 Financial position.

8 Sales trend, earnings, growth.
9 Research activities.
10 Advertising programme and marketing policy.
11 Relationship with union(s).
12 Company policies – on safety, industrial relations, etc.
13 Expansion plans (or contraction plans – usually a very sensitive issue).
14 Relations with the community.
15 Official views on current issues – pollution, energy conservation, etc.

This is obviously not an exhaustive list but it does provide the basis for giving employees a 'better insight into their work, and its relation to the work of others in the firm' and for giving them 'a sense of belonging to the firm'. Certainly if there is a willingness to communicate on controversial or sensitive issues, the organization is saying to the employee: 'We recognize you as an important part of the organization and as an individual. We, therefore, want to share with you important news which concerns the organization and therefore concerns you.' Thus the very act of communicating is likely to 'improve their status and importance as individuals in the firm'.

Why won't people pass information down?

Before we look at the methods available to an organization for communicating the kind of information that people need and want to know, we should first consider how people – and it is mainly managers who must accept the responsibility – can be persuaded and encouraged to communicate, to share their knowledge, discuss the issues affecting the organization.

Lack of knowledge

. . .the problem of communication between managements and shop floor frequently stems from a failure of communications *within* management. When front line managers are accused of poor communications the truth is often that they cannot communicate because they don't know much themselves [Speech given by HRH The Prince of Wales at the Parliamentary and Scientific Committee Luncheon, Wednesday 21 February 1978].

One of the reasons people may not pass on information is, of course, that they themselves have not been communicated with. However, if an organization can establish a climate in which everyone is *expected* to communicate downwards properly, starting with the man at the top, then at least this should help to ensure that the supervisor at the bottom of the management chain is sufficiently informed himself to be able to pass on the information. Later in this chapter we will look at how a company communication programme can encourage downward communication.

Lack of confidence

Another reason why people may not be eager to take their part in the communicating process is that they are simply not sufficiently skilled themselves at communicating: they don't know *how* to do it, or rather, they feel they don't have the confidence to do it. Part of any organization's responsibility for improving downward communication must be to provide the employee with communication training which covers the processes which we are exploring in this book; training which includes not only the skills involved – more effective reading, writing, speaking and listening – but also some guidance on the kinds of methods which are available with which he can communicate, from audiovisual aids – the hardware of communication – to more effective use of meetings, noticeboards, memos, interviews and so on.

Lack of guidance

Above all, perhaps the main reason managers do not communicate as often or as much as they might is because they are not sure what to communicate, how much to communicate, and in what way to communicate.

Let's look at an example. The company has just acquired another company or site, or a new piece of equipment, or a more advanced production method. Should the manager explain to his staff what the company hopes to do with this new acquisition? Left to his own devices, one manager may decide to tell his staff as much as he knows, as honestly as he can; another manager may choose to pass on only some of the facts 'because otherwise they will get involved in things that aren't their concern'; a third manager may decide to say nothing because he feels it is too risky. The result in a case like this will be rumours – to explain the situation and fulfil everyone's need to know; these rumours will inevitably distort and exaggerate the truth and lead to anxious, unhappy, possibly disgruntled employees. In other words, a recipe for strikes, grievances, work slowdowns and, at the very least, poor morale.

The grapevine

If an organization does not accept its responsibility to communicate down the line, or if some managers in the chain of communication cause a blockage because they don't want to or cannot communicate the things people want to know about, then people will find a way to get answers to their questions. Rumours will fly: those people who know a little will pass it on and, as the story passes from person to person, it will, as usual, get distorted and exaggerated until the message people are getting is the wrong message. The company will suffer because the rumour leads to uncertainty, uncertainty leads to fear, and fear to the inability to work effectively. If people are anxious about their future, their need to find out exactly what is happening will take over, and become more important to them than their jobs.

Management must recognize that if they won't communicate, someone will. And the grapevine (opposite) is the fastest, most efficient form of communication in any organization, but particularly in an organization which fails in its formal duty to communicate in an honest and open manner.

The need for a communication policy

The organization's management must beat the grapevine at its own game. It must have a consistent communication policy in all divisions, branches and locations. In other words, it must have a *philosophy of communication* which, like the grapevine, spreads throughout the organization. Just as an organization needs policies for marketing, finance, personnel and industrial relations

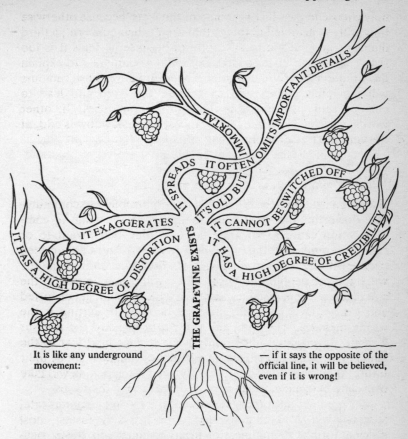

IT OFTEN OMITS IMPORTANT DETAILS

IT'S OLD BUT IMMORTAL

IT SPREADS

IT EXAGGERATES

IT CANNOT BE SWITCHED OFF

IT HAS A HIGH DEGREE OF DISTORTION

IT HAS A HIGH DEGREE OF CREDIBILITY

THE GRAPEVINE EXISTS

It is like any underground movement:

— if it says the opposite of the official line, it will be believed, even if it is wrong!

and production as we have seen, so too it should have policies for communication. These policies will provide evidence to everyone that the organization is serious in its intention to communicate; that those at the top are behind it. Stated policies for communication will also provide guidance to everyone on what is to be communicated, how much is to be communicated and how and by whom it is to be communicated.

Self-check

Can you suggest how people are likely to behave if they are not given this guidance on what, how much, how and by whom information should be communicated.

When people don't know what the organization's philosophy on communication is, they will play safe with the result that:

● there will be little or no discussion of sensitive or controversial issues (industrial relations problems, salaries, promotions, layoffs, etc.);
● the communication that does take place will concern the superficial and pleasant but innocuous areas – marriages, retirements, holidays, social activities and possibly the state of the company's industry;
● similar issues will be handled differently throughout the organization.

So if an organization genuinely wants to improve its communication climate – to establish an atmosphere of truth and honesty which will not only encourage everyone in the organization to discuss openly and frankly the things people need to know, but make people feel that communication is just as much a part of their job as running a production line, keeping the accounts, buying materials, promoting the goods or services or whatever – it must start by publishing its philosophy so that everyone knows what the organization's attitude is to the business of communicating.

A philosophy of communication will obviously differ from organization to organization and will depend on the aims and objectives of the particular organization, but it will obviously need to contain a positive intention to communicate as a matter of course on those topics suggested on page 87. However, to be a true philosophy it will need to go further than a mere list and might include points stated rather like this:

● Inform all employees about organization goals, objectives, plans and directions.
● Inform all employees about current activities of the organization.

- Inform all employees of the various aspects of sensitive, controversial and negative issues affecting the organization.
- Encourage a regular flow of communication up, down and across the organization – two-way communication.
- Guarantee that all employees get a regular periodic chance to discuss their performance with their superior.
- Hold meetings which will explore important areas and where free expression is encouraged.
- Communicate important events and situations as quickly as possible to all employees.

You can see that a philosophy like this begins to give people a very clear indication of how far the organization expects them to go. Words like 'all employees', 'regular', 'guarantee', 'two-way communication', 'free discussion' and 'communicate as quickly as possible' are all keywords in helping all managers in all sections of an organization to know what, when and how to communicate. A checklist might be even more specific:

- Be frank.
- Be timely.
- Be clear.
- Be constantly aware of your employees' needs and wants.

Self-check

When might it be sensible for a manager *not* to communicate?

WHEN NOT TO COMMUNICATE

Of course, encouraging managers to be frank does not necessarily mean that everything should necessarily be communicated to everyone. There will be occasions when there must be some constraint, some limits. Telling everyone in an organization right at the outset that there is a possibility of getting such-and-such an order might well mean that competitors get to hear about it. This could be harmful and against everyone's best interests. Obviously then, some issues will need careful judgement at the time, but top management again should be prepared to give specific guidance to those below. Even if a decision is made not to say anything for the time being then employees should at least be given the reasons why some facts are held back. Employees arc reasonable people and will usually be prepared to accept that there are good reasons for information being withheld if there is a feeling of mutual trust; but that atmosphere of trust and honesty can only be gained by evidence that top management is prepared to pay more than lip-service to improving communication. It must be seen to be demanding good communication from everyone right down the line, to be showing by its actions that it is prepared to be open and honest, quick to give employees all the information they need when they need it, and willing to support its policies with the funds, the time and the personnel necessary to carry out these policies.

Review

1 What factors discourage subordinates from being open with their managers?
2 What sorts of action can bosses take to encourage openness and therefore effective upward communication?
3 What are the three main types of information employees need?
4 What are the main reasons why people may be unwilling to pass information *down* the line?
5 Why can management not afford to ignore the grapevine?
6 What points might a communication philosophy include?

ANSWERS

1 • Fear that if he admits he has a problem, his boss may think he is not as capable at his job as he should be.
  • Fear that if he is honest and gives his real opinion the boss may disagree and become hostile.
  • Fear that if he admits his real opinions, feelings and difficulties the boss may penalize him in some way.

- Knowledge that his boss has the power to sack him, block a pay rise or block promotion.

All these factors are based on a fear of what might happen, and will therefore discourage a subordinate from communicating truthfully. If, of course, the manager actually does do any of these things, then the subordinate's fear is justified and he will be even less likely to be honest and open.

2 He could start by telling his subordinates that he expects them to tell him about their difficulties, and to disagree with him from time to time.

When they are honest and open, he must reward their behaviour by accepting their disagreements without becoming hostile or defensive; he must help them with their problems and difficulties, not criticize them or hold it against them in some way. In other words, he must back up his words with actions, so that his subordinates find that honesty really is the best policy.

Lastly, he could try setting an example by behaving in the way he expects them to behave; in other words, taking them into his confidence by revealing his own feelings, opinions and difficulties.

3 Employees need *personal*, *job* and *organization* information.

4 Lack of knowledge, lack of confidence and lack of guidance may all discourage people from passing information down the line.

5 The grapevine cannot be ignored because:
- it exists;
- it cannot be switched off;
- it is old but immortal;
- it has a high degree of distortion;
- it has a high degree of credibility;
- it exaggerates;
- it spreads; and
- it is the fastest, most efficient form of communication but, like any underground movement, if it says the opposite of the official line, it will be believed, even if it is wrong!

6 See pages 92–3.

Activity

Find out in your organization if there is:

1 a written communication policy;
2 someone at top level who is responsible for internal communication;
3 a staff handbook;
4 an induction course for new staff;
5 written job descriptions for all jobs (or only some – if so, which ones?).

Start by asking the personnel manager if he can help you.

Want to read more?

C. Northcote Parkinson and Nigel Rowe, *Communicate – Parkinson's Formula for Business Survival*, Pan Books, 1979.

6 | The tools of the trade

A large manufacturing company had suffered from strikes, working to rule and overtime bans for years. Eventually, following a crippling strike which almost put the company into receivership, it was decided to launch a communications policy. A budget was allocated and a director made responsible full time. Within a few months, regular filmed reports on the company's progress were being shown to employees, a whole series of new factual publications about many aspects of the company's business was being distributed, and a family of joint committees at junior and senior level was dealing with such issues as the five-year business plan, and discussing such subjects as where to produce which products.

Less than a year after the communication policy had begun, the union convener who had led all the major strikes was quoted in the national press as saying, 'If I'd known a few years ago what I know now about how the company works and how its been doing I'd never had led all those strikes.'

In the last chapter, we saw that in order to improve communications in an organization it is necessary to encourage information to flow in all directions, not just upwards – though this is essential for good decision-making – but also downwards and horizontally across the organization. In this way people will generally have a better idea of what is going on in their organization and why; and above all, how they fit into the overall scheme of things and how they can therefore best contribute.

This chapter will look at the main methods organizations can use to communicate with the public and their employees, and at the advantages and disadvantages of each. It will also provide some tips on how to use each successfully, and a note towards the end on the dangers of leaving people out of the communication process.

You will probably be familiar with some of these methods already. So you may prefer, rather than giving each the same amount of attention, to skim quickly through the chapter, trying each of the activities perhaps, but only paying particular attention to those types of communication which you have not properly examined before. You can then use the chapter as a directory, referring back to specific methods of communication whenever you feel it would be helpful.

In any large organization, whether there is a communications manager or not, there should be one person responsible for ensuring that the communication policy is being carried out. He should have various specialists available to help in executing certain parts of the policy, for example a personnel manager and a public relations manager. However, as we have seen, whatever role you play in the organization you too will inevitably have a part to play in the communication system. You will not only be on the receiving end of much of the communication, but you will probably also be involved from time to time, and in one way or another, in creating communication which will go to other people.

You may be a manager who sends memos and letters, writes reports, drafts notices, chairs meetings to pass on and discuss news of current activities; you may be a member of the public relations staff and help to compose advertisements, posters or news releases; you may be a secretary who types memos, letters, reports, material for company newspapers or magazines, or agendas for meetings; you may be a supervisor in a production department who must introduce new members of staff to the department and the company, brief staff on instructions and procedures, or make announcements on the public address system. Whatever you do, you will probably have some experience of the methods of communication used in most organizations.

Communicating with the public

Any organization is in constant communication with the public – customers, suppliers, government agencies and so on – by means of letters, reports, forms and telephone calls. As we have seen, this communication serves a very significant function in creating and maintaining an organization's chosen image in the eyes of its public, but these methods of communication are explored in more detail in separate chapters elsewhere in the book and in its companion, *The Business of Communicating*.

What we are more concerned with here is the kind of communication that tells the public about the organization, its products, its activities, its interests and, of course, its views.

|| *Self-check*
||
|| List as many different methods as possible that an organization can use to communicate with the outside world.

The ways in which an organization communicates with its external environment are almost too numerous to mention, as you may have discovered. They would certainly deserve a book all to themselves. Since the functions of public relations, advertising and marketing are now well-established professions in their own right, there are many books already on the subject of external communications.

However, no book on communication in business would be complete without at least a brief word on the main methods of communicating with the public.

In fact, there is a close link between what a company says internally to its employees and what it says externally to the general public. After all, its employees are also members of the public. Their view of the organization they work for will be conditioned not only by what they hear officially when at work, but also by what they read in the newspapers and see and hear on television and the radio. The credibility of the mass media is very high: people are more likely to believe what they read in the local press about the company they work for than what they read in the company newspaper. Many surveys have shown that there is a great deal of scepticism about house newspapers – they are seen as propaganda.

The methods which companies use to communicate to the world outside include:

- press releases $\Big\}$
- press conferences

national newspapers
local newspapers
national television and radio
local radio
magazines

- offers of press interviews with executives
- advertising in the mass media
- leaflets and brochures
- films
- sponsorships
- exhibitions
- circular letters to MPs and local councillors
- annual report
- open days

Employee communication

Employees are just as likely as anyone else to receive information about their organization from these methods of communicating with the public; but some of these methods can be used specifically within an organization as a means of communicating the kind of information we discussed in the last chapter.

Self-check

What would you say is the biggest limitation on the effectiveness of these methods of communication? There is one characteristic that is common to all of them.

Yes, they are all one-way methods of communication and therefore the company has no real way of determining how effectively it has communicated its message.

Self-check

How many of the methods listed above could a company use for communicating with its employees? (Tick them.) Can you think of any other methods it could use? Which of these methods only communicate with particular groups of people?

See how many of these methods you identified:

TWO-WAY: UPWARDS AND DOWNWARDS

Briefing groups (1)*
Interviews (3)
Walking the floor (4)
Employee councils (5)
Consultative committees (5)
Collective bargaining negotiations (5)
Induction programmes (6)
The grapevine (7)
Response systems (8)

HORIZONTAL OR SIDEWAYS

Reports (10)
Memos (11)
Telephone
House journals (12)

ONE-WAY: DOWNWARDS

Mass meetings (2)
Notices, posters and public address systems (9)
Briefing meetings (1)
House journals and newspapers (12)
Bulletins (13)
Company handbook (14)
Annual report to employees (15)
Pay packet inserts (16)
Personal letters (17)
Exhibitions and films (22)

ONE-WAY: UPWARDS

Suggestion scheme (18)
Union newsletter (19)
Response to surveys (20)
Industrial action (21)
Labour turnover (21)
Absenteeism and lateness (21)

Activity

Which methods has your employer or college used?

Since this is a fairly comprehensive list of the current methods, your organization may not use them all. You may like to consider whether you think it uses too few methods or the wrong methods, and whether you think it ought to consider being more adventurous.

* The numbers after each method refer to the order they are dealt with later in this chapter, so you can use this list as an index.

Activity

Looking at the list above, through which of these channels
do you prefer to receive information? (Write them down.)
    Which do you like least?

In Chapter 3 we looked at some of the advantages and
disadvantages of the major categories of communication.

Self-check

For each of the channels or methods listed above list *all*
the advantages and disadvantages you can think of from
your point of view.
    When you have done that, try listing the advantages and
disadvantages from management's point of view. (If you
are a manager, think of your own boss and everyone
above him as 'management'.)

Now read on. As you read the sections on each form of
communication, compare the advantages and disadvantages set
out with those which you listed.

Face-to-face communication

There really is nothing to beat direct face-to-face communication. It allows a genuine two-way exchange of information and
views to take place. It allows really up-to-date news to be
presented. It is personal. It is direct. But it can go badly wrong.
To be effective, not only does the communicator (the transmitter) have to be well prepared, well informed and a competent
speaker, but the audience has to be willing to listen, ready to
believe what they are told, and feel sufficiently confident to ask
questions and request explanations of points they have not
understood. Let us look at some of the face-to-face methods
currently in use in business:

1 Briefing groups

The team leader (foreman, section leader, office supervisor, managing director) holds a short meeting with those who report directly to him. The military have relied on this method since time immemorial. When it works well it has all the advantages of face-to-face two-way communication, but it can suffer from many of the hidden dangers (see Chapter 3) and therefore often goes wrong in industry. It goes wrong because the team leader is often not, himself, well enough informed either to tell his team anything which they do not know already, or to cope with many of their questions. This is often because he has not been briefed by *his* boss. If you follow the management chain back, you will find that the person who has to start the briefing process is the managing director. If he does not set the example, no amount of exhortation will induce managers and supervisors at lower levels to brief. Another defect of the briefing system (often called the cascade system) is that it is ephemeral: it requires reinforcement with a written bulletin or notice.

2 Mass meetings

Some companies have experimented with holding large meetings: 300 or more employees in a canteen, addressed by a senior manager, perhaps using visual aids, like slides or a film. If the senior manager is a good speaker these meetings can be highly effective. They let everyone see and hear their ultimate boss, who may spend much of his time away from the business talking to customers and suppliers. And today, every manager should learn to speak effectively: it is a tool of his trade. It is, however, difficult to make even the best-handled mass meeting a genuinely two-way event.

3 Interviews

Obviously the personal one-to-one interview is the best way of dealing with individual problems and queries; but perhaps because they are so time-consuming, formal interviews tend not to be used as much as they might and are reserved for the exceptional problem. The main types of interview with employees therefore tend to be these:

Grievance interview A chance for an employee to air complaints about his job, conditions of work, other employees or other dissatisfactions which are bothering him. Grievances will undermine morale and the sooner they are dealt with the better.

Disciplinary interview Used when it is necessary to reprimand an employee for some breach of rules or code of behaviour, e.g. lateness, absenteeism, disobeying instructions, disregarding factory act requirements or safety rules and regulations.

Appraisal interview Often not popular with subordinates or managers mainly because they are very difficult to conduct well and can therefore create conflict. Their main purpose is to appraise the subordinate's performance on the job, identify areas of difficulty and agree on future action by the subordinate. They therefore need to be carried out in an objective and friendly manner which will encourage the subordinate to improve.

Termination interview Any company will be concerned when an employee decides to leave, not just because it will be necessary to select and train someone else, but because of the reasons that lie behind the resignation. However, if these reasons can be elicited in an interview before the employee leaves, they may indicate a need for action to remove the causes of dissatisfaction which may be encouraging labour turnover.

Activity

Find out if your organization operates a performance appraisal system. Are people generally satisfied with it? If not, what are their reasons?

4 Walking the floor

Every boss should know his team; he should go out to where ˙y are and meet them. With a section of twelve machinists, it's easy. With a motorcar company with several plants employing 100,000 staff, it is a daunting task, and unfortunately many managers seem to think it is not worth the time. Yet I know a general manager of a plant employing 20,000 people who walks round and talks to some of his people for the first hour of every morning he is at his factory. He reckons to talk to everyone once in ten years this way. They adore him because he takes the trouble to do it. In fact, if he stopped tomorrow, his reputation for walking the floor would be undimmed ten years from now.

5 Councils, committees and collective bargaining

I've lumped these together because they are not really channels of communication with employees. They only communicate with the representatives who are elected to attend council or consultative committee meetings, and with the shop stewards who bargain over wages and conditions for their members. In theory, these representatives should communicate with their constituents; in practice, some do and some do not. Shop stewards certainly do when the subject of the meeting is a wage claim. But all these meetings are not really channels of communication; they are rather a part of the representative system.

6 Induction programmes

Induction is not in itself a communication medium, but it is mentioned here because it plays a crucial role in communication with employees. The induction programme should get new members of staff as far as possible to the same level of knowledge as existing staff about their employer. If the induction programme does not succeed in doing this, the communication gap is in effect being widened every time a new employee is recruited.

Activity

If you are a comparatively new employee, try to list the things you learned when you were inducted into your company, and then list, separately, the things you have picked up since. You may be surprised how little you learned during your induction period.

7 The grapevine

'If you don't tell people the truth, they will invent the truth for themselves.' Of course the grapevine which exists in every organization does not carry only invented truth – although I do know a shop steward who reckons that if he wants to find out something that management doesn't want to tell him, he just plants a rumour about it in the grapevine, and waits to see whether management denies it. The grapevine can be highly distortive, or highly accurate. It depends on the nature of the information. You can be sure that the fact that the chairman kissed the canteen girl on the cheek on her birthday will be boosted by rumour into a grand passion, with the chairman caught with her in the company limousine by his wife. But you can equally guarantee that a boardroom leak that the annual pay offer is to be held down to two per cent will go right round the company totally unaltered.

Written communication

Written communication, with one notable exception, is one-way. It can be downward, in the form of a newspaper, notice-board or report, or upward, in the form of letters to the editor or response to a survey questionnaire. We shall begin by looking at the notable exception.

8 Response systems

This is an idea which is so simple and so effective that it is astonishing that it has not been more widely used. At its simplest, forms are made freely and permanently available to all employees on which they can write a question about the company's operations. The employee puts the form in a special collection box, from where it goes to a central administrator who approaches the appropriate person in the company to obtain an answer. The rule of the system requires an answer within one week, and the administrator is given sufficient muscle to extract it. Having obtained it, he sends the answer to the employee who asked the question. Periodically a summary of all the questions and answers is published.

Note: this is not the same as a suggestion scheme, which tends to be one-way (upwards).

9 Noticeboards

This is the traditional method of getting a message quickly and cheaply to a large number of people, but it only works if those people want to receive the message. Most school students will cluster around the noticeboard to find out who has made the first eleven. However, few employees will gather round to read the safety regulations, or to study the company's quarterly performance results. Apart from the unkempt state of noticeboards in most factories and offices, many adults appear diffident about standing to read a notice at work. News of anything that matters – like a pay increase or a redundancy – will reach them on the grapevine long before a notice about it reaches the noticeboard. Yet, used intelligently, a noticeboard can be a powerful channel for communication; it can even be made to work two-way, and be used as a motivator. Let's simply list its advantages and limitations:

Advantages
- Can address all employees or groups.
- Cheap.
- Immediate (if read regularly).
- Easy for receiver to recheck message later.

Limitations
- Dependent on the receiver wanting to receive.
- Requires constant attention to keep tidy and fresh.
- Easily sabotaged.
- There are *never* enough drawing pins.

Self-check

How can a noticeboard be made more effective? (Try listing your own ideas on this before reading on.)

Here are some of the ways that have been used successfully:

- Give each notice a date by which it is to be removed.
- Colour code notices (e.g. safety: red; industrial relations: blue; social: green).
- Pay a small retainer to someone to maintain the noticeboard's appearance.
- Run a 'best noticeboard' competition.
- Provide a section (or separate board) for 'small ads' for articles for sale.
- Provide a 'gripe board'.
- Have a special 'subject of the month' exhibit with photographs (e.g. on an item of company history).
- Offer a reward to the person finding their payroll number hidden in a notice each week.

Public address systems really serve the same purpose as noticeboards but although they have the slight advantage of being oral, in companies where they are used regularly, people become so used to them as background noise that they stop paying attention. However, they are effective in reaching all employees at the same time and for this reason can be very effective when, for example, a senior executive wants to address all employees on a matter which requires urgency.

10 Reports

Although primarily a medium used by managers, the formal written report is one of the foundation stones of communication in organizations in commerce, industry and in local and national government. Its function is to allow a comparatively large number of people to receive the facts and arguments relating to an issue on which a decision has to be made. Although it may be laborious for the person who produces it, the report has major advantages over other methods (such as meetings) of getting a large number of complex ideas across to several people:

- it does not require everyone involved to arrange to be present at once;
- it is quick for the receiver; reading is at least twice as fast as speech;

● it tends to remove any heat and emotion from a subject.

The disadvantage of reports is that they do not allow an effective dialogue to take place: a meeting is still required to achieve that.

11 Memos

Memos (short for 'memoranda') are merely internal letters. They are often used unnecessarily to communicate information which could have been more quickly and cheaply dealt with through a short telephone call. They are useful for ensuring that important messages get passed between busy managers who are constantly in meetings or away from the office. They are also useful occasionally as a record of an arrangement made during a telephone conversation – although they often reflect 'back-protection' (the desire to prove oneself not to blame if anything goes wrong!) rather than a genuine need for confirmation. Many companies still use many more typewritten memos than they need. A short handwritten note is usually adequate, and lightens the typing load. Pads of forms with carbonless copy sheets are ideal, and often have space on the form for the reply so that the note can go backwards and forwards. They are often known as 'ping-pong' memos.

12 House journals

Almost all medium and large companies now run a house journal of some sort, whether in the form of a quarterly magazine or monthly newspaper. Typical contents include reports on:

● recent sales successes;
● staff appointments;
● retirements;
● sports and social events;
● customer satisfaction;
● company performance – financial and productivity figures;
● awards for suggestions, prizes for apprentice and safety competitions;
● profiles of company personalities;
● new machinery installed;
● new products.

It is rare to see reports on industrial relations issues, and even rarer to see articles which in any way criticize the company or its management. Many house journals do not even have a letter page. The reasons given by directors for this restricted coverage are usually centred on the risk that a customer may see the paper, and that they should not be allowed the opportunity to hear about the less glorious aspects of its business.

Yet some companies have taken the risk of telling the whole truth, 'warts and all'. *Ford News* has for years regularly published vitriolic articles attacking the competence of management (and equally strong counter-articles emanating from management), yet the Cortina is still the best-selling motorcar. However, more and more companies are coming to realize the limited value of the traditional house journal; attitude surveys have shown time and again that employees regard them as management noticeboards, and do not take them seriously; many do not read them at all.

Producing a house journal is an expensive business. In a well-known multi-site company with 50,000 employees, the monthly paper takes six staff and an annual print bill of £100,000.

At the other extreme, the house journal may be run off on a duplicator by an experienced employee with no knowledge of journalism at all. Some companies have their journal produced by one of the publication agencies which specialize in this kind of work. An agency can provide a highly professional product with minimal trouble and cost.

The technical quality of the newspaper is dependent on the ability of its editor. The level of objectivity and independence that he exercises is dependent on the amount of licence which the board of directors is prepared to allow him.

Activity

Get hold of your company's house newspaper, or get one from a friend, and analyse its contents. Work out how many column inches are allocated to each subject area mentioned above, and any others that seem appropriate to you. Translate the resulting numbers into percentages. Then ring up the editor (who may, like you, be a company employee, but in a small company, work for an agency) and ask him what the newspaper's policy is on reporting criticisms of the company, and on reporting industrial relations, accidents at work and ecological problems with which the company or its products may be associated.

13 Bulletins

The distinction between a house journal and a bulletin is perhaps a fine one. Technically a journal is a news report, often independent, whereas a bulletin is an official announcement. In a company which has a thriving independent house newspaper, there can be an important role for publication of a parallel official bulletin which concentrates on facts, on the company's progress and performance, and which tells employees that the directors think they ought to know, rather than what a newspaper editor judges to be newsworthy.

Growing use is being made of the 'management bulletin'. One of the fundamental problems which has emerged from recent analysis of employee communications is the lack of information available to middle managers and supervisors. This prevents them fulfilling their role as the principal communications link between senior management and the shop and office floor. Many companies have responded by launching management bulletins. These rarely contain information which cannot be made available to all employees, but they do provide a digest of material which is particularly relevant to managers, and which equips them better to brief their employees, and to discuss company performance with them.

14 Handbook

The company handbook began as a means of providing employees, and in particular new employees, with the basic information which they need to survive in the company. A typical contents list covers:

- company rules;

- contract of employment particulars: hours of work, holidays, notice entitlement;
- medical services;
- safety standards and procedures;
- disciplinary procedure;
- pay query procedure;
- grievance procedure;
- unions and union recognition;
- expenses when travelling on company business.

There is, of course, no need for the handbook to be limited to this basic set of information. Some companies see the handbook as an opportunity to provide employees not just with what they need to know, but with background information which it is nice to have. Such information might include:

- an organization chart;
- photographs and 'who's who' biographies of directors and senior executives;
- pictures and facts about the company's products;
- customer profiles – who buys what;
- company history;
- for a large company, a map showing what products are made where.

One of the main problems with company handbooks is that it is expensive and time-consuming to keep them up to date. A looseleaf design and the issue of regular amendment sheets is one solution that is often used, but in practice the issue of amendment sheets is often intermittent, their distribution haphazard, and the readiness of people to add the amendment sheets to their handbook almost zero. A better solution, although expensive, is a regular update and reissue – possibly every five years.

15 Annual report to employees

The annual report which companies are required by law to issue to their shareholders, although often available to employees and to the general public on request, does not make much sense to those of us with little understanding of accounting conventions. It has therefore become the practice for a special annual report to be prepared for employees. Some eighty per cent of publicly quoted companies are now said to produce such reports.

Reports to employees began as merely popular versions of the shareholders' report. They contained the same (or less) information presented in the form of charts and graphs, simplified as far as possible. This kind of report, although still used by some companies, was not a really effective communication medium, largely because many employees are just as unfamiliar with understanding histograms and graphs as they are with understanding accounts. Some of these early employee reports were illustrated with piles of coins and pound notes cleverly converted into charts: striking to look at, but difficult to make sense of.

Good employee reports are now more closely tailored to the information needs of employees; the company's annual financial results are only a small part of what they report on. A well-thought-out report is likely to have in it:

An employment report This aims to give employees the facts that will tell them whether their jobs are secure, and whether the company manages its people (its most valuable resource) effectively. It may be divided into sections on:

a Manpower:
- numbers employed;
- how numbers have changed over the year;
- the proportion of employees in particular groups, e.g. management, skilled workers, women;
- a breakdown of numbers by age and length of service.

b Attendance:
- lateness;
- time lost through sickness;
- time lost through absenteeism;
- comparative attendance of different groups of workers.

c Industrial relations
- time lost through industrial action;
- important agreements made with trade unions.

d Employment costs;
- wage and salary payroll costs;
- changes in pay rates over the year;
- costs of running canteens, welfare scheme, etc.;
- report on the pension scheme.

e Health and safety
- numbers of accidents and amount of time lost;
- new materials introduced during the year.

A review of the year Many employees, unless they work for a small organization, only get to know about events which directly involve them. A summary of what the company as a whole has been doing during the year, and of how well it has succeeded, can make a significant contribution to a feeling of belonging to something more than an impersonal institution. Typical subjects covered are:

a New products launched during the year; what they look like, how they were developed, how well they are selling and performing.
b Sales successes during the year
c Honours and awards made to company employees.
d New machinery and plant installed, and how it is performing.
e Performance of the company during the year:
- financial results;
- achievement of production and sales targets;
- productivity performance.

Annual reports usually focus on past performance. Yet for most employees it is not the past which is important, but the future. They want to be able to assess how secure their jobs are. A well-designed annual report should therefore go to some lengths to demonstrate what conclusions about the future can be drawn from what has happened in the past, and to present and explain the company's plans for the coming year, if not even further ahead.

The annual report should also set the information it contains in a context which employees can understand. It is no use stating baldly that the company's sales amounted to £2.5 million. Most of us on incomes of under £10,000 cannot tell the difference between £2.5 *million* and £2.5 *billion*. They are just large figures. For them to mean something, we need to be told that turnover last year, after taking out the inflation factor, was £2.7 million, and that the year before it was £2.9 million. We then need to be told that this is happening because the world demand for our products is falling, and that the company must respond by developing new products for which there is an expanding or steady market. This in turn will mean that we as employees must be ready to accept new machinery and to learn new skills.

All this needs explaining in straightforward words, not solely in pictures. Yet many employee reports consist largely of diagrams, pictures and cartoons, almost as though its readers were barely literate – despite the fact that almost everyone reads a daily newspaper. Newspapers, including the tabloids, are mostly words, not pictures.

There is no reason why employee reports should be annual: they can equally well be six-monthly or quarterly. Neither need they be printed: they can often be more effective on film or video-tape. Talbot Motors, for example, produce a quarterly report on film. Shoe manufacturers Clarke's produce an excellent tape/slide annual report. There are specialist contractors who are in business to produce such packages for companies.

Activity

Try getting hold of a company's annual report to employees, preferably that of your own company, or failing that, its report to shareholders. List its strengths and weaknesses against the points covered in the last few pages.

16 Pay packet inserts

This is a cheap and readily available medium that is far too little used. If a company is to pay the cost of giving an envelope containing a payslip to each employee every month or every week, it might as well let the envelope be used for carrying other information, either in the form of a separate enclosure or as a message printed on the packet itself. The letter is the only method available if a company is using preinserted computer stationery.

17 Personal letters

Employers rarely send individual letters direct to every employee: it is an expensive business, unless the pay packet is used for delivery, as suggested above. The most common regular use of direct letters is for the announcement of a redundancy or lockout, or to persuade employees not to go on strike. But letters can also be used in a positive way, even in small companies, to explain the company budget for the coming year, for example. The direct letter can very effectively reinforce the oral briefing, by giving people a chance to digest and look again at what they have been told.

18 Suggestion schemes

Suggestion schemes are probably the most traditional method of trying to encourage upward communication, by inviting employees to submit suggestions on improving efficiency, and rewarding those suggestions which are implemented. Perhaps because they are so traditional they are often ignored by employees and regarded as a waste of time. Imaginative ways of injecting new life into a tired scheme may be necessary.

To work successfully a suggestion scheme must ensure that:

● it is seen to be fairly administered;
● suggestions are all considered and some form of reply sent back to the employee (even when the suggestion cannot be implemented) giving the committee's reaction and their reasons;
● the financial reward is related to any cost savings which result from the suggestion – usually this is done on a percentage basis.

19 Union newsletter

Any newsletter produced by a factory shop stewards' committee for the union members it represents should be required reading for all managers in that factory – provided they can get a copy. Equally valuable can be the district or regional newsletter produced by some unions: the *T & GWU Record* is an example. One of the aims of communication in industry is to encourage better relationships between management and workforce. To achieve this, it is just as important that managers understand how their employees think, as it is for employees to understand how their managers think.

20 Surveys

In a small organization it is easy for the manager to get to know and understand what his workforce is thinking: he can talk directly to a good proportion of them and find out. In medium-sized companies, however, this is more difficult, and in large ones it is impossible. An alternative which is not used enough is the professionally conducted survey of employees' opinions and attitudes. Such surveys are often regarded with suspicion by those who take part in them. They smack of market research and of prying. Yet in fact they are nothing more nor less than a highly structured form of upward communication. They present an opportunity for people to state their views privately and confidentially, and often therefore more honestly than they might when talking to their bosses.

This is not the place to deal with the details of how a survey is conducted. Suffice it to say that, although a very effective means of doing what is often called 'collecting feedback', surveys need to be handled with care. In particular:

- the design of questionnaires is a skilled job which requires a knowledge of psychology. It is very easy to get a highly inaccurate response simply because a question was loosely phrased;
- the selection of a representative sample of employees to be surveyed requires a knowledge of statistical methods;

- experienced and trained interviewers are needed;
- processing the results of a survey can be complex and time-consuming, and may best be accomplished with the aid of a computer. The processing system should be designed at the same time as the questionnaire;
- gaining the acceptance and commitment of management, trade unions and employees to participating in the survey and to accepting its results is best handled by someone who has conducted surveys before, and can answer the very real worries and suspicions of those who are to be involved, by describing their first-hand experience of similar situations.

There are many excellent consultancies and survey firms with long experience of this kind of work: it is always advisable to approach one of them, or a social science research expert at a university or polytechnic. Almost all will offer you a free appraisal and estimate.

Communicating with your feet

21 Industrial action, labour turnover, absenteeism and lateness

At first sight, strikes, high labour turnover and high levels of absenteeism or lateness may not sound like forms of communication. Yet they all say to a company, 'Things have gone far enough; we cannot get our feelings through by using the proper channels (perhaps there aren't any) so we're taking the law into our own hands.' Management's response is often to hit back, when its response ought to be to listen even harder, and to recognize that it has failed to understand something that someone is trying to say.

Visual communication

22 Exhibitions and films

I have put these together because they suffer from three common disadvantages:

- they are expensive to produce (typically £10,000 for a twenty minute film);
- they cannot be shown to employees at their actual work station; and
- they communicate only downwards; they are not two-way.

They also, however, have three common advantages:

- they are the most vivid form of illustration available;
- they are a readily acceptable medium: it is less hard work to watch than to read a book
- like the printed media, they are consistent: they give everyone the same information.

For most of us, they cannot be regarded as a readily available way of sending a message. But for the senior executive in a large company, they can often be the best and most cost-effective means of doing so.

Bypassing middle management

Many of the communication channels described above carry information direct from senior management to shop floor, without going through middle management and supervision. House newspapers are in this category, as are annual reports, noticeboards, personal letters, films and joint committees and councils. Attitude surveys also bypass, in an upward direction. This bypassing effect, if not carefully handled, can lead to serious problems with the motivation of middle management. Many companies have suffered serious crises because the growth of direct channels between board room and shop floor has been seen as an expression of lack of confidence in middle management.

A conscious effort therefore has to be made by those responsible for planning a company's communication programme to ensure that middle managers and supervisors are not frozen out of the system, and do not *feel* frozen out of the system. They are the people, when all is said and done, who perform one of the most difficult management tasks of all: working at the interface between management and the workforce. To ensure that they are able to carry out this difficult task, and feel encouraged to carry it out enthusiastically, the designer of a communications strategy should pay attention to the following points:

- the foundation stone of the communications programme should be regular briefing of each departmental team by its manager or supervisor. This in turn will require the establishment of suitable arrangements for making sure that managers are themselves well informed;
- middle management should be involved in the design of the communications programme, possibly by forming a small working party to design the annual report, or to advise on the house newspaper, or to go through the proposed survey questionnaire;
- when an important piece of information is to be divulged, managers should be told first, even if it can only be minutes before the rest of the workforce;
- the communications programme should include such arrangements as a management bulletin, designed to give managers a deeper knowledge than their subordinates of the way the company operates. Management training courses also have an important role to play in this respect.

Bypassing the unions

In an organization with recognized trade unions, it is important to ensure that employee communication arrangements do not cut across long-established practices. Most shop stewards are in fact prepared to confine their role to the traditional area of collective bargaining (although this area is being constantly extended). Shop stewards do not usually see it as their job to act as a communication channel between management and their members on subjects other than pay and conditions. Neither do their members want them to act as such a channel: a survey in 1976 showed that almost all wanted to hear about the performance of the company from their supervisor, not from their shop steward. It is still of course necessary to run joint communication and consultative meetings with trade union representatives, but they should not be expected to pass on the information they receive; that is management's job.

Reinforcement

None of the institutional systems of communicating with employees can survive in isolation: each is dependent on the other. One of the earliest lessons learned by students of human behaviour was that we do not absorb information at a single sitting. We need to have it fed to us over and over again in different forms until we firmly take it aboard and it becomes part of our personal fund of knowledge. This process is called reinforcement; it is the basis of all effective teaching and of all effective communication. Thus the company's annual results should be reported not just in the annual report, but also in the house newspaper – not in the same form, but in different, perhaps more journalistic words, with some comment and elucidation of the more interesting and contentious points. The annual results should be presented in a different way again at each departmental briefing meeting. The sales force might be told, for example, that the contracting market for the company's products will mean that they will have to learn to sell new products, or to sell the old ones harder; the packing department may be told that they will see a smaller throughput of work for a period, which may mean redeploying some of them to other work, or buying a film-wrapping machine to make the product more attractive than that of a competitor.

Conclusion

Much of what we have looked at above applies only to companies which employ around 100 or more people. Below that number there is usually no need for more formal arrangements – although if they exist they can do only good, not harm – because there are good informal arrangements at work.

Activity

If you work in a small firm which does not yet need any sort of more formal system, try thinking about where the need for a more structured one might arise if the company were to expand.

Part 3:
On the receiving end

So far we have looked at communication from the
point of view of the process and the organization
– identifying general principles as a means of
setting the scene in which we, as individuals,
communicate. It is now time to begin to focus
more closely on the particular skills of
communicating. In Part 3 we will start by looking
at the skills involved in being an effective
receiver.

7 | Listening

We have all met them:

- The person who looks at you with glazed eyes, so intent on working out what he's going to say next that he hears nothing you say and cuts you off in mid-sentence to say something that bears very little relationship to what you have just been saying. . .
- The manager who says: 'Never hesitate to come and see me if you've got any problems,' and when you do make an appointment to see him, he spends all the time talking about *his* problems. . .
- The student who complains about every lecture, switches off after about the first five minutes, barely stays awake and says everything is boring and a waste of time. . .
- The person next to you at the conference, who, as the last speaker sits down, says: 'Well, that was pretty awful. The man didn't know what he was talking about and anyway I can't stand people who wear handkerchieves in their top pocket!'

. . . perhaps *you* are one of those people!

So how good at listening are you, and why is listening important anyway?

The neglected skill

We have already seen that in an attempt to meet the increasing demands of people to be kept informed, and in an attempt to improve morale and productivity, there has been a fever of activity in many organizations aimed at increasing the quality and quantity of written communications. Yet we have also seen that merely subjecting people to more and more information does not necessarily improve the communication climate in organizations.

Much of this activity stems from two beliefs. First, to judge from the contents of most training courses aimed at improving communication skills, the answer lies in improving people's ability to *transmit* information more effectively – to write more clearly and concisely and to speak with more confidence and sensitivity to their audience; and yet those who study the way in which human beings communicate have discovered that it is our ability to *receive* information which is just as much in need of improvement.

Listening tests have shown that the average person can remember only half of what he has heard immediately afterwards, and only about twenty-five per cent two months afterwards. Worse still, the US army has shown that only one tenth of the original message remains after three days!

The second belief, very commonly held though perhaps unconsciously, that has led to this concentration on producing more and more written and printed information, is the belief that the higher up the ladder of success we go and the more we find ourselves in positions of responsibility, the more our activities shift from listening and receiving messages to giving out and telling others what to do and even how to do it. In fact, this is exactly the opposite of the observable facts.

One study which looked at how white-collar workers spent their day, by logging them at intervals of fifteen minutes over a two-month period, discovered that: seven out of every ten minutes awake were spent in some form of communication activity. And it broke down like this:

9% writing
16% reading
30% speaking
45% listening!

If this statistic is correct, and there have been many other studies which support it, the average white-collar worker spends forty-five per cent of all communicating time listening and about thirty one and a half per cent of all time awake listening.

It is listening, then, which in most organizations carries a large part of the communication burden.

If we compare the rather alarming findings about the quality of our listening with this tendency to rely more and more on oral methods for transmitting information both in our social lives and at work, we can see that, far from being an unimportant and automatic skill, it is perhaps the most important area in communication, and desperately in need of some attention.

Did you get taught to listen?

'I do wish you'd listen!' 'Do you ever listen to anything I say?' or just simply 'Listen!' probably sum up, for most of us, all the help and instruction we were ever given in this very important skill.

At school, you were probably taught to write, from the first day to the last; you were taught to read and speak, at least up to a basic level of ability. Whether you received any more instruction on reading and speaking once you could 'do it' probably depended on the particular school you went to, but most of us were left to our own devices, perhaps refining our skills a little, more by luck than judgement.

As for listening, it seems to be assumed that so long as we don't have a physical hearing deficiency, we are automatically capable of listening from the day we are born, and do not therefore need to be taught. Yet a few minutes thought will probably enable you to recall many instances when people you talk to, and you too (if you're honest), seem to go through the motions of listening but, in reality, are either thinking of other things or, more particularly, thinking of what they are going to say next.

Listening, therefore, seems to be sadly neglected, and is sometimes written off as a merely passive skill, about which we can do very little. But it is crucial to good communication, for as we have seen it is really the receiver, the listener, who communicates, rather than the speaker: unless somebody listens to the message and understands it, there is no communication, only noise.

Why should you improve your listening?

In the final analysis, effective listening produces many salutary results:

Encouragement to others When others note that you listen to them in a non-threatening manner, they in turn lose some or all of their defensiveness and will usually try to understand you better by listening more effectively to you. Thus your effective listening often results in making others good listeners.

Possession of all the information We have already seen that to solve problems and make decisions more effectively, it is necessary to obtain as much relevant information as possible. Good listening helps you to get as much information as the speaker possesses. Your careful listening will usually motivate him to continue talking and to cite as many facts as he can. When you have as much information as possible, you are in a position to make accurate decisions.

Improved relationships Effective listening usually improves relationships between people. It gives the speaker the opportunity to get facts, ideas and hostile feelings off his chest. You will understand him better as you listen; he appreciates your interest in him; and friendship may therefore deepen.

Resolution of problems Disagreements and problems can best be solved when individuals listen carefully to each other. This does not mean that one must agree with the other's point of view; he must merely show that he *understands* the other person's point of view. Remember the picture of the young lady/old hag in Chapter 2. It was important to discover that not everyone saw the same thing as you and that even if you felt that what you saw was the more obvious, or the right one, someone else had different ideas for reasons that seemed very obvious and sensible to him. It was no good saying, 'No, you're wrong! It's not a picture of. . . it's a picture of . . .' and refusing to listen to his explanation of what he could see. You needed to be able to listen to his explanation in order to be able to see the picture from his point of view. Everyone wants understanding, and there is no better way of expressing this quality than through sensitive listening.

Listening may also help the other person see his own problems more clearly. Usually when any of us can talk through a problem, we can more easily work out possible solutions.

Better understanding of people Listening carefully to another will give you clues on how he thinks, what he feels is important and why he is saying what he is saying. By understanding him better, you will be able to work better with him, even if you do not particularly like him. Knowing that Tom is an extrovert, that Jim is an introvert, or that Mike needs frequent praise, leads to better understanding and thus harmony.

In other words, the good listener gains:

- information
- understanding
- listening in return
- cooperation

We all need to listen

Finally, then, listening is vital for the student whose success depends on how well he retains ideas, and for the manager who must know what is taking place in many areas if he is to make intelligent decisions and ensure the morale of his staff. The salesman must listen to his customers. The parent must listen to his child. And there are several professional areas where effective listening is the main stock-in-trade: psychiatry, educational and marriage guidance, personnel interviewing. In medical training, too, increasing emphasis is being placed on the skills of listening, since the patient is the main source of information on which the doctor bases much of his diagnosis.

This is not to say that we should all become full-time listeners, or that those who tend to be very quiet, diffident people can afford to pat themselves on the back, for as one writer commented:

A man who listens because he has nothing to say can hardly be a source of inspiration. The only listening that counts is that of the talker who alternately absorbs and expresses ideas.

How, then, can we train ourselves to really listen to what we hear? Or, perhaps, you think you already do!

Are you a good listener?

Activity

If you are interested in finding out how well you listen as a matter of habit, answer the following questions. This 'test' is easy to 'beat', and if you are happy to cheat, go ahead, but don't be fooled by your answers. However, if you are honest with yourself, you have a chance of estimating your listening ability. Just answer 'yes' or 'no'.

1 Do you place yourself in the room so that you are certain you can hear clearly?
2 Do you listen for underlying feelings as well as facts?
3 Do you take no notice of a speaker's appearance and watch out only for the ideas he is presenting?
4 Do you 'pay attention': do you look at the speaker as well as listen to what he has to say?
5 Do you allow for your own prejudices and feelings as you evaluate what the speaker has to say?
6 Do you keep your mind on the topic continuously and follow the train of thought being presented?
7 Do you try consciously to work out the logic and rationality of what is being said?
8 Do you restrain yourself (you do not interrupt or 'stop listening') when you hear something you believe to be wrong?
9 In discussion, are you willing to let the other speaker have the last word?
10 Do you try to be sure that you are considering the other person's point of view before you comment, answer or disagree?

• If you answered all the questions with a definite 'yes', then you were not being honest with yourself. You may like to believe that you do all those things, always, or you may intend to do them, but – be honest! – listening as well as that is hard work and none of us can keep it up all the time.

- If your score was around five then you were probably being honest and are prepared to admit that even the five that you answered 'yes' to can't be maintained without frequent lapses when you forget to try. However, you obviously make some attempt to remember that, despite what your real opinions are, everyone is entitled to a reasonably fair hearing. Which ones did you answer 'no' to? What does that signify about you as a person? Do you find it difficult to concentrate? Can you only listen effectively when you like someone or agree with their views? Do you tend to switch off if you don't like their appearance, or at least tend to let their appearance affect your assessment of their ideas?

- If you scored under five then you are either being disarmingly honest or falsely modest, but you are in danger of being the sort of person you don't like – self-centred, only interested in his own ideas, narrow-minded and unwilling to accept that other people's views may be just as valid as his own, unprepared to recognize his own prejudices and . . . well, just not very keen on making much effort to listen to other people.

Activity

Now, go back to those 'listeners' at the beginning of the chapter and use your imagination about how *they* might have answered the questions or, rather, since they may not be too honest, answer the questions on their behalf.

As you work to improve your listening performance, the preceding ten questions should be your guides, for they include the most significant listening problems which occur in personal and organizational communication.

However, here are some practical suggestions which, if seriously practised in organizations, might double or treble communication effectiveness, and help you to become a more effective part of any organization.

Aids to good listening

Perhaps the simplest way of ensuring good listening is to concentrate. 'Easier said than done,' you might say; 'but how does one concentrate?' The guidelines suggested below include ways of improving concentration.

Be prepared to listen Listening is not a passive skill but one that requires active hard work. Communication is a two-way process and so we must share the responsibility for effectiveness with the speaker: try to think more about what the speaker is trying to say than about what you want to say.

Being prepared also means getting into the right mental attitude – ready to maintain attention, increase awareness and elicit comprehension – and having the right background knowledge to understand what's being communicated. This means doing some homework for the meeting, the interview or the lecture, so that you start off with a common frame of reference.

Be interested 'If he can't make it interesting, he can't expect me to listen!' is a comment frequently heard after lectures or speeches. Remember – the listener is equally responsible. Look for ways in which the message might be relevant to you, your job, your interests. Any message, any time, could be relevant. Ask questions like, What is being said that I can use? How can I use this information to produce more goods, improve morale, be more efficient, learn something about myself or other people?

And look interested – after all no one wants to speak to a 'blank wall'. Put yourself in his shoes and imagine how you'd feel.

Keep an open mind Being open-minded means being aware of your own prejudices, or you may 'tune out' those messages that don't fit your bias. Don't feel threatened, insulted or resistant to messages that contradict your beliefs, attitudes, ideas and values.

Being open-minded also means trying to ignore a speaker's appearance and manner of presentation. Just because you don't like the look of him, don't be put off his ideas. If you know your own prejudices, you are more likely to control them and take them into account.

Don't jump too quickly to conclusions about the speaker's personality, his main message and your own response. You may be wrong and if you make up your mind too soon, you may block out any chance of hearing the truth. In other words, delay judgement.

Listen for the main ideas Poor listeners are inclined to listen for the facts only. Learn to discriminate between fact and principle, idea and example, evidence and argument.

The ability to extract the main ideas depends on your ability to recognize the conventional methods of structuring a message, transitional language and the speaker's use of repetition (the next four chapters should help you with this). The main points can come at the beginning, middle or end of a message, so you must always be alert. If the speaker gives a preview or a summary listen especially carefully.

Listen critically You should be critical, in an unbiased way, of the assumptions and arguments the speaker is using, and weigh up carefully the value of the evidence and the basis of the logic behind the main message.

Resist distractions Concentrating is only another way of saying 'resist distractions'. Attention, as we have seen, is fluctuating and selective. Your own experience will tell you that it is very easy to 'switch off'. Of course the speaker has a very real responsibility to attract attention and to keep it. But the best orator in the world can fail if the listener is not prepared to make an effort.

The natural attention curve for most people begins quite high, drops off as the message continues and increases again at the end. You should try to combat this tendency by making a special effort in the middle of the message and trying to keep it constant.

Don't be distracted by the speaker's dress, appearance, vocabulary, style of presentation, use of visual, oral and written aids. Above all, don't let other people in the audience distract you. They may not be good listeners; prove you are.

Take notes If the message is essential to you, you will need to make an outline of the speaker's main ideas and particular examples which you might otherwise forget. But, remember that note-taking can be a distraction, so be flexible. It might be better to listen attentively and then make notes after the speaker has finished.

Help the speaker We have already noted that it helps the speaker if we try to look interested, but in conversation there are other ways in which we can encourage the speaker. These 'listener responses' are very brief comments or actions that the listener makes to the speaker, which convey the idea that you are interested and attentive and wish him to continue. They are made quietly and briefly so as not to interfere with the speaker's train of thought – usually when the speaker pauses. There are five types of listener response.

Self-check

Can you think of what they are? Picture the last conversation you had. What did you do while you were listening?

POSSIBLE LISTENER RESPONSES

- nodding the head slightly and waiting;
- looking at the speaker attentively;
- remarking 'I see', 'Uh-huh', 'Really?' etc.;
- repeating back the last few words the speaker said (but be careful. If this becomes a habit, it can be irritating);
- reflecting back to the speaker your understanding of what has just been said ('You feel that. . . ').

How many did you get? The value of listener responses is that they provide feedback to the speaker and tell him that you are still with him and want him to continue.

(Chapter 15, 'The silent languages' will tell you more about the way in which the listener and speaker synchronise their conversation.)

Play back This is another way of describing the last of the listener responses mentioned above but it is such an invaluable tool for the good listener that it is worth a special mention.

If you don't understand what has been said or you want the speaker to elaborate on a point, try to introduce the thought with a reflecting phrase, such as 'you said', 'you mentioned', 'you suggested before', or 'you described'. After repeating the idea, follow with a question beginning with 'who', 'what', 'where', 'when', 'why' or 'how'. Reflecting phrases are designed to give you a second chance of receiving something you missed the first time round.

Playing back the speaker's own ideas in this way has the added advantage of showing the speaker that you are really listening to what he is saying. In addition it allows you to check that you have really understood what the speaker meant to say. Most of us are so intent on how we are reacting to the speaker's words that we don't really listen to them. One psychologist, Carl Rogers*, was so aware of this problem that he developed a game to delay argument and encourage people to really listen to one another. He suggested that before people can make a point in a discussion, they should first be able to summarize the last person's contribution to that person's satisfaction. Try playing this game and see for yourself how very difficult it is not to prepare mental arguments while the other person is talking, with the result that you miss most of what is really being said.

Hold back Perhaps the hardest thing about being a good listener is trying not to interrupt. Even when there is a pause, it doesn't always mean that the speaker has finished, so be patient.

Listening is a process of self-denial! [A. C. Mumford.]

Review

1 What percentage of communicating time does the average white-collar worker spend listening?
2 What proportion of the original message is remem-

* Carl R. Rogers and F. J. Roethlisberger, 'Barriers and Gateways to Communication', *Harvard Business Review*, vol. 30, 1952.

bered after three days, according to US army research?

3 List and explain the five results of effective listening.

4 List and explain at least five ways in which you could improve your listening.

5 Now look back at the four 'listeners' at the beginning of the chapter. Which of the aids to good listening would be particularly helpful for each one?

ANSWERS

1 45% listening (9% writing; 16% reading; and 30% speaking).

2 One tenth of the original message is remembered after three days.

3 See pages 128–9.

4 See pages 132–4.

5 The person who tends to concentrate on his own thoughts and interrupt might do well 'playing back' and 'holding back' the ideas of others before making his own contribution. He would probably find the game suggested by Carl Rogers extremely difficult but very instructive.

The manager who tries to appear a good listener but ends up talking about his own problems might also benefit from 'playing back' and 'holding back' but could also try 'helping the speaker' by more use of listener responses.

The student needs to be alert for messages which affect him, constantly asking himself, how can I make use of this? 'Being interested' is not something that just happens, it requires hard work, preparation and a readiness to listen and show he's interested. He might also make a real effort to 'resist distractions' and increase his concentration in the middle of a lecture. 'Listening for the main ideas' would help his concentration.

And finally, the person who is quick to judge a person's ideas on the basis of superficial things, like the appearance and dress of the speaker, needs above all to 'keep an open mind' and 'resist distractions'.

Summary checklist

Results of effective listening
1 Encouragement to others.
2 Possession of all the information.
3 Improved relationships.
4 Resolution of problems.
5 Better understanding of people.

Aids to good listening
 1 Be prepared to listen.
 2 Be interested.
 3 Keep an open mind.
 4 Listen for the main ideas.
 5 Listen critically.
 6 Resist distractions.
 7 Take notes.
 8 Help the speaker.
 9 Play back.
10 Hold back.

Activity

For your next face-to-face listening situation, write down the ten aids to good listening on a card and intentionally practise each and every one. Try the same exercise on a televised party political broadcast, preferably that of a party you would *not* normally support.

Activity

Read the article in the journal *Harvard Business Review*, vol. 30 (1952), called 'Barriers and Gateways to Communication' by Carl R. Rogers and R. J. Roethlisberger.

Try the listening game suggested in this article. Have a discussion with a friend but institute the rule: 'Each person can speak up for himself only *after* he has first restated the ideas and feelings of the previous speaker accurately and to that person's satisfaction. . .'

At the end of twenty minutes, discuss the difficulties of

this method and the advantages in terms of effective listening.

8 | Read faster. . . read better

From: Head of department
To: You
Date: Monday

I have to attend a meeting on Wednesday afternoon at which I gather there will be a discussion on the possibility of introducing a 'Flexitime' system. I gather there are several magazine articles available on the subject, but I shan't have time to read them as I shall be away at the planning conference and won't be back until late on Wednesday morning.

Can you read through them and let me have a summary of the main points and your comments so that I can read it through quickly just before the meeting? I will get my secretary to give you copies of the articles.

Your reputation is at stake here: you are ambitious and keen to get on. This gives you the chance to make a good impression by showing you can handle any situation, so it's not just a case of skimming through the articles and handing them back with a short note. You will need to read them carefully, analyse them and make valid comments, but today is Monday and you have your own job to do as well, so you haven't much time. How would you react to this task? How would you go about it?

Perhaps you feel that this is an unlikely assignment to be given, but even if you feel this now in your present circumstances, things change; and one of the purposes of this book is to provide you with skills in communication, so that when the opportunity to use them arises, you will be well equipped not only to cope, but to do well.

Even if you are not faced with a task quite like this, for many of us the problem of reading a great deal of material in too short a time is fairly common. As has been mentioned, we seem to be living through an information explosion or a 'paper avalanche'.

For students on courses, it is a problem of tutors recommending books and articles faster than they can read the ones already recommended. Many students do not read quickly or retain what they read, so reading becomes a chore and their courses become more difficult than they need be.

For people at work, it is often a problem of finding the time to read all the things they know they ought to read – minutes of meetings, piles of letters and memos, articles which might be helpful, copies of this 'for information', copies of that 'for information', as well as wanting to keep up with newspapers and perhaps even the occasional novel.

So, what's the problem? After all, most of us have been reading since we were five or so, and for many of us that is quite a long time. But despite all this experience few people read as well as they might. They read too slowly, they cannot concentrate and they don't retain what they've read.

The average adult reads at a speed of between 200 and 300 words per minute (w.p.m.) but some people read at 600 w.p.m. and John F. Kennedy is reputed to have been able to read at 1000 w.p.m. Why do people read at different speeds? How is it some people are three times more effective than others when it comes to reading?

It certainly doesn't appear to have anything to do with intelligence, or education, or status, or occupation or sex. There are many wives whose jobs require little reading, who infuriate their husbands by being able to read much faster than their husbands, despite less experience and less practice. Similarly, there are many brilliant men and women who are outpaced by their subordinates.

No one seems to know why faster reading comes more easily to some people than to others. What we do know is that more effective readers read in a different way from slower readers.

If you feel you do read more slowly than you would like, perhaps it isn't your fault. Certainly, the best of readers can be slowed down by things like:

- the complexity of the material;
- the author's style;
- typeface which is hard to read;

- monotonous layout and presentation (e.g. 'solid blocks of print weary the eye');
- unfamiliar words and expressions.

However, these may be just excuses. It is equally possible that it could be your fault, in the sense that we do know that slow readers tend to have developed some bad habits, whereas effective reading calls for certain techniques. These techniques can be learned and practised. You could very probably read at least half as fast again as you do now and still understand as well; many people who either attend an 'effective reading' course or are conscientious enough to teach themselves with the aid of a book like *Read Better, Read Faster* by Manya and Eric de Leeuw (Penguin) are usually able to double their reading speed without any drop in comprehension. Some people's comprehension level actually increases.

In this book it is not possible to allow enough space to give you a structured training course. What we can do, though, is explain why people read slowly and ineffectively, find out how you read at present and then suggest some techniques which, if you really want to improve your reading, you can practise perfectly well on your own.

Self-check

The first thing to discover is *how* you read. As with other exercises in this book, it is important to answer questions honestly. You will gain nothing by trying to guess what you think the answer should be.

How do you read?
In order to assess how effectively you tackle serious reading, put a tick ('usually true') or a cross ('seldom true') against the points below.

1	I skim over reading material before studying it.
2	I tend to go back over words and phrases I have not understood, before going on.

3	I find it difficult to pick out the main idea of a passage.
4	I read different types of reading material at different speeds.
5	I pronounce words to myself when I read.
6	When I have a lot of reading to do, I try to stick at it for as long as possible, before having a break.
7	I always skim over the entire questionnaire, exam paper, etc. before starting to answer the questions.
8	I have a tendency to daydream when trying to study a report, article or section of a report.
9	I prefer to read slowly and carefully through a fairly difficult article, rather than read it quickly two or three times.
10	I find it easy to understand and remember what I read.
11	Generally, I am a rather slow reader.
12	I skimmed quickly through all these questions before I started to answer any of them.

If you put a tick for **1, 4, 7, 10** and **12** then you have probably already been through an 'effective reading' course, or you have developed good reading habits naturally, or you have cheated yourself by trying to guess the right answers!

If, however, you put a tick against any of the other points, you have developed some bad habits and could probably improve your reading considerably by practising conscientiously some of the techniques suggested in this chapter.

Different material – different speed

At the moment, it is very likely that you read practically everything you read in much the same way and at much the same
speed. A moment's thought will tell you that you are spending
too much time on the easy material, which doesn't leave you
enough time to spend on the more difficult stuff. Improving your
reading speed is, therefore, mainly intended to increase the
range of reading speeds available to you, so that instead of
reading everything at the same fairly slow speed, you can be
more flexible. With practice you will probably end up reading
everything rather faster than you do now, even the very difficult
material.

Reading is rather like driving: when you are learning and
rather lacking in confidence, you drive fairly slowly and you
don't get much above second gear. When you are more experienced, you can change up and down through all four gears at
will, almost without thinking about it, in order to suit different
road and traffic conditions. So it is with reading. If you can gain
confidence by employing advanced techniques, you will be able
to adapt your approach to reading to suit the material and your
purpose, at any given moment.

Purposes of reading

There are three basic reasons why we read:

Pleasure Many people read for no other reason than the sheer
pleasure they gain from a good story or the sound of the words.

Information This type of reading is perhaps the most basic
reason. Whether we like reading or not, most of us have to read
in order get facts – about our job, our interests, our lives in
general. It covers everything from recipes to nuclear physics;
from instructions on forms, to guidance on operating machines
or gadgets.

Judgement In this type of reading, you are interested in people's
ideas and opinions, in order to come to your own opinions and

conclusions. You therefore need to be able to evaluate critically the arguments put forward, and be alert to the presence of prejudice or bias, or the use of emotive arguments intended to manipulate you.

This book is not intended to enable you to change your style of reading for pleasure or to help you to get through a novel in one sitting, since much of the pleasure of reading comes from savouring the words and images the author uses to create particular effects. What we are concerned with is making the serious business of acquiring information and reading for judgement purposes a more efficient process; in other words, making better use of your time.

Comprehension and speed

Reading *faster* is not the only problem. Although it is obviously important to eliminate bad habits and increase your reading speed, this is only part of developing a more effective approach to reading.

The other dimension is, of course, concerned with understanding, for it is no good simply increasing the rate at which you read if in doing so you gain less from what you read. In fact, these two aspects of efficient reading are inextricably linked, as we shall see; it is certainly true that many people discover that their comprehension improves as their speed increases.

The physical process of reading

Eye movements

Many people read inefficiently because of faulty eye movements, of which they are not even aware.

When you read, your eyes do not move smoothly across the page from left to right without stopping. If they did, all you would see was a blur. Try moving your eyes from one side of the room to the other without letting them stop. What did you see? blur? You can only keep your eyes in focus while they are moving smoothly without stopping if the object you are looking at is also moving. Since the words on the page are stationary, your eyes can only focus on the words when they, too, are stationary. So when you read, your eyes stop to take in a word or phrase and then move on to the next. These stops are called 'fixations'. It is estimated that each fixation that our eyes make lasts approximately $\frac{1}{4}$ to $1\frac{1}{2}$ seconds and then the eyes move on. At each fixation, the eyes read a word or perhaps several words.

The number of words you focus on and take in or recognize at one fixation is called the 'recognition span'. Some people appear to be able to read straight down a printed page. In other words, they fixate only once on each line and, at each fixation, take in or recognize the whole line. Their recognition span is large.

Now it is obvious that the bigger your recognition span, the fewer fixations you will need to make, and so, the faster you will read – since it is the fixations that take up the time.

Poor readers tend to make a large number of fixations and have a small recognition span, but they also tend to have other habits associated with the eye movements and the brain's activity while reading.

'Regression': poor readers, who tend to focus on each word, are actually making life more difficult for themselves than they realize, because individual words do not convey very much meaning until they are joined to other words. So as the slow reader plods steadily from word to word, trying to join the idea of one word to the idea of the next, he finds it difficult to grasp any overall meaning from the individual words. After three or four words he probably finds he has forgotten what the first was and has to go back to the beginning again, rather like this:

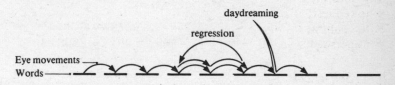

Because this process is so slow, much slower than his brain can actually perform, the brain finds something else to do. In other words, he gets easily sidetracked or distracted by what we tend to call daydreaming or thinking about something else.

Activity

Let's look at an example. Read the sentence below very
slowly word by word, using a finger to cover the word in
front each time, but gradually uncovering each word.

Though . . . there . . . are . . . no . . . doubt . . . some
. . . people . . . who . . . think . . . words . . . must . . . be
. . . read . . . one . . . at . . . a . . . time . . . they . . . are
. . . wrong . . . because . . . meaning . . . tends . . . to
. . . come . . . from . . . groups . . . of . . . words.

Like this: 'Though' . . . 'Though there' . . . 'Though there are'
. . . 'Though there are no' . . . Though there are no doubt' . . .
etc. At each stage the words do not convey very much meaning,
do they? Not until we get to 'people' does it begin to make some
sense.

A good reader, then, with a bigger recognition span and fewer
fixations, not only reads faster, but also makes the business of
comprehension easier, and is less likely to be distracted because
his brain is being pushed to keep up with the eye movements.

A good reader's reading pattern might look like this:

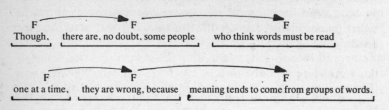

So the good reader tends to select his recognition spans on the
basis of their meaning. He reads 'thought groups' rather than
single words.

Activity

Find out the pattern of your eye movement. Ask a friend
to stand behind you while you read from a book, holding a
mirror in front of your face so that the friend can see your

eyes. Then ask whether your eyes tend to regress from time to time, whether they stop to focus many times along a line or only two or three times.

Sub-vocalization and visualization

Another habit of the slow reader is the tendency to register the sound of the words as he reads, either by physically mouthing them, or internally acknowledging the sound of the words in his head.

This is often a legacy from the days when we learned to read, first aloud and then 'to ourselves'. Small children can certainly be seen mouthing the words as they read, and though this is less common in adults, either externally mouthing or internally acknowledging the sound will inevitably slow down your reading speed.

Reading aloud, the average reader can only read at about 125 w.p.m. Mouthing the words or acknowledging the sounds inside your head would be bound to limit your reading speed to something below 200 w.p.m.

This habit also has consequences for the idea of reading for meaning, which we have just looked at. If you mouth the words or hear them inside your head, you are concentrating on the words themselves, not on the meaning of the ideas you are reading.

Activity

There is a simple test which you can try, to check, whether you mouth the words. Place your index finger vertically over your lips while you are reading. If your lips are moving, you will feel them moving with your finger. This test is also a cure because if you do find that your lips are moving, all you have to do is to press your finger harder against your lips and they won't be able to move!

Finding out whether you tend to register the words separately by *internally* acknowledging the sound of each word, is more difficult. There is no real test other than just consciously thinking about the danger, perhaps while you are reading this, and trying to discover whether you tend to do it or not. If you are a slow reader, the chances are that you are almost bound to be doing it. If you push up your reading speed you won't be able to mouth the words or visualize them – it will become physically impossible.

Comfort

Physical discomfort can also affect the ease and fluency with which you read. But too much comfort can reduce your concentration.

- Position: a comfortable (but not too comfortable!) chair, which is the right height, at a table, is probably the most suitable position for a serious reading task.
- Lighting: good lighting is essential. Although desk lights are commonly accepted as the best form of lighting, a light source falling over your shoulder is better, since it reduces glare.
- Eyesight: Have you had your eyes tested recently? Your eyes can deteriorate without your realising it, since the muscles work harder to compensate for any deficiency in vision. Similarly, the lenses in spectacles can become unsuitable. Pride often prevents people going to the optician, but even if you aren't suffering from any physical effects like tired eyes or headaches, your reading could still be suffering.
- Rests: whilst you should avoid being distracted by noise, other people, hunger or thirst and should give yourself a chance to get stuck into a reading or studying task, you should allow yourself reasonable breaks. Short, frequent breaks are probably more helpful than a longer break caused by exhaustion, after trying to stick at a reading task for hours without a break.

Vocabulary

Obviously if you are having to go back to words or ponder over them because your brain can't assimilate them because they are unfamiliar or you don't understand them, your reading speed will inevitably be held back. Although writers should try to avoid using unnecessarily complicated and unfamiliar words, if your own vocabulary is weak you should work to improve it.

Quizzes designed to test your wordpower like those in the *Readers' Digest* are a useful method of measuring your vocabulary from time to time.

Self-check

Test your vocabulary
In the list below, underline the word or phrase you believe is nearest in meaning to the keyword. Answers are on the next page.

1 NEFARIOUS	a dangerous b suspicious c evil d distant		**6** PREMISE	a basic assumption b a building c foreword d abstract idea	
2 CENSURE	a suppress b reject c blame d delete		**7** CREDIBLE	a superstitious b sceptical c praiseworthy d believable	
3 NEBULOUS	a transparent b vague c fat d luminous		**8** INVALIDATE	a overwhelm b cancel c injure d verify	
4 SALUTARY	a beneficial b courteous c respected d respectful		**9** BIZARRE	a odd b a market c comical d colourful	
5 TORTUOUS	a arduous b cautious c slow d winding		**10** DEFUNCT	a wicked b forbidden c extinct d hopeless	

ANSWERS

1 NEFARIOUS **c** evil; vicious, villainous; e.g. a nefarious plot (Latin: *nefas* – 'wrong, crime').

2 CENSURE **c** to blame; criticize; reprimand officially; e.g. to censure a member of Parliament (Latin: *censere* – 'to estimate').

3 NEBULOUS **b** vague or unclear; hazy; cloud-like; e.g. a nebulous statement (Latin: *nebula* – 'mist').

4 SALUTARY **a** beneficial; promoting health; wholesome; e.g. a salutary exercise (Latin: *salus* – 'health').

5 TORTUOUS **d** winding; full of twists and turns; e.g. a tortuous path; also, devious; e.g. a tortuous argument (Latin: *torquere* – 'to twist').

6 PREMISE **a** basic assumption; proposition from which a conclusion may be drawn: 'He started with the premise that 'All men are mortal' (Latin: *praemittere* – 'to place ahead').

7 CREDIBLE **d** believable; apparently worthy of belief or confidence; e.g. a credible story (Latin: *credere* – 'to believe').

8 INVALIDATE **b** cancel; render of no force or effect; e.g. to invalidate a will (Latin: *invalidus* – 'weak').

9 BIZARRE **a** odd; eccentric; fantastic; strikingly out of the ordinary, or at variance with accepted standards; e.g. bizarre behaviour (Italian: *bizzarro* – 'gallant, brave').

10 DEFUNCT **a** extinct; dead; e.g. a defunct system (Latin: *defunctus* from *defungi* – 'to finish, discharge').

How did you get on? If you got nine to ten correct, your vocabulary is excellent; you probably need no encouragement to continue learning new words.

Eight right: good – a very creditable score, but make the effort to look up the odd word you come across that you're not sure about.

Six to seven: you have a fairly good vocabulary, but try some of the exercises suggested below.

Five and under: your vocabulary is rather limited and this will inevitably slow down your reading. Make a resolution to practise the exercises suggested below.

Ways of increasing your vocabulary

Read widely Apart from reading tasks for work or study, you should try to read as much as possible: books and articles on other subjects than your own; a newspaper regularly (preferably one of the 'quality' newspapers, which tend to use a more varied vocabulary than most of the popular newspapers – but any paper is better than none). You might also try reading magazines like the *New Statesman*, the *Economist, New Society* and the *Listener.*

Word of the week Try choosing one word each week, which you have come across but don't know or would not naturally use. Then use it in speaking and writing as much as possible throughout the week. Your friends may find it amusing but will soon envy your wide vocabulary.

Get the dictionary habit If you hear a word you are not familiar with, ask the user what he means and/or make a note of it and look it up in a dictionary later. If you don't possess a good dictionary, i.e. at least two inches thick, buy one *now. Chambers Twentieth Century* and the *Concise Oxford English* are both good but any good bookshop will help you choose one.

Latin and Greek roots. Many English words, even those that come from other languages, are formed from Latin and Greek words. Although very few people now learn Latin and Greek at school, it is well worth learning some of the more common affixes (parts of words which usually appear at the beginning or end of a word), e.g. 'auto' comes from Greek and means 'self', giving us words like 'automatic', 'autobiography' and 'autograph'.

Self-check

How many of these Greek and Latin roots and affixes do you know? (You should know all of them. If not, learn them – now is as good a time as any.)

Root or affix	Meaning	Example
ante (L)	before	antecedent
amphi (G)	around, both sides	amphitheatre
aqua (L)	water	aquarium
audio (L)	hear	auditorium
bene (L)	well	benefit

bio (G)	life	biography
circum (L)	around	circumference
corpus (L)	body	corporate
dia (G)	across, through	diameter
graph (G)	write, record	photograph

Activity

Exercises to help you read faster

The purpose of rapid-reading exercises is to get your eyes used to moving quickly and smoothly across the page, and your brain used to searching for the meaning of what you are reading, rather than concentrating on single words.

Most of the exercises will feel awkward at first, and you may well find that you are concentrating more on the mechanics of the exercise than the meaning of the words. However, as with any skill, you will find that actions that seemed awkward to start with soon become automatic.

You may find that one or two of the exercises don't work for you at all, but give them a really good try before you reject them.

Pointer

Follow the words across the page with your finger or a pen: try to move the finger or pointer at a steady speed along each line.

At first, you will find that you are tending to concentrate on the pointer rather than taking in the words, but gradually with practice you should find that you are forgetting the pointer.

Now gradually increase the speed but keep the movement smooth and regular. Then try following only the alternate lines: then every third, then every fourth line.

You may feel foolish doing this exercise, but it is one of the good habits which unfortunately children are taught to drop. In fact, this method of using a finger or pointer is only a simpler copy of the method used in more sophisticated rapid-reading training courses, which use some form of moving light on film to encourage your eyes to move at a smooth but increasing speed.

Tapping a rhythm

Since the aim in rapid reading is to obtain a steady rhythm, it is helpful to use a rhythmic sound as well as the sight of a moving pointer. This can be achieved by tapping the page lightly with a finger or pen down the margin at the end of every line, or every alternate line or less often. Practise for a while until you find a sound and frequency which is comfortable for you. Then, when you have found a comfortable speed, gradually increase it slowly, as in the previous exercise with the pointer.

The sound and sight of the tapping finger act rather like a musician's metronome in improving your rhythm.

Read everything faster

Try practising reading everything you read that much faster.

9 | Why start at the beginning?

Imagine you are faced with an in-tray containing an assortment of letters, memos, articles, reports and so on. Some of it will be important, requiring urgent attention; some of it will be interesting but could afford to wait. Some of it will be easy to read; some of it will be difficult and very time-consuming. Or imagine that as a student you have been told to read a certain book and have just settled down to start the task. In both cases, particularly if time is short (and it usually is!), the temptation is to start reading and keep going until you run out of time or stamina, which is usually before you have finished the pile of paperwork or reached the end of the book.

Some of what you read turns out to be *essential*: perhaps only a small fraction of the total amount, but nevertheless the vital stuff, without which you can't do your job – but it may be halfway through or even at the very end of the pile or the book. Some of it is *useful*: it includes interesting background information, not absolutely essential, but useful to know. It needn't be read immediately and could probably wait until you are less busy. The rest is *irrelevant*: this type of material may have been sent to you in error, or incorporated with the useful and essential stuff, or it contains things you already know. You don't want to waste time reading this at all.

Ineffective readers not only read everything at the same speed, but they also tend to wade straight into their reading at the beginning – which in this case is not necessarily the best place to start. This tendency to jump straight in – either at page one of the book or at the top paper on the pile in your in-tray if you are a businessman – leads to two problems:

- you don't read things in the most sensible order;
- you don't know what to expect when you start reading.

Walking over a strange track is always more difficult than walking along a track you're vaguely familiar with.

In this chapter we will look at how you should approach your reading tasks so that you do read things in a sensible order. You should devote just as much time as, and no more time than, the nature, difficulty, and your purpose in reading the material requires. You should read material only after you have gained an overall idea of what it is about and how it is structured; this will make reading not only easier, but also faster. The suggested approach is dependent on two essential skills – scanning and skimming – which are both a form of reading, as we shall see, but which allow you to alter your reading speed in relation to your purpose at any given moment.

But let's go back to that overflowing in-tray, or the weighty recommended textbook with which you are confronted.

Determining reading priorities

If you do have a tendency to start reading at the beginning and work steadily through the material, the trouble is that you have to read right through everything before you find out what is essential, what is useful and what is irrelevant. But all this material takes the same amount of effort and concentration to read. A moment's thought will make you realize that this is obviously inefficient. But how can you find out how valuable the material is until you've read it?

Scanning

What you need is a method of reading which allows you to get a broad view of the whole piece of reading material *before* you read it properly, so that you can assess its value to you and get some idea of when you need to read it and how much effort it will require.

Scanning is one of the techniques of reading which allows you to do just this. Strictly speaking it is not really reading at all, but it is an essential part of the reading process.

In fact you probably do it occasionally now: when you are

looking for a number in a telephone directory, for example. Certainly, having the names in alphabetical order helps, but if you are looking for a friend's name amongst a lot of Browns, you will probably scan the list looking first for the right initials and then the right address. You don't *read* every address, but because you know what you are looking for, the address you want seems to stand out on the page when you get to it.

Self-check

How would you find the radio and television programmes in a newspaper if you were not familiar with its layout? Or the classified advertisements for cars for sale?

Well, you would probably look first of all on the front page, to see if there was a list of contents. Your eyes would range over the entire front page, in a rather random fashion, not really reading anything, but looking for the one area relevant to your purpose. Your eye and brain would register only those words which seemed to contain clues to what you were looking for: 'television', 'radio', 'programmes'. Your eyes might be attracted to the word 'television'. Your eyes would stop ranging, or scanning, far and wide, and come to rest focusing on that word. You might then discover that the word following 'television' was 'reviews' – not what you're looking for. Your eyes would then start ranging again, until they found what they were looking for. If the 'contents list' then directed you to a particular page, you would ignore all but the page number on each page until you came to the one you wanted, and then begin the ranging or scanning process on the relevant page until you again found what you wanted.

This process of scanning involves blotting out everything but the few key words related to your purpose, and a constant coming-in and narrowing-down to what you need.

Scanning has two main advantages in helping with the process of all your serious or work-related reading:

● *assessment*: allows you to 'read' rapidly through a text looking for key words, which will give you enough of a taste of the whole thing to assess its value to you;

- *introduction to the structure*: it provides you with a rough idea of the material, how the author has structured it, and therefore you will know what to expect when you come to read it properly.

Categorization

Now, if your purpose has been to gain an overview of the material in order to assess its value to you, and determine whether you need to read it at all – only part of it or all of it in some depth – you should now be in a position to assess it against these three categories:

- essential – to be read with maximum attention;
- useful – to be read when you have the time, after you have read the essential stuff;
- irrelevant – in this case, if you are a businessman, one writer has suggested that you file it in the wastepaper bin!

    Warning! If you are a student and have judged as irrelevant something recommended by a tutor, you will still need to read it through critically in order to be able to support your judgement with well-argued reasons and evidence. Alternatively, you should consult your tutor and discuss your initial reaction with him. But be prepared to accept that since you are learning, the tutor may know better than you at this stage and his advice to read it conscientiously should be taken, particularly if it is essential reading for the course. In this case, you are going to have to think hard and find the relevance.

You will find this process of scanning is needed on and off throughout the process of reading, not only when sorting through material. It is rather like the highest gear imaginable on a very fast car – not useful when you are negotiating steep hills or difficult winding roads, but very useful when you want to get from A to B as fast as possible.

Getting an overall idea of the material

If we continue the analogy of the car, you know that it is far more difficult to travel along a route which is totally new to you. In view of this, most people before setting out on a journey which is unfamiliar will attempt to find out where they are going and how they are going to get there, by either seeking directions or looking at a map. In just the same way, reading any new material is made considerably easier by having an overview of what the material is about and how the author has structured or organized his ideas.

In scanning the material in order to carry out an initial assessment, you will already have picked up some clues and you are now ready to start reading – but still not in the conventional sense of the word. First you need to become familiar with the route, where you will have to make changes of direction, where you will have to slow down and where you can expect to find signposts to help point you in the right direction. Gaining this overview will require another rate of reading, in which you are not concerned with taking in all the words and all the detail, but only the author's major ideas so that you can get a feel for his structure and treatment of the material.

Skimming

Skimming is one of the techniques of reading which allows you to do just this. It is a kind of rapid reading *par excellence* where you are reading right at the top end of your range, as fast as you possibly can, gaining a broad outline and ignoring the detail. It is probably the ability to skim well which accounts for the sometimes incredible speeds at which some people are reputed to be able to read. They skim through large chunks of the material, only slowing down for the bits which they need.

Since skimming is a technique intended to help you pick up the main ideas and the structure of the material, the process is considerably helped if you are aware of the way in which English writing is structured and where you might expect to find the main ideas; in other words, the way in which sentences are put together to form paragraphs and the way in which 'signposts' are used to help the reader know what's coming. So before we discover more about the technique of skimming itself, let's look at these two aspects of structure.

Self-check

In a paragraph of technical or business writing (i.e. not fictional writing) where would you expect to find the main idea?

Topic sentences

Most paragraphs in factual, explanatory or discursive writing contain *one main idea*. Normally, one sentence contains this idea and is, therefore, known as the 'topic sentence'. It is usually the first sentence or the last sentence in the paragraph.

First sentence: the author uses it to state his main idea and then the rest of the paragraph is devoted to material which illustrates, supports or elaborates on this main idea.

Last sentence: the author uses the first part of the paragraph to lead up to his main idea in the last sentence.

Exceptions:

* occasionally the topic sentence is in the middle of the paragraph;
* fiction or descriptive writing is produced for very different purposes and will, therefore, be structured differently;
* poor writing: you may well come across badly written material which does not obey the rules of clear writing; and, of course, the best of writers will go astray from time to time. This will just make your job that much harder.

Self-check

Look at each of the following paragraphs and find the topic sentence:

1 'Getting an overall idea of the material', paragraph 1, pages 157–8.
2 'Getting an overall idea of the material', paragraph 2, page 158.
3 'Skimming', paragraph 1, page 158.
4 'Skimming', paragraph 2, page 158.

In both the paragraphs under 'Getting an overall idea of the material', the topic sentences are the last sentences, though you may have been tempted to think that they were the first. However, even if you had, in skimming through the paragraphs you would have paid some attention to both the first and last sentences and would therefore have picked up my main ideas. In the two 'Skimming' paragraphs the topic sentences are both in the first sentences, with the rest of the paragraphs providing elaboration and details of the main idea.

Activity

Look through other sections of this book and see if you can find the topic sentences in paragraphs. If you find it very difficult too often, it's probably my fault, not yours!

Self-check

An author has at his disposal various devices – some visual and some verbal – for indicating to his reader which direction his line of thought is taking and which ideas he considers are important. Can you think of any examples of these 'signposts'?

Signposts

Visual signals Most textbooks and writing for business purposes will make use of *headings* and *subheadings* which indicate to the reader what is to follow. Other devices which act as visual signposts are:

1 Words and phrases underlined.
2 Words written in **bold face type**.
3 Words written in *italics*.
4 Lists using numbering, as in this example, or alternatively, lettering.

Verbal signals In addition to visual signals, there are also signal words to look out for, which suggest to the reader what is to follow; e.g. 'firstly' should prompt you to be on the look-out for 'secondly', 'thirdly', etc. later in the text; 'for example' will introduce some supporting detail which, at the skimming stage when you are only aiming for the broad picture, you can afford to skip over rapidly; and 'therefore' may introduce an important conclusion of what has gone before, so at the skimming stage you would want to read a sentence with 'therefore' in it.

These signal words act rather like traffic signals telling you to slow down or speed up and can therefore be classified accordingly:

- Slow-down words – these words signal that you should slow down because a change in ideas is about to occur:

however	but	nevertheless
although	despite	rather
yet	in spite of	on the other hand

- Keep-going words – these words signal that there is going to be more of the same:

furthermore	and	moreover
also	more	more than that
in addition	likewise	similarly

- Here-it-comes words – these words signal that a summary or conclusion is about to be stated:

therefore	consequently	thus
in conclusion	so	then
accordingly		

All these words help you through your reading like signposts. It is worth learning them and watching how they are used from now on. Then use them to help you read faster and better (and to help you write more clearly).

Bearing in mind the importance of topic sentences, and visual and verbal signposts, these are the rules of skimming which you should always follow when faced either with a pile of paperwork to read or before starting to read a textbook.

The method of skimming

1 Use your fastest possible reading speed – this is one of its main purposes. Since you are concerned with gaining an overview you can afford to go fast; you can read the detail later – if you need to.

2 Don't stop when you get to an interesting bit; it will only destroy your concentration on evaluation of the text. In any case, you will understand it better later on after you have formed a general view. Keep going!

3 Read the title, contents list and summary where they exist. If the document or book has headings and subheadings, skim rapidly through it reading them all before you go back to the beginning and continue with the rest of this method.

4 Read the *first paragraph* of the document or chapter. This will introduce the main topics and will state the assumptions on which later information is based. If the first paragraph is very general, you may need to read the second. Use your judgement.

5 Read the *first sentence*, and only the first sentence, of each subsequent paragraph. This should state the topic of the paragraph and should give the basic information about it. Don't read the paragraph itself – that's where the detail is, and you'll be coming back to it later if you need it.

6 Normally when taken in order, the first sentences of consecutive paragraphs should follow one another logically, without gaps. If they don't, try the last sentence of the paragraph you're on; if that doesn't work, try the last sentence of the preceding paragraph; if that still doesn't work, go on to the first sentence of the next paragraph. Though you may be left wondering – no writing can consistently stick to the rules – it is usually better to go on.

7 Near the end, read the *last two or three paragraphs* completely at a slower speed. They should contain deductions, conclusions and results from the preceding material. They may also contain a summary of the whole document or chapter, even though there is no heading to that effect.

Just as scanning is a technique of reading which you need to be able to call upon whenever it is appropriate to your reading purpose, so the ability to skim efficiently, when reading in more detail is not required, will extend your range of reading speed. Depending on your purpose and the nature and difficulty of the material, you should be able to slow down and speed up at will.

Activity

Turn to a chapter in this book which you have not already read. Chapter 11, 'Acquiring and organizing your material', would be a suitable one because much of the material is related to the ways in which material is structured to enable the reader to follow the writer's train of thought; it will therefore supplement the points we have looked at in this chapter. Skim through the chapter following the procedure recommended above. Remember – your purpose is merely to get an overall idea of the way the chapter is structured and a rough idea of what it is about. Keep your speed up and don't stop to consider detail or to carry out any of the self-checks or activities.

How did you get on? Don't be disappointed if you found that from time to time you were slipping back to reading at a fairly slow speed. Like everything else, it takes practice. It also takes a fair amount of self-discipline to drive yourself on, and the constant reminder that if your purpose does not require you to get a good grasp of the detail, then why hang about?

Now let's assume that you have scanned through the material in your in-tray, or found a book or an article which you now need to read thoroughly. Let's see how the skills of scanning and skimming can be used along with other techniques to approach your reading task in a systematic and active way, so that you will get the most possible from the material, in the shortest possible time, and in such a way that you can remember what you need to remember after the task is finished.

The approach has five stages and is called the SQ3R method after the initial letters of each stage.

First stage of reading – SURVEY!

If you only want to read a particular section of the document, you will need to scan the table of contents and possibly the index, if there is one, to find the particular reference you are interested in. If you are reading the whole document then you will need to survey the whole thing using the method suggested for skimming. This is an essential first stage in reading any fairly lengthy or complex material. Don't be tempted to skip sections like the preface or a synopsis, as they will usually contain valuable clues about the purpose of the document, the way it is organized and the overall idea of the whole document.

Second stage of reading – QUESTION!

In order to read actively and purposefully, you need to think continuously about what you are reading – in other words, concentrate. One of the best ways of concentrating and thinking about what you are reading, rather than just being like a piece of human blotting paper sopping up the ideas in a completely passive way, is to question what you are reading, just as you might question a speaker. Since the author is not with you, you must ask yourself questions:

- What is all this about?
- In the preface (or introduction) he said he would cover such-and-such an area. It doesn't seem to appear amongst the main headings. Has he linked it with something else under a different heading? He said at the beginning that he would make four points. I can only find three. What is the fourth point? Do I agree with these points?
- That seems to be rather a far-fetched conclusion. Has he got the evidence to support that view?

Many of these questions should occur to you while you are doing the initial survey, and will provide you with a basis for reading the text more actively and critically. But when you come to the actual reading, you should continue this questioning:

- Did he really back up what he said?

- That opinion seems to conflict with my opinion/my tutor's opinion/another author's opinion. Is his evidence better than that of others? Why?
- Is that what he really means, or is he being sarcastic or ironic?
- How many people did he interview to arrive at that conclusion?
- He seems to be using emotive arguments here? Is he trying to manipulate me?

Active participation in the reading process like this will help you to understand and retain what you are reading. It is therefore one of the most important reading skills and although it is suggested here as the second stage, you should constantly practise it throughout the whole process of reading something – just as skimming is a skill which, though used particularly at the survey stage, you should be prepared to use whenever it is appropriate.

Third stage of reading – READ!

'At last,' you may be saying, 'we are going to get down to the real business'. Yes! But like every other skill, it is not enough just to wish you were a more effective reader. It is necessary to analyse what good readers do, and be prepared to try out the various stages and techniques in the process – at first very slowly and then, as you become more skilled, the whole process becomes automatic.

Your initial survey will have provided you with some questions to which you are probably seeking the answer, and also an outline of the whole document or the first chapter which has suggested the main ideas the author is trying to communicate. As you now start to read, you will be looking to confirm the main ideas of each section, and find the main ideas at a lower level than you found in your survey. For instance, if you are reading an article or a short report, you will have skimmed through at the paragraph level looking for the main ideas in each paragraph. You will now be reading to confirm these ideas and to search for the supporting detail, the examples and illustrations which you ignored during the survey.

If, however, you are reading a book, your first survey will have been of the entire book, reading the chapter headings and section headings, the first and last paragraph of each chapter, and the whole of the preface and the last chapter to get a good general view of the whole book. You would then have to do a slightly closer survey of the first chapter along the lines suggested in the method of skimming; now you would be ready to start reading the chapter properly, looking for the supporting detail.

At this first reading, don't take notes – it will only break your train of thought and you would probably end up copying out large chunks of the author's original prose anyway.

Now, if what you are reading is fairly complex it is better to read it twice fairly fast rather than once slowly. At this second reading, provided it isn't someone else's book, underline the main ideas and the supporting detail, if you want to, but still don't take notes.

Fourth stage of reading – RECALL!

Now you can take notes! But not by copying. Try to recall the main ideas and the supporting detail contained in the section you have just read. 'Ah,' you say, 'but I can't!' If, after really trying, you can't remember what you've read, then you haven't been reading effectively. Go back and try again. This time the knowledge that you are going to have to recall what you are reading will probably help you to concentrate and read more effectively. There is nothing concentrates the mind so well as a test!

If retaining what you have read is your problem, then this is the most essential step for you – you can't afford to skip it. If, however, you find this step easy, then it won't take you long.

Fifth stage of reading – REVIEW!

This is the final stage – the chance to check that you haven't missed anything essential, that you have found the answers to the questions you've been producing, that you have been able to recall and make a note of all the main ideas and the important supporting detail without missing anything.

The review stage consists of going back very rapidly over the previous four stages:

- Survey – quickly survey the whole chapter or report again, checking that you are completely clear about the way the author has structured his material and that there aren't any loose ends that you can't explain. (There may still be some that *he* hasn't explained!).
- Question – remind yourself of the questions that you had after doing the survey and while reading the text. Have you found all the answers? If not, can you find the answer in the text, or should you make a note of them to get the answer elsewhere!
- Read – you may need to read through the text again. This is where your skill at rapid skimming will again be useful. Have you noticed something important this time, which you haven't made a note of before?
- Recall – this is your chance to check your notes. Fill in any gaps and make sure that your notes reflect the balance that the author gave to his material. Have you got very lengthy notes on a section to which the author devoted very little space? You may have a very good personal reason for this being so, but at least think about it!

Explained in detail like this, the process may seem time-consuming and off-putting. But remember, like any skill, reading takes longer to write about it than to actually do it. Learning to ride a bike can be rather painful at the beginning but now you can't remember what it felt like *not* to be able to do it. So it is with effective reading – hard at first, but worth it in the end.

Review

If you were normally in the habit of skimming through a book before you started to read, then you would probably have come across the following questions *before* you started reading this chapter. In that case if you didn't know the answers already, you would have been looking out for the answers as you read through the chapter which would have meant you would have been reading actively, and will mean that you will now find the questions very easy to answer.

If, however, you started in at the beginning and this is the first time you have come across the questions for this chapter, then you may find them a little more difficult to answer, but now is your chance to assess your comprehension of this chapter.

1 What are the three categories into which you could group your reading material, in terms of its value to you?
2 Suggest at least one advantage of skimming.
3 Apart from fictional writing, where would you expect to find the main idea of the paragraph?
4 Give an example of a 'slow-down' word, a 'speed-up' word and a 'here-it-comes' word.
5 List the five stages of reading.
6 At which of these five stages should you start making notes?

ANSWERS

1 The value of reading material can be assessed against these three categories: *essential, useful* and *irrelevant*.
2 Skimming helps you with the final reading task because at each level of depth of detail it familiarizes you with the structure of the material you are about to read, before you read it.
3 In discursive or factual writing the main idea is usually contained in a 'topic sentence' which is normally the first sentence of the paragraph, but is sometimes the last.
4 For examples of 'verbal signposts' see page 161.
5 The five stages of reading are: *survey, question, read, recall* and *review*. This method of reading is usually referred to as the SQ3R method.
6 You should not start taking or making notes until you start the *recall* stage. Having to make notes at this stage helps you to recall what you have read.

Activity

Carry out a chapter survey. Using an article or the chapter of a textbook fill in the following survey outline:

1 Title of the journal or textbook: _____

2 Title of the article or chapter: _____

3 List at least three questions the title suggests to you:

   a _____

   b _____

   c _____

4 Skim through the article reading the first paragraph, the headings and subheadings, the topic sentence of each paragraph and the whole of the last two paragraphs. What is the article/chapter about?

_____

_____

_____

_____

5 How much do you know already about the subject?

_____

_____

_____

6 What reading aids does the article/chapter contain?

   _____ bold print   _____ summary

   _____ italics   _____ bibliography

   _____ graphs, charts   _____ questions

   _____ picture   _____ other: _____

7 How valuable is the article/chapter to you?

   _____ Essential

   _____ Useful

   _____ Irrelevant

8 How long will it take you to study it properly?

_____

9 If you will need to divide the article/chapter into sections to study it, where are you going to divide it? (Name page numbers)

_____

10 List at least four questions you are going to read to find answers to:

   a _____

   b _____

   c _____

   d _____

Activity

Carry out a survey. Using this book, another textbook or a fairly long report, fill in the following survey outline:

1 Title: _____

2 List at least three questions or thoughts which the title suggests to you:

    a _____

    b _____

    c _____

3 List at least two major points the author makes in the preface/introduction/foreword

    a _____

    b _____

4 Take at least five chapter or section titles listed in the table of contents and turn them into questions:

    a _____

    b _____

    c _____

    d _____

    e _____

5 If there is an appendix, what does it contain?

_____

_____

6 Does the book/report contain a glossary?_____ An index?_____ If the answers are yes, look over the glossary and/or the index looking for familiar names, places or terms. How much do you think you are going to know about the contents?

_____

_____

7 Look through the first two chapters and tick any of the following reading aids used in them:

_____	headings	_____	footnotes
_____	subheadings	_____	pictures
_____	graphs, charts	_____	italics
_____	bold print	_____	bibliography
_____	study questions	_____	other

Part 4:
Preparing and planning
to communicate

In the last three chapters we looked at the skills and techniques involved in being an effective receiver of other people's communication. Indirectly we inevitably touched on principles which are the responsibility of the communicator. Using your insight into the difficulties of being a receiver, we can now turn in Part 4 to the ways in which you, this time in the role of communicator, can anticipate some of these difficulties and by careful planning and preparation try to avoid them.

10 | The essential questions

A rotten picture! *You own a Zanig television set which has just broken down for what seems to you to be the umpteenth time in its so far very short life – three and a half years. You returned it to the service department for their diagnosis and an estimate of the cost of repairing it, and you have just received a letter from the service manager telling you that the tube has gone and it will cost £150 to repair it.*

Your immediate reaction is anger and frustration and you are determined to write a letter complaining. The set is no longer under guarantee but it has so far been back for repair twice: once under guarantee after one year (selector unit faulty) and once outside the guarantee (tuner faulty, loss of colour: cost £7.65). Since each of these repairs, the picture has not been completely satisfactory but you have put up with it, partly because it was so inconvenient to return it to the service department and be without it, and partly because you couldn't really believe that there was something wrong again with what was supposed to be such a reliable set.

You bought the set after doing a fair amount of research – asking friends, reading consumer reports, talking to TV retailers – and were so convinced that it was probably the most reliable set on the market that you decided not to pay for a service contract. In fact, you already owned one or two other products made by Zanig with which you were very satisfied to the extent that you had become very loyal to the brand of Zanig.

However, your experience with the television set has worn your patience down. You are tempted to cut your losses and buy a new television made by a different maker and, furthermore, never buy anything made by Zanig again. At any rate you decide to write to the service manager and let him know how you feel.

Activity

Write the letter. Make up any other details you think you need.

Before we start to look at the process of writing that letter and the techniques which you can use to improve your chances of communicating what you really intend to communicate, why not think about some of the material you have read or listened to recently.

Activity

Go over what you read or listened to yesterday – a talk or a lecture, letters, reports, some articles in a newspaper, a chapter or two in a textbook perhaps, or an article describing some new process or idea in a magazine. Now think carefully of your reaction to each of these:

● Was what you read easy to follow even though the content may have been new to you?
● Were you given all the information you needed in order to understand what was being said?
● Did you feel the writer was well organized so that you didn't have to waste time sorting things out?
● Did he irritate you because he 'talked down' to you?
● Did he give you too much detail?
● Was this detail irrelevant?
● Did you feel agreeably disposed towards the communicator?

In these situations you have been the *receiver*, responding to the communication of others, and in such situations you can learn a great deal about communication in general before you ever get to your feet or put pen to paper. This is why this chapter comes after those concerned with receiving other people's communication and before we get down to the basics of writing letters and reports, and speaking in formal and informal situations.

The techniques described in this and the next few chapters are based on principles which apply to all communication, whether spoken or written. However, you will have had more experience in speaking situations all your life, and may find speaking, at least in informal situations, easier than writing. And yet it is obviously important for the modern businessman or woman to be able to write well. So much business is transacted in writing that very frequently you will be required to put your ideas on paper in the form of memos, instructions, notices, reports and letters. Incompetent writing and insensitive speaking can be responsible at best for misunderstandings but, at its worst, it can have an adverse effect on a person's career. It is important, then, that we do not rely on hit-or-miss tactics. We must know what we are doing and why, as well as how to achieve the best results.

The overall purpose of communication

Whenever we communicate we should have two purposes in mind:

• Transmitting a clear message.
• Maintaining or promoting a good/harmonious relationship with the receiver.

However, as we have seen it is all too easy to fail to communicate because the receiver doesn't understand the message which we thought was so clear, or because he becomes hurt or offended by something we have unwittingly communicated. How can we try to prevent these misunderstandings occurring?

There is no easy answer. It is simply a matter of thinking in advance about the message you want to convey. But not just vague, general thinking. The thinking and planning need to be purposeful and structured; otherwise it is all too easy to kid ourselves that we have thought about the message when, in fact, all we have really done is thought about what we want to say in the barest outline. Instead we need to consider, above all, the receiver and the situation in which the communication is going to take place. Just as communication is a two-way process so the thinking about it must be twofold. Of course, we need to know what we want to say; but we must also think about the person or persons with whom we want to communicate. This is essential if what we have to say is to be within the understanding of the receiver, and so that we get the right tone.

How can we give our thinking about the message a framework? Perhaps the simplest guidelines are expressed in Rudyard Kipling's poem:

> I keep six honest serving men
> (They taught me all I know)
> Their names are *what* and *why* and *when*
> And *how* and *where* and *who*.

Although I would not argue that those six words – what? why? when? how? where? who? – form the basis of all the questions we need to ask when we are about to communicate, I would ask them in a different order. After all, *what* we want to communicate is usually uppermost in our minds, and many a poor communication is the result of never getting beyond this question. No, I would leave consideration of what to communicate until later in the process of planning.

Why? Know your purpose

Why do I want to communicate? That is the essential first question you should ask. What exactly are you trying to achieve? Sometimes you will have a free choice in this matter of purpose; but more often than not in your job, someone else will give you an assignment which will determine your purpose. In other words, you are told what to do.

The purpose of most communicating that you do at work will be:

- to inform;
- to request;
- to confirm;
- to persuade.

> ### Self-check
>
> The following sentence fragments illustrate different purposes. Which?
>
> **a** Jim, I just wanted to let you know. . .
> **b** I would greatly appreciate it if you could. . .

c This note will confirm our telephone conversation. . .

d Therefore, the project will satisfy two very pressing needs. . .

a is a simple example of the most common purpose in business communication – informing; b indicates a courteous way of requesting; c's purpose is obviously confirming and d is obviously part of a message intent on persuading.

All fairly straightforward but, of course, it is not always quite this simple.

Self-check

Now look at these three assignments. What is the purpose behind each assignment?

a 'Write a memo to John Eden and tell him we won't be able to complete the job before the end of the month. . . .'

b 'Have a look at the Gasco job and let them know what has to be done. You might give him some idea of what it'll cost and how long you think it'll take.'

c 'That chap from MacDonald's has written about his central heating again. Says the same thing's gone wrong again. Give him a ring and tell him we'll call in next Friday on our way to Leicester.'

In each of these assignments you would have to pass on some information, and in b at least in some detail. But you must do more than that. In a and c, for example, you have to influence John Eden and the chap from MacDonald's so that they won't feel that they're getting a poor deal. In b you not only have to give Gasco a clear account of what the job involves, but you also have to make them feel that the job has been analysed by a competent person (i.e. you), that the quote is reasonable and that they'll get value for money. In other words, as well as informing them you must concentrate on convincing them of your sincerity and credibility as well.

There is another purpose for which much communication takes place, and that is to entertain. However, our purpose in business communication is not usually to entertain. But it is worth remembering that if, in achieving our main purpose, we can do it in such a way as to make it a pleasant experience to read or listen to our message, we have prepared the ground for easy acceptance of what we have to say.

Your purpose, then, is the first thing to be considered. What are you doing, and why are you doing it? Why are you writing or speaking, and what do you hope to accomplish by writing this particular memo or report, making this particular telephone conversation at this time and to this person?

The answers to these questions will determine your choice of material, the amount of material you will use, your organization of that material and even your style of writing or speaking.

Remember that since you will always affect your receiver in some way, you might as well ensure that you affect him in precisely the way you want.

To clarify your purpose, you should think carefully about it. Sometimes this will be easy as in the fairly simple cases above, but in others you may need to give the matter quite a lot of thought.

It helps to write down your purpose in a simple sentence or two; for a fairly long assignment like a report or a talk, this is essential, if you are not to lose track of your objective. This statement will probably form a part of the introduction to your message, in other words it is your *public* objective. But it is also useful sometimes to have a *private* objective which it might be tactless to reveal to your audience.

Self-check

Compare these two objectives. Which is 'public' and which is 'private'?

> The purpose of this report is to describe the range of word-processing systems available and recommend a suitable system for XYZ.

> To persuade the company board of directors to adopt the Kwik-word word-processing system.

The first one might well serve as a public objective and could be written into the introduction of the report, but the second is the real objective which you would keep constantly at the front of your mind when writing the report.

The statement of your purpose will not only serve as a guide, as you prepare an outline of what you want to say, but it will also limit your treatment of the subject. Everything you say must have some bearing on this statement of your purpose. If anything doesn't, then it must be ruthlessly rejected, however interesting it may be.

Now let's go back to that letter you wrote to the service manager about your television set. What was your objective?

Activity

Write down in one or two sentences your objective.

Look at the letter again. Does it indicate that you know your purpose? If you think it does, ask yourself whether it was the right purpose/objective.

FIRST POSSIBLE OBJECTIVE

To let the service manager know exactly how annoyed I am.

This is likely to be the first objective which comes into your head – or something like it. It is therefore very likely that you would reel off a list of what has gone wrong in a tone which makes it quite clear how angry you feel.

But what will this achieve? Certainly it will let him know exactly how you feel and it will probably do you good to air your frustration. However, it is very likely that this is all it will achieve. He will probably reply in a rather more polite tone, apologizing on behalf of the company and giving you all sorts of reasons and explanations as to why you have been unlucky enough to be 'the only one' to have had such an unfortunate experience. If the tone of his letter is conciliatory and polite, it will probably be because he has received complaint letters before, and is therefore used to suppressing his own indignation at being attacked in this way, when the cause of your complaint is after all not his personal fault. The reply you receive may of course be the work of someone else – a clerk whose job it is to

reply to complaint letters, who sees you not as a real individual
but as merely a faceless writer of a complaint letter, one in a pile
to be answered that day. If the service manager is responsible for
dictating his own letters, then you may have made him so
defensive that he will be likely to search for any possible way in
which he can attack you: you should have complained before;
the guarantee is meant to cover you against breakdowns soon
after you bought it, but you can't expect any product to be
guaranteed reliable for four years; you may have been unwittingly responsible for causing the breakdown and since 'they'
cannot be sure how you have treated the product over the years,
'they' cannot be held responsible . . . and so on.

SECOND POSSIBLE OBJECTIVE

To complain and get something done about it.

Exactly what you're not sure, but you feel you are entitled to
some sort of recompense.

This objective does go a little further than the first objective
but you are still likely to fall into the same traps and get a similar
reply to that suggested above.

Surely your objective is really to get the service manager to
understand and sympathize with your complaint to the extent
that he feels strongly enough that you deserve some positive help
from him in getting things put right, ideally without causing you
any expense.

THIRD POSSIBLE OBJECTIVE

*To persuade the service manager that your complaint is justified
and deserving of some special effort on his part to get things put
right for as little cost to you as he is authorized to allow.*

This objective – and it could obviously be expressed in various
ways – does begin to define more precisely what you want to
achieve and what you want the service manager to do and feel as
a result of reading your letter. We have gone further than just
thinking about ourselves and what we want to say in the heat of
the moment and begun to think about the receiver and how he
might react.

This brings us to the second question it is always necessary to
ask before attempting to communicate.

Who? Know your audience

Who exactly am I communicating with? It is possible that you have met the receiver, in which case you may know quite a lot about him. However, more often than not when we are communicating in business we have not met the receiver; even if we have, we do not really know him well, as we would a friend or relative to whom we are writing. How, therefore, can we answer the questions which we must think about whenever we are communicating?

Is he the right person to communicate with? Without a little thought it is easy to write to the wrong person, especially when we are contacting an organization and we don't know who does what, who is responsible for which department or operation in the organization.

A little research can often uncover the title of the right person to write to and sometimes even his name. A casual conversation in a shop with an assistant or perhaps the shop or departmental manager can often reveal something about the way the company organizes things like aftersales service, complaints or whatever aspect you are interested in. If a personal visit is impossible then make a telephone call to the organization in which your aim is to talk to the telephone operator himself. It is true that not all switchboard operators are as knowledgeable or even polite as we would wish, but if you are polite and friendly and can get them to talk (after asking them first whether they can spare you a moment!) it is surprising how much you can find out about an organization from the switchboard operator. After all, second only to the post-room staff, they probably know the name, position and general responsibilities of more people in the organization than anyone else.

Armed with some possible names and positions, the second thing you need to consider under this question is: who is the best person to communicate with in the sense that they will know something about the subject of your communication and, more important, will be able to do something about it? For example, it is often useful to aim at someone who has sufficient authority to deal with the matter constructively without being so lofty in status that either he will never see your letter because it will be opened by a secretary and dealt with by clerks in the department as a matter of routine, or he will be irritated because it is too insignificant a problem in his scheme of things to be worthy of his attention, and he will immediately re-address it to someone lower down the hierarchy.

At this stage it is easy to stop thinking about the receiver and assume that, since you don't know him personally, there is nothing else you know about him. But there are some general assumptions we can make about people. The receiver is after all bound to be a human being and yet all too often we communicate as if there is nobody at the other end.

Let's go back to the service manager and the television set. The service manager is not only an employee of Zanig, he is also a consumer, someone who buys products like television sets himself – products which sometimes break down and about which he needs to complain.

There are therefore at least two things to bear in mind when you communicate with him:

- He is an employee of the company. Your complaint is with the company, but it is not necessarily his fault that you have unfortunately bought a troublesome set. There is little point in getting rude and aggressive in your letter; in fact there rarely is. It will only antagonize him and you run the risk of losing a potential ally.
- He is a human being with feelings who may well be capable of feeling sympathetic to you and your problem if you can get him on your side. With the right approach, he can be motivated like anyone else to want to help you; in which case he may want to use whatever power and influence he has within the company to get you satisfaction.

How is he likely to react to the communication? In thinking about the objective and the receiver, we have already begun to answer this important question. One way to think intelligently about the receiver is to imagine how you might feel and react if you were in his position. How do you react when you receive a rude aggressive attack, even when you are to blame? Most people's immediate reaction is to go on the defensive; in doing so, they often become aggressive in turn, and certainly do not feel very willing to be calm and helpful. Most employees have some loyalty to the organization they work for and if they feel the organization is under attack, this loyalty can work against the attacker – the complainant. However, this same loyalty can be made to work in favour of the complainant. If the employee feels sympathetic towards you, and that the complaint is justi-fied, he may want to protect the reputation of the organization, but this time by doing everything possible to put the matter right and leaving you feeling as warmly disposed towards the organi-zation as possible.

Putting yourself in the receiver's shoes is not the complete answer, though. *You* might be an extremely patient, tolerant person able to remain calm and understanding even in the face of a torrent of abuse, and expecting other people to be equally tolerant and understanding. You should therefore be aware that not everyone may react in the same way you would.

Activity

From your knowledge of people, their personalities and attitudes, try to make some predictions about the way your receiver might react.

He might well be quick to take offence, so you must avoid giving him the chance; he might be very busy so you should keep your communication as brief as possible while still telling him every-thing he needs to know – and that brings us to the next question we need to answer.

How much does he know? How much does your receiver know about the subject of your communication? When you are prompted to start communicating about something, the subject and its background are uppermost in your mind. It is all too easy to assume, without thinking, that the receiver is in the same position as you; but remember, your communication is likely to come out of the blue. When he receives your letter, report or spoken words, he will almost inevitably have been involved in thinking about something completely different. So you will have to 'fill him in', not just about the immediate facts of the subject, but enough details of the background to the subject or problem for him to get to the same position of understanding as you.

It is also easy to err the other way and launch into a catalogue of minute details which leaves him feeling even more confused.

You must therefore work out in advance as precisely as possible what he knows already and what he needs to know in order to deal with your problem.

Our service manager will obviously know about the products his organization produces and sells – at least, those that he is required to know about in order to repair them. If the television has previously been repaired in the department he works in, there should be records of the previous repairs. But when he opens your letter he will not be able to call your particular television and repairs instantly to mind, so help him by giving him dates and details of repairs and invoice numbers if you have them, so that your letter conveys enough detail to give him an outline of the subject, and allows him to get more information from his files if he needs to.

Activity

Now go back to your letter. Does it indicate that you have thought carefully about your reader?

In thinking about your audience you need to ask the following questions:

- Who is he? What is he like?
- Why will he read or be listening to what I have to say?
- Can I expect him to study the material carefully or will he read or listen to it superficially?
- How much does he know about the subject? A great deal? A little? Nothing at all?
- If you are communicating to a group, do they have any common interests?

If you consider your audience in this way before you communicate, you are more likely to be effective and thus avoid the three major faults:

- the tendency on the part of the writer or speaker to omit essential details simply because he is so familiar with them that he takes it for granted that everyone else is familiar with them too;

- the use of specialized vocabulary when writing for the general public without explaining what the words mean;
- the use of too much detail because either the audience does have the background knowledge and there is no need to supply it, or the communicator can't discipline himself enough to omit what is unnecessary but what he thinks is interesting.

Give your audience the information it needs – no more and no less – in the language it understands

So far, then, we have already got some ideas about what we want to say, what we need to say and how we should say it, but we are still not ready to tackle the problem of *what* we are to say and *how* we are to say it.

First we must consider the *when* and *where* of Rudyard Kipling's poem.

When and where? Know your context

No communication takes place in a vacuum. It is always a part of, and therefore affected by, the surrounding situation – the context.

We have probably all suffered from having something we have said repeated out of its original context with the result that the message, or that part of it, is distorted or misunderstood.

While we are aware of the importance of context in relation to parts of a message, we sometimes overlook the fact that the *entire message* is bound up with its context. If we are to communicate effectively we must be fully aware of the physical and psychological factors which make up the context in which that communication will take place.

Physical context

Surroundings Will the communication take place in a plush-carpeted, panelled office with one communicator sitting behind a massive leather-covered executive desk? Or will it take place over coffee during a hurried fifteen-minute break? Is the message communicated in a lift or car park at the end of a hard day at work? Or does it take place in leisurely, relaxed surroundings – or on the golf course? Will that letter be read in the peace and quiet of an individual office, or on the train, or in the hubbub of a busy department with typewriters or other machinery causing a distraction?

Depending on the particular location where the communication takes place, there will, as we have seen earlier, be varying degrees of stimuli competing for attention and creating an atmosphere which will affect the way a communication is received.

For example, the specific arrangement of seating affects the communication process.

Seating arrangement In large group meetings, rows of seats facing a platform will create a very different context from a semi-circle of seats with the speaker standing near the middle. Low chairs and a coffee table may create a more relaxed setting for an interview than office chairs either side of a big formal desk.

Number of receivers The total number of receivers involved in a communication must be considered. In oral situations, there is a difference in the amount and kind of interaction that occurs in, for instance, an interview (maximum interaction and feedback) and a presentation to fifty or more people (minimum interaction and feedback).

Time Will the communication occur in the morning, in the afternoon, or in the evening? Too early in the morning and the receiver may not be as alert as later in the day. Too late and the reception of the message may be influenced by receivers who are simply too exhausted to receive and decode the message accurately. After lunch and they may feel too relaxed to concentrate.

Adolf Hitler suggested evening meetings for his rallies, because he felt the people would be so tired that they would 'succumb more easily to the dominating force of a stronger will'.

Wherever you are able to control the physical context of your communication – choice of room, seating arrangements and time of day – take advantage of organizing the context to suit your purpose.

Where you have no control over the context, at least think about the possible effects and they will influence what and how you communicate.

Think about how *you* feel in different contexts and let that be your guide.

Self-check

Which of these settings –

a the communicator's office
b the board room
c at the work station (where the employee normally works)
d a room usually used for training courses and joint consultative meetings

– might be the best physical setting for each of the following messages?

1 A talk by the managing director to all first-time supervisors as part of an efficiency drive.
2 A word of warning to an employee who has been persistently late for work.
3 A presentation to senior executives to persuade them to accept a new idea you have been asked to investigate and report on.

In principle, any setting could be suitable for any message, since it would depend on the real purpose of the message, the anticipated attitude of the receiver(s), the background of the message and the skill of the receiver in counteracting any potential disadvantages of the setting.

While no setting is probably ever ideal in all respects, a sensitive communicator should be able to adapt the style of his message to suit the circumstances. So if he is forced, for example, to talk to a small group in a very large room, he should realize the likely effects of this setting and perhaps arrange the seating so that only a part of the room is being used. He might also try, by adopting a friendly intimate style and tone, to indicate to the group that though the room is large and formal, he does not intend the occasion to be formal.

Similarly, a manager in reprimanding an employee may want to summon the offender to his office and sit behind a desk with the employee on the other side. This seating arrangement would reinforce the idea of the manager's authority and the seriousness of the offence. On the other hand, he might want to create a less forbidding atmosphere and conduct the interview with both of them on the other side of the desk, perhaps sitting in low chairs at a coffee table. He might want to go still further in removing the idea of being 'sent to the headmaster for a ticking-off' by speaking to the employee casually at his work station; though, depending on the nature of the message, it might be advisable to avoid the conversation being overheard.

This principle of 'going to them' is, in fact, a good rule of thumb if you anticipate an adverse reaction to your message and want to seek cooperation, because people usually feel more secure on their home ground. Consequently, the managing director would be advised not to intimidate the supervisors by summoning them to the board room and should consider using the meeting room which both he and the supervisors should be used to and see as neutral ground. However, if he thought that they were very unlikely to feel that they were being criticized and likely to feel instead that they were being taken into the managing director's confidence, then meeting in the board room might help by enhancing their status in the eyes of their colleagues.

Similarly, although it might be more difficult for you, the presentation to senior executives might best take place in the board room, in which they would feel at home and possibly therefore more receptive to your views. Taking them off their home ground into a neutral setting would tend to weaken the strength that would otherwise arise from their outnumbering you.

There is never any hard and fast right way to do things. The important thing is to be aware of the various factors involved and the 'signals' that various settings may give out.

Psychological context

Expectations In reality it is difficult to separate the physical context from the psychological context because they operate interdependently; the way we feel in a particular context is inevitably affected by our feelings and attitudes towards the physical surroundings. For example, the number of receivers influence the psychological as well as the physical communication context. If only fifteen people attend a meeting for which over one hundred were expected, interaction between the speaker and the audience may increase, but the effectiveness of that increased two-way communication may be reduced by the psychological impact on everyone of the low attendance. On the other hand, if many more people than anticipated attend a meeting, there may well be an atmosphere of excitement and satisfaction which may enable those communicating to overcome the problems created by the physically crowded conditions.

The influence of others Anyone who has ever been part of a mass meeting or a mass audience will know how powerfully the reactions of each receiver can affect and influence others. We get caught up in the mood of the crowd and are therefore likely to regard a speech as a great speech if the reactions of others around us are sufficiently positive. On the other hand, we may regard a very good speech as a poor speech if other audience members are extremely negative and unreceptive.

Similarly, if on reading a notice or a letter sent to many others as well as you, you find the other receivers are reacting in a particular way, you are very likely to react the same way.

Timing Choosing the right moment to communicate something can be crucial to its success. In a conversation with someone you have just met, you may be able to say things just before you part company that would be inappropriate during the first few minutes of the conversation.

Similarly, the way in which a message is received will be influenced to a certain extent by the mood of the receiver at that particular moment, and by the background or history of the subject and your relationship up to that moment. For example, turn back to cases 1 and 2 at the beginning of this book. In both cases, the way in which the words were received was heavily influenced by what had happened before, between the participants.

Now let's turn to the television service manager again. When you wrote the letter, did you picture the receiver in a physical setting? If you did, did that influence the way you wrote the letter? And did you bear in mind the time context? The fact that until then your relationship with him had been fairly distant, impersonal and straightforward. Set against this, a sudden volley of abuse might have come as rather a shock which, since he wasn't prepared, might have made him react adversely to your complaint. On the other hand, if you could remind him that until now you have not complained and have shown exemplary patience and tolerance, this might provide some justification for a rather stronger letter than would have been appropriate on the first occasion that the set broke down.

Another aspect of time that should be considered when planning a communication is, of course, the duration of the message. How long will it take? How long *should* it take? How long have you been given to speak? How busy is your receiver? Points to consider:

- The average adult can concentrate only for about twenty minutes.
- For most people time is a very valuable asset – there is never enough of it.
- Public and individual ability to retain information is notoriously short. Important information is best repeated several times (ideally using different media). In other words, several short messages may be more effective than one long one. A message given too early may be as ineffective as one given too late.

By this stage, after answering *why? who? when?* and *where?*, we are well on the way to knowing *what* we are going to say and *how* we are going to say it.

How you organize your material and the style and tone you will adopt will come later, but at this stage you should consider *how* you are going to communicate in terms of the methods of communication available – a letter? a telephone call? a personal interview or visit?

> ### Activity
>
> You have been asked to write an article to be included in a booklet to be sent to applicants for jobs/places in your organization/college. You were told: 'Say something about what it's like working for us (or being a student at this college).' First think about the questions *why? who? where? when?*
>
> Then list the steps you would take in the process of preparing the article.

Having answered the four essential questions *why? who? where?* and *when?* you should be well on your way to knowing what you are going to put in your article and how you are going to organize and order the material. The next chapter will look at techniques which help in the rest of the process of preparing a message.

11 | Acquiring and organizing your material

In the last chapter we looked at some of the essential questions that it is necessary to answer before you even start the process of communicating. This chapter carries on exploring the process of preparing and planning by asking the questions *what* and *how?* It will therefore look at what you are going to include in your message, where you can get the material from, how you can record your notes and then how you can organize the material so that it will best achieve your objective.

What? Know your subject

What exactly do I want or need to say? Unfortunately, it is often tempting to start with this question without considering the four previous questions. Answering these questions, as you will have seen, not only helps to reduce unintended misunderstandings, but also helps you to answer the question, what exactly do I want (or need) to say?

> *Self-check*
>
> Your department has received a cheque without a signature in payment for goods already dispatched. You need to send back the cheque with a covering letter explaining the problem and asking the receiver to put things right.
> What steps would you take in preparing and planning the letter?
> Draft the letter message.

Your mental notes might run something like this:

- Why? To get the customer to sign the cheque and send it back *immediately*.

- Who? A customer who has caused you inconvenience but not intentionally (at least we assume not!).
- When? The customer does a lot of business with the company, so may need to be reminded exactly which order the cheque was in payment for.
- Where? Probably not a very important question this time since the message is fairly routine and you don't expect the receiver's reaction to be anything other than cooperative.

Short messages

Whenever you are fairly familiar with the subject you are going to communicate about, the message is a fairly short one – a brief note, telephone call or letter – and you have made sure that you have to hand any details you might need – dates, names, reference numbers, etc. – you can now take pen to paper.

- Jot down in note form what you want to say, perhaps with a reminder alongside of how you want to say it.
- Organize these notes in a sensible order.
- Write the first draft (if it's a written message).
- Check your draft for errors – grammar, syntax, spelling, etc. – and for any possible ambiguities of content or tone.
- Re-write the final draft – if necessary.

If you are not really sure how to put things into a logical order, or if your message is a reasonably long one and you're also interested in how to put the words together in the most effective way possible – read on!

Understand what you're trying to communicate You can't write about a subject unless you know something about it. There is nothing more frustrating than trying to write about a subject you don't understand thoroughly. You will probably know what I mean if you have ever had to answer an essay question in an exam on a subject you are not prepared for. In fact, one of the reasons people sometimes write badly and incoherently is that they don't really understand what they're trying to say. It's no wonder that the reader is left rather puzzled too.

Communicate correctly and completely The material you use must be correct and complete. This means that before beginning to write anything you must be sure that you have all the facts you need and that they have been checked. In business writing, you are more concerned with facts than with opinions, although opinions can be important especially when they are based upon careful investigation of all the relevant and available facts.

The importance of communicating only adequate and accurate material should be obvious. Even a simple piece of communication like an ordinary business letter will contain facts: figures, quantities, qualities, times, dates, prices, names of people, organizations, addresses and places. In each case, errors can be made unless the information is checked before it is passed on.

Reports and articles are more complicated and require a great deal of investigative research and checking to make sure you are not misinforming your reader. It is better to hold off writing or speaking until you have completed your research than to rush in with inadequate and inaccurate information, which will mislead your audience and do nothing to improve your reputation for being reliable.

Longer messages

Selecting the subject If you have been asked to give a talk or write an article and have any choice in the matter, select a subject you know about. If you are interested and enthusiastic, this will help you to communicate in an interesting and enthusiastic way.

However, in business we usually have our subjects imposed on us, either by circumstances or by someone else. But beware; frequently the instructions given are very vague and usually very wide:

'Write a letter to Milfords telling them all about it.'

'Find out about this new idea for cutting office costs. Oh! and you'd better let me have a report on it.'

Limiting your subject You think you know exactly what you have to do until you come to do it. Only then the subject seems to get bigger and bigger, as more and more things seem relevant.

Go back to your purpose – to the objective you have written down. As we have seen, it is essential to know why you are communicating so that you can limit your subject to only those matters which are essential to your purpose. If you are working on someone else's instructions and you realize they are vague, go back and clarify them.

If you have suggested the subject yourself, don't take on the whole world. Limit it to one aspect which you can handle, in the time and the length you are allowed or which suits the circumstances.

Acquiring the information

You need information to write a letter, a report or give a talk. Where can you get information?

Primary sources

This means getting your material 'straight from the horse's mouth' so to speak. It will therefore involve you in interviewing or writing to the experts, the people who you suspect have information you need. You will need to consider these points:

- What do you need to know?
- Who is the best person to give you this information?
- How are you going to persuade them to be interested in helping you?
- What sort of questions are you going to ask and how are you going to frame them to make is as easy as possible to be given the right answers?

The ability to ask the right questions clearly is a great asset and should be cultivated. No one can answer questions satisfactorily if they are ambiguous.

Secondary sources

These sources, as their name suggests, mean that you are getting your material second-hand – usually from things other people have written, e.g. books, articles, reports. Again you need to know what you are looking for, and where is the best place to find it. This will vary with the particular subject you are tackling, but being able to work out where you will find the information you want will depend largely on how well you have kept your eyes and ears open in the past. For example, if you have been rather lazy in the past about familiarizing yourself with libraries and what they have to offer in terms of reference books, then now is the time to start.

If you are working on an unfamiliar subject and can't think where to start then ask a librarian, either in a public library or the local college library; alternatively you may find there is a library at your place of work which will specialize in work-related material and general reference and statistics.

It is really rather like being a detective at work. All you need is one clue to start you off and the curiosity and tenacity to keep following up leads. As any detective will tell you, the best clues often turn up in very unlikely places and at very unexpected moments.

Self-check

Your company frequently sends people to work for periods of a year or more to Nigeria. They are allowed to take their families if they wish, but in the past these arrangements have not always worked as well as the company would wish, since the employees have not had access to suitable information on which to base their decision to go with or without their family; and if they have taken their family, life in a strange country has not always turned out the way they expected.

You have been asked to do some research on life in Nigeria, and to produce an information pamphlet which briefly covers matters like climate, geography, the political and economic position, schooling, opportunities for wives to work, food, customs and practices for shopping, entertainments and social life generally.

Make a list of possible sources of information.

Well, your first move might be to track down employees who

have already been to Nigeria and ask them, and possibly their families too, about their experiences and what sort of information they would have found helpful before they went. These sources of information might well lead to others – for example, there is an organization which puts wives who are about to go abroad in touch with someone else in Britain who has already spent a period living in the country concerned.

You might also try the Nigerian Embassy in London. Travel agencies would also be able to give you quite a lot of general information, certainly about climate and geography, customs and practices.

Your next stop would be the local library for reference books which would provide some of the hard facts. It must be possible to find out almost anything from reference books – if you can find the right book. The following list represents only a small selection of the sort of reference book which you should find helpful for business purposes, but you should always assume that the information exists – somewhere! Your job is to find it.

A general guide to reference material

Guide to Reference Material (A. J. Walford: Library Association, 1970 edition in three volumes).

Guide to Reference Books (American Library Association, 1967). These two books provide a helpful starting point if you are completely at a loss. But the following list represents a list of general reference books which you might find useful.

General *Annual Abstract of Statistics* (HMSO, published every year). Statistical information supplied to the Central Statistical Office by various government departments.

Britain: An Official Handbook (HMSO, annual). The national economy and administration of the United Kingdom, e.g. industry, labour, finance.

Chamber's Encyclopaedia (Pergamon Press, fifteen volumes, periodically updated).

Complete Atlas of the British Isles (Reader's Digest, 1977). As well as the usual atlas information, this is also a useful source of facts on nature, population, health statistics and physical characteristics of inhabitants of Great Britain, religion, language and dialects, machinery of government, crime trends, agriculture, recreation, trade, transport, communications, industry resources and products, building and architecture, Britain's world military commitments, etc.

Encyclopaedia Britannica (twenty-five volumes). Be wary of encyclopaedias as they quickly become out of date. However, this one is being revised continuously and each volume is periodically updated and reissued.

Geographical Digest (George Philip, annual). Useful for details of administrative and political changes.

Great World Atlas (Reader's Digest, 1978). Comprehensive maps on population, natural history, food patterns and health as well as the usual physical maps.

Keesing's Contemporary Archives (weekly). This summarizes news and each issue contains an index. Cumulative indexes appear every six months.

Kelly's Directories.

Social Trends (HMSO, annual).

Statesman's Year Book (Macmillan, annual). This not only contains statistical information on the countries of the world but also provides sources of that information.

Titles and Forms of Address: A guide to their correct use. (A. & C. Black, 1978 edition). Titles and forms of address plus abbreviations and pronunciation of difficult surnames.

Whitaker's Almanack (annual). Government, commerce and finance and general world statistics.

Who's Who (A. & C. Black, annual). Several thousand short biographies of notable persons.

Dictionaries *The Shorter Oxford English Dictionary* (Oxford University Press, 1933). Not small, as its name might suggest, but it gives examples of usage as well as definitions, etc.

The Concise Oxford Dictionary (Oxford University Press, 1976 edition).

Chamber's Twentieth Century Dictionary (Chambers, 1977 edition). It is worth having one of these last two dictionaries at home.

Brewer's Dictionary of Phrase and Fable (Cassell, 1970 edition). A fascinating source of meanings of phrases and 'words that have a tale to tell' which are not usually found in conventional dictionaries.

Self-check

Do you know the meaning and origin of the phrases 'beyond the pale' and 'like the curate's egg'?

Business *Bankers' Almanac and Year Book* (Skinner, annual). Detailed information about all kinds of financial institutions.

Directory of Directors (Skinner, annual). Who holds which directorships. A useful supplement to *Who's Who*.

Kelly's Directories (of merchants, manufacturers and shippers) (annual). Firms listed alphabetically and by trade.

Register of British Industry and Commerce (Kompass, annual). Information about hundreds of British manufacturers and their products.

Register of British Manufacturers (Iliffe, annual). Lists member firms by product and services; also lists trade associations and British trade unions.

Stock Exchange Official Year Book (annual). Financial information concerning all British companies quoted on the London Stock Exchange.

Which Company?: 'Daily Telegraph' Guide to Job Opportunities and Employers (Kogan Page, 1977).

Who Owns Whom? (Roskill, 1972).

Government *Civil Service Year Book* (HMSO, annual). Replaced *Imperial Calender* from 1974. Summarises functions of government departments, and lists ministers and civil servants down to Assistant Secretary level. Updated four times a year by Her Majesty's Ministers and Senior Staff in Public Departments.

Municipal Year Book (Municipal Journal, annual). Lists local authority council members and principal officers; addresses and telephone numbers of local departments throughout the UK. Includes brief descriptions of services operated by each authority and information relating expenditure on these services to the population served.

Parliament *Dod's Parliamentary Companion* (annual). Everything you need to know about parliament, MPs, officers, constituencies, ministers and heads of government departments, the judicature, the government of London, British Parliament, overseas government and biographical details of members of both the House of Lords and the House of Commons.

Vacher's European Companion. Addresses, membership and senior staff of the various European Economic Community institutions.

Travel *ABC Rail Guide* (monthly).
ABC World Airways Guide (monthly).

Self-check

Exercises in reference work: in which reference book(s) would you expect to find the following information:

1 Information about premium bonds.
2 Details about council building last year.
3 The number of deaths in the UK for a particular year.
4 The value of a particular country's exports or imports.
5 Names of holders of the Victoria Cross who are still alive.
6 Lists of householders in a particular area.
7 The currency of Qatar.
8 The chief imports of Thailand.
9 The MP for Bristol West.
10 Conditions for sending foodstuffs.
11 The salutation and complimentary close for a letter to a bishop.
12 The meaning of *op. cit.*
13 Where the island of Leros is situated.
14 Who said: 'We stand today on the edge of a new era.'
15 The origin and meaning of: 'on the nail'.

These are reference books you can use: **1** *Post Office Guide;* **2** *Municipal Year Book;* **3** *Annual Abstract of Statistics;* **4** *Statesman's Year Book;* **5** *Whitaker's Almanack;* **6** Electoral Register (or *Kelly's Local Directory);* **7** *Statesman's Year Book;* **8** *Statesman's Year Book;* **9** *Whitaker's Almanack;* **10** *Post Office Guide;* **11** *Titles and Forms of Address;* **12** *Chamber's Twentieth Century Dictionary* or a dictionary of abbreviations; **13** an atlas; **14** *Penguin Dictionary of Modern Quotations;* **15** *Brewer's Dictionary of Phrase and Fable.*

Recording the information

Normally you will make notes as you go along.

Tip 1: You never remember what you think you'll remember, so always make brief notes. Keep a very small notebook in your pocket or handbag. You never know when something useful is going to turn up.

Tip 2: Develop your own system of shorthand. It doesn't matter if no one else can understand it – as long as you can.

Keeping notes

Self-check

Before we look at the skills involved in taking and making notes, think about the various methods you could use to store your notes, and the advantages and and disadvantages of each.

NOTEBOOK

While this has the advantage of storing all your notes together, it makes the job of organising more difficult because you cannot change the order of the material – everything remains in the order you write it down. When you come to prepare your draft, your notes are confusing and you will have to write everything out again separately so that you can put it in an appropriate order.

LOOSELEAF FILE

The use of loose sheets in a ring-binder is probably the best method because you can add and take out notes at will, and store the notes in sections according to their subject matter. Use cardboard sheets (dividers) to separate the various sections.

CARDS

Cards are a very useful method of storing brief notes and references. But put only one item on each card. This allows you to reorder the information over and over again until you get it into the right order.

Probably the best solution is a mixture of cards and looseleaf sheets. Cards can be used for references, quotations, statistics and main section headings which can then be amplified in your more comprehensive notes written on looseleaf sheets.

Tip 1: Write on only one side of the paper and leave lots of space. It's expensive but it's worthwhile in the long run. You can add to the notes easily and cut the sheets and stick them together again in different ways to suit your purpose.

Tip 2: Always make a note of the source of the various bits of information, otherwise when you come to writing the final product and giving the references, you won't remember them. You will also need to know the source if you have to go back to it for clarification, or for more information.

Taking notes from spoken sources

It's worth bearing in mind that with the arrival of small but efficient tape recorders it is now possible to make verbatim recordings. Most people will not object if you record the lecture or conversation, as long as you explain your reasons and ask their permission first. You can then take notes from the recording afterwards at a more leisurely speed.

> ### Self-check
>
> If you cannot tape record the discussion, there are often ways of overcoming the problem of trying to ask questions, listen to the answers and make notes all at the same time. Think of four methods.

1 Take someone with you (one asks the questions and listens; the other listens and makes notes).
2 Write your questions down in advance. Then you only have to make notes of the answers alongside.
3 Make notes immediately after the interview or lecture.
4 If you must make notes during a talk or lecture, only note the essential points and fill in the outline afterwards.

Taking notes from written sources

- Always read the material first and then make notes.
- Use the structure of the original as a guide, e.g. headings, first and last sentences, first and last paragraphs (see Chapter 9).
- Look for relationships.

A list of points, however comprehensive, will not provide a complete record of a lecture or speech, the chapter of a book, or an article. You need to appreciate the relationship between the points expressed. Which are major points? Which are minor points? Which points are related? As the theme develops through the main points, and through the subheadings and minor details, a definite pattern should emerge.

The introduction may give you some clues about what is going to be dealt with and how the author or speaker intends to present his ideas. He will almost certainly refer to the major sections of his message.

Outlining

A well-planned talk or piece of writing will have a logical development and your notes will need to reflect this layout:

```
I  .......................................................................................
   A  ...................................................................................
   B  ...................................................................................
      1  ................................................................................
      2  ................................................................................
      3  ................................................................................
         a)  ...........................................................................
         b)  ...........................................................................
   C  ...................................................................................
      1  ................................................................................
      2  ................................................................................
II  ......................................................................................
   A  ...................................................................................
      1  ................................................................................
      2  ................................................................................
      3  ................................................................................
   B  ...................................................................................
      1  ................................................................................
      2  ................................................................................
   C  ...................................................................................
      1  ................................................................................
      2  ................................................................................
      3  ................................................................................
   D  ...................................................................................
      1  ................................................................................
      2  ................................................................................
         a)  ...........................................................................
         b)  ...........................................................................
```

The relationship between the ideas and their level of importance is shown by the system of numbering, lettering and indenting, so that all the ideas which start at the same imaginary vertical line have the same weight. The ideas alongside I, II, III, etc. all have the same weight; the ideas alongside A, B, C, D all have the same weight and so on. Thus, I, II and III are main divisions of the overall theme (the theme would normally be expressed in the title). A, B, C and D represent in each case an important breakdown of these main divisions in smaller units, or subdivisions; and 1, 2, 3 and 4 represent subdivisions of A or B or C.

Let's see how it works out in practice.

Self-check

Look back over this chapter and produce an outline for 'The Process of Writing an Article for a Journal'.

The simplest way of breaking down the subject 'The Process of Writing an Article for a Journal' might be as follows:

   I Selecting the subject
  II Limiting the scope
 III Acquiring the information
 IV Organizing the material
  V Writing the article

An expanded outline might look like this:

   I Selecting the subject
  II Limiting the scope
 III Acquiring the information
    A Reading
    B Note-taking
 IV Organizing the Material
    A Dividing it into logical sections
    B Putting the sections into a logical order
  V Writing the article
    A Making an outline
    B Writing the first draft
    C Editing the draft
    D Writing the final draft

Activity

Turn to Chapter 7. Using the headings as the main outline make notes of the contents of the chapter. You will have to produce some subheadings of your own.

Now find a chapter of a textbook which has very few or no headings and subheadings to help you and make notes of the contents of the chapter.

Summarizing

So far we have looked at extracting information and recording it in an intelligible outline. This outline is a form of summary and is useful for recording the contents of lectures, talks and speeches, discussions, meetings and interviews as well as reports, articles, books and letters.

Often, however, it is not sufficient to make an outline and just leave it at that. For one thing, an outline is written in note form which may be very difficult for someone else to understand – since if they did not hear or read the original they cannot fill in the details as you can.

If someone else may have to refer to what you have written, you will have to turn your notes into complete sentences and continuous prose. To distinguish this kind of summary from the outline explained in the last section, it is usually known as a précis or paragraph summary.

Now, perhaps because of the unfortunate memory many people have of labouring over précis-writing tasks at school, the word 'précis' often induces the shudders and is regarded by many people as both difficult and of no value outside the school room. But before you turn on to the next chapter, just think for a minute. If someone asks you about a film you've seen, you have no difficulty telling them. In the course of everyday conversation both at work and at home you recount quite happily things people have said and incidents that have taken place. You don't pass on all the details – you pass on a summarized version. So don't be put off by the word 'précis' which only means 'to abridge' or 'to shorten'. However, use 'summary' if you prefer. The important thing is that you do it, frequently and regularly;

the art of good summarizing is therefore an invaluable skill which is worth devoting some efforts to acquiring.

A précis (or summary) is a piece of connected and easily readable writing which expresses concisely and clearly the main ideas of any message, spoken or written.

Although it is inevitable that you will use the précis in the course of your everyday life, you probably do so without too much conscious thought. However, in business writing there are countless occasions when a rather more formal précis is required. You may be asked to summarize an article or report for a boss; you may have written a report yourself which will have involved summarizing, and in addition you may want to include a summary of the whole report at the beginning (this is standard practice at the beginning of a long report); or you may be asked to summarize some correspondence for your boss or for a meeting.

Self-check

So how do you go about it? Can you remember the steps in producing a précis?

The most important thing to remember is that a précis is not a paraphrase, i.e. it is not a mere selection of phrases and sentences lifted piecemeal from the original and glued together with your own words. It should *all* be written in your own words. It is essential to bear this in mind because it will help you to see the justification for the essential steps in précis writing. If you cheat, and skip these steps, you will produce poor summaries which are not well balanced and therefore not true reflections in miniature of the original. There are seven steps:

1 Listen carefully to the speech or read twice through the material you are going to summarize. Determine the overall theme – this forms a possible title.

2 Take outline notes or underline the important points if you prefer.

3 Write a rough draft from your notes. Don't look back at the book or you will be tempted to lift large chunks of the original. It is uncanny how when you are able to refer to the expressions

in the original, 'that' seems to be the only possible way to say it. So shut the book and find your own words to write this first draft.

4 Now check what you have written against your notes and against the original, if it is written material.

- Have you included all the essential points?
- Have you included any inessential points? Any examples, illustrations and quotations should be omitted.
- Have you changed the author's meaning in any way?
- Have you introduced ideas of your own? (You shouldn't.)

When, and only when, you have completed these steps satisfactorily you are ready for the final three steps.

5 Write the final précis. Remember, the purpose of a précis is to save the reader's time.

- It should be much shorter than the original. (Approximately one third is a good guide.)
- Write concisely using short, simple terms and sentences, and short paragraphs.
- The précis should be in the form of a paragraph which presents the ideas in a logical order, similar to that of the original.
- Avoid expressing your own opinions. You are summarizing the ideas of the author.
- Write in the past tense if what you are summarizing has already occurred and turn direct quotations into indirect speech.

6 Edit the précis – correcting grammar, sentence structure, spelling, punctuation and so on.
7 Now review the theme sentence. Is it still appropriate to use as a title?

It is not good enough just to know the steps in producing a précis. The only way to improve your skill is to practise – and keep practising. How about starting now?

Self-check

1 Prepare an *outline summary* of the following article.

‖ **2** Using this outline, prepare a *précis* of the article in about 160 words.

Professor George Miller's Granada lecture on Tuesday on 'Computers, Communication and Cognition' was salutary for those pessimists who dread the impact of automation on our social and economic institutions. He took a different view from the British physicist who predicted that twenty years from now electronic engineers might become 'conscientious objectors' to prevent their pernicious machines from wrecking the structure of society. Automation need not mean future unemployment if plans are made *now* to adapt our educational system to the new age and to redistribution of the labour force in new occupations. Professor Miller feels anyway that centuries of work will be needed to achieve full automation of industry.

The chief interest of the lecture, however, was the professor's approach to the relation between men and machines. In his view, the old question of whether machines are superior to men is irrelevant; a machine can work faster than a man in some spheres, but since man has the computer to help him, man and machine can together make a powerful team. What interests Miller is the nature of those systems of communication which mechanical and human brains have in common. By comparing, for instance, the modes of operation used by man and machine in answering questions, he hopes to gain insight into how we think. To what extent does the human brain function in the same way as the machine in processing information? If a question has to be answered by man or computer, the answer can be obtained either by consulting some memory store or by reconstruction of the known facts. In most cases, both techniques are used – but a machine can make use of its memory more efficiently than man. Furthermore, it can be designed to interrupt its main task to perform several subsidiary operations such as deriving answers from the given facts.

Miller's experiments are designed to find out to what extent humans use similar techniques in processing information – specifically in understanding the meaning of complex sentences. Harvard students were required to listen to sentences such as this: 'The story that the book that the man whom the girl that Jack kissed met wrote told was about a nuclear war.' This sentence, in spite of its unusual form, is perfectly grammatical (according to contemporary linguistic theorists such as Chomsky at Harvard). It consists of a number of clauses within clauses. It is necessary to interrupt the analysis of the main sentence in order to comprehend the inner clauses.

Miller measured how well students could remember such sentences. The results indicated that the ability of students to perform analysis of subsidiary clauses and at the same time carry out the main analysis of such sentences was rather limited. In a task such as this humans are less efficient than computers. Miller considers that experiments like this can help to tell us which tasks are best done by humans and which by computers. Perhaps he is being visionary, but his ideas are certainly worth attention.

[About 480 words. © New Society, London. Reprinted by permission.]

Here is my suggested version – not perfect, and not the same as yours no doubt, but it does seem to convey the basic idea of Professor Miller. However, compare your version with mine and think about the differences. I am sure, in some cases, your version will be better than mine.

Man and machine

(1) In his recent Granada lecture, 'Computers, Communication and Cognition', Professor George Miller differed from pessimists who argue that automation spells doom for society. He feels that since full automation is in the very distant future, plans made *now* to adapt education and the distribution of labour can prevent automation causing unemployment.

(2) He is more concerned with the way in which man and machine can work together as a powerful team and is therefore interested in comparing the way man and machine each process information. In answering questions man and computer both consult a memory store and reconstruct facts, but the computer can both use its memory more efficiently and perform these other operations concurrently.

(3) & (4) His experiments with Harvard students have concluded that in tasks which require the interruption of one thinking process by another, humans are less efficient than computers, and he considers that experiments like these can suggest which tasks are best performed by humans and which by computers.

[160 words]

This was quite a difficult passage to summarize, because the ideas are quite complex. In trying to remove the detail and examples there is a danger that the whole thread of the argument is lost. The important thing is that the theme – that by finding out what computers do best and humans do best we can help them work together as a team, which can prevent unemployment – is not lost sight of in the final précis and that all the major sections of the original are given proportional weight in the précis. The numbers beside my précis refer to the paragraphs in the original and you can see that I have combined the ideas of the third and fourth paragraphs.

As well as trying to summarize the ideas by standing back, as it were, and saying What is all this detail really getting at? you can also reduce the number of words by changing constructions wherever possible. For example, 'he took a different view from' can be expressed as 'he differed from' without really changing the sense. However, sometimes the one word alternative is more foggy than the simple phrase of several words it replaces. For example, I do not like 'concurrently'. 'At the same time' would probably be better, if the exact number of words was not crucial. Incidentally, 'concurrently' is anyway not really the right word since the computer does not carry out the two different operations absolutely at the same time. But it can alternate from one operation to another so fast that, compared with the speed of a human, to all intents and purposes it does perform the operations 'concurrently'; so I decided that word was better than any other I could think of.

Finally, I omitted any summary of the final sentence of the article because it seemed to be the personal opinion of the article writer. However, if you felt it was essential to include it then this might serve the purpose –

'Visionary ideas perhaps, but worth attention' – as a separate one-line paragraph.

Summarising a series of letters

You may be required to bring someone up to date on a particular matter which necessitates summarizing the correspondence so far.

The procedure is the same as that suggested above, but you may find the following additional points helpful.

1 The title of the summary should read:
   'A summary of the correspondence between (name) of (address of organization), and (name) of (organization), concerning (subject or theme of the correspondence)'.

2 Make your notes of each letter under the appropriate letter dates.

3 In your summary, include the dates, but not the letter form.

Self-check

Write a summary of the following three letters in about seventy-five words (not including the heading).

29 Purdown Avenue,
Lenton,
Frewshire.

22 February 19—

The Manager,
Sharpe's Garage,
Fore Street,
Lenton,
Frewshire.

Dear Sir,
I understand that the car I have just bought from your garage – a Stanton Special Mark 2 – has now been serviced and is ready for collection.

There are, however, two other jobs which I would like you to carry out before I collect the car. I understand that undersealing would provide worthwhile protection and that an aluminium exhaust system is likely to last longer.

Will you please proceed with these two jobs and let me know when I may collect the car.

Yours faithfully,

Matthew Benedick.

Sharpe's Garage,
Fore Street,
Lenton,
Frewshire.

26 February 19—

M. Benedick, Esq.,
29 Purdown Avenue,
Lenton,
Frewshire.

Dear Mr Benedick,
Thank you for your letter of 22 February, asking for further work
to be carried out on your Stanton Mark 2 car.

I have given instructions for the car to be undersealed and it
should be ready within four days. However, I should tell you that
there will be an extra charge of £5.60 for cleaning before the
underseal is applied.

I am afraid that although we normally hold a complete range of
aluminium exhaust systems, there has been a delivery delay on
the one best suited for your car. We have been told to expect
delivery within a week.

I therefore suggest that you collect the car after it has been
undersealed and I will notify you when the exhaust system arrives
so that you can arrange to bring the car in again.

Yours sincerely,

P. DENTON
Manager

29 Purdown Avenue,
Lenton,
Frewshire.

27 February 19—

P. Denton, Esq.,
Manager,
Sharpe's Garage,
Fore St,
Lenton,
Frewshire.

Dear Mr Denton,
Thank you for your letter of 26 February 19— regarding the
undersealing and exhaust system of my car. Please telephone me
at Lenton 4460 when the undersealing has been completed.

As you will know, there is no immediate urgency for the new
exhaust system and I will wait to hear from you.

Yours sincerely,

Matthew Benedick.

Example summary
A summary of the correspondence between Mr M. Benedick of 29
Purdown Avenue, Lenton, Frewshire, and the manager of Sharpe's
Garage, Fore Street, Lenton, Frewshire, concerning work to be done
on a recently serviced Stanton Special Mark 2 car.
   On 22 February, Mr Benedick asked for an aluminium exhaust system
and undersealing for the car.
   On 26 February, the manager promised undersealing within four
days, with an extra charge of £5.60 for preparatory cleaning, but quoted
a week's delivery for the exhaust. He suggested the car be collected
after undersealing.
   On 27 February, Mr Benedick asked to be telephoned when undersealing was finished and said the exhaust was not urgent.
[71 words]

Review

1 What are the steps in preparing short messages, once you have determined your purpose, your audience, the context and the subject?

2 You have been asked to investigate a matter about which you know very little, so you are going to have to interview people who do know about it. What questions should you ask yourself in preparing for the interview?

3 List three reference books which might be useful to you, but which you had never heard of before reading this chapter.

4 Is this statement true or false: You should always take comprehensive notes while you are reading a book, otherwise you will forget what you've read.

5 When taking notes you should reflect the . . . . between the ideas and their . . . .

6 Give two occasions when being good at summarizing would be an advantage.

7 List at least two points you should remember when summarizing correspondence.

ANSWERS

1 After you have answered the questions *why? who? when?* and *where?* the steps in preparing a short message are fairly simple:

- jot down your ideas in note form;
- organize these ideas into a logical order;
- write the first draft (or make the telephone call);
- check the draft for errors;
- write the final draft.

2 In preparing for an interview where you will be the one asking the questions, you should prepare by considering the following questions:

- What do I need to know?
- Who is the best person to provide this information?
- How shall I persuade them to be interested in helping me?
- What sort of questions shall I ask?

- How shall I frame the questions to make it easy to be given the information I need?

3 See 'A general guide to reference material' on page 197.
4 False: while it is essential to make notes of material you read (or hear) because your memory is unreliable, you should always make notes *after* you have read through the material twice.
5 The essential art of note-taking consists in distinguishing the main ideas from the details but your notes need to reflect the *relationship* between the ideas and their *level of importance*.
6 There are obviously countless occasions when summarizing proves to be a useful skill, for example:

- summarizing articles, reports, books for study purposes or for someone who hasn't time to read the original;
- summarizing a meeting or an interview or a discussion for someone who was unable to be there;
- summarizing a report so that you can provide a synopsis at the beginning of the report.

7 When summarizing correspondence you should:

- provide a title which includes the names, organizations and addresses of the correspondents and the subject of the correspondence;
- include letter dates;
- discard the letter form;
- write in the past tense.

Organizing your material

Clear thinking about what you are going to say or write involves much more than considering:

- the purpose;
- the audience;
- the context; and
- the subject.

It involves organizing this material so that you can set down your ideas in an orderly fashion. If you have ever listened to a child recounting an incident or the story of a film you will remember not only how amusing it was but also how difficult it was to follow and make sense of what the child was saying. If a letter or a report is as badly organized as this, it would be completely unacceptable in an adult situation. When you are taking notes from someone else's material you have to rely on their ability to organize their own material; recognizing the pattern they have used helps you to take sensible useful notes.

However, when you have to *make* notes – that is, design the pattern of a message of your own, from a huge assortment of information – the task is more difficult and you need to know how to find relationships between information so that you can put it into logical groups and then put those groups into a logical order, which the receiver can follow easily. Read this letter:

Dear Sir,

I am writing to complain about the price of my television. This is absolutely ridiculous. I only bought the set three and a half years ago and it is always going wrong which is very inconvenient for my wife and for my children, who keep taking it to the service department. I am also concerned that my friends may have reason to complain because I advised them to buy my set. I don't want them to have to pay £156.29 as well, although they have had the first thing go wrong with it.

Actually it was always a very good television with a very reliable and good picture and I am very pleased with the clock radio and the cassette player which I also have. In fact I am quite a fan of Zanig and always buy your products. The other television was made by Onyan and is still very good and I am so angry about this one that I am tempted to buy another one and never buy any more of your products. I cannot afford £156.29 and would therefore be grateful if you could do all in your power about it. At least let me know if you think it is worth repairing since it has been repaired three times already. Once the colour went funny. You didn't charge me for that and then again when the colour went it cost me £7.65 and now you are asking me to pay £156.29 for a new tube. The other one has had the same tube for twelve years and it is still perfectly all right. If I thought it was going to be unreliable I would have taken out a service contract but I didn't because everyone I asked – magazines, TV shop assistants said it wasn't necessary. I feel really cheated and I think you should do something about it.

Yours faithfully,

I. M. MOANIN

Since you already know something about the story of the television set which needs repairing (again!), you will probably have been able to sort some sense out of this muddle of ideas, but imagine if you were the service manager and this was the first you had heard of this complaint. How might you react?

Self-check

What is wrong with the letter?

The writer has literally written down his ideas as they came into his head, and this is where the problem lies. When we speak or write we are forced to utter one word after another in a linear fashion, but current knowledge about the working of the brain when we are thinking suggests that this is not really a linear process at all: we are often 'thinking' of a lot of ideas at once. Since we have to utter those ideas in a linear manner, it is all too easy to try to deal with more than one idea at once by uttering a bit of one idea followed by a bit of another unrelated idea and then another, and then going back to the first one again. We may be reflecting the mass of thoughts in our head but the result for anyone else is confusion.

We therefore need to break down the total idea into the various parts of which it is composed, then organize those thoughts into related 'chunks' or groups, and only then put them into a sensible order. The whole art of organizing our ideas consists therefore in:

• analysing the total material;
• classifying the material into logical groups;
• choosing the best order in which to present those groups.

Analysing and synthesizing

'Analysing' is the process of breaking down down a complicated whole into the various parts from which it is made. It is possible to analyse anything into its constituent parts, and examples of this process of analysing are easy to find. The table of contents in a book represents an analysis of the whole book.

Self check

What has been analysed to produce this list?

cherries   milk
eggs   baking powder
flour   margarine

And this?

yeast   barley
malt   hops

In deciding what whole these constituent parts make, i.e. a cherry cake and beer, you have reversed the process of 'analysis'. This reverse process is called 'synthesis'.

Self check

But let's go back to the process of analysis. Look again at the letter on page 216 and analyse that letter, or the whole idea expressed in the letter, into its constituent parts.

Since it is such a confusing letter you probably found the task of analysing it very difficult but you will probably have a list which looks rather like this:

complaint
television
quote of £156.29
ridiculous price
set bought three and a half years ago
history of breakdowns
inconvenience
friends bought the same set

Classifying

Strictly speaking, to analyse, or break down, that letter into its smallest constituent parts we could reasonably have produced a list of all the black letters:

I, a, m, w, r, i, t, i, n, g, etc.

Because I am sure you didn't analyse the letter in that much detail I can be equally sure that you went through the process of 'classifying'. In other words, you mentally joined some of the very small parts together to form bigger 'chunks' which were easier to manage. You discovered that some things had characteristics in common which meant that they could be grouped together or classified (put into classes). So we could have analysed the letter by classifying the parts in different ways.

The way you analyse and classify things will depend on:

- *why* you are classifying them – your purpose;
- *who* you are classifying them for – your audience;
- and, of course, the nature of the subject.

So why did you analyse the letter in the way you did? Perhaps because I asked you to analyse the 'whole idea', and this may have prompted you to list all the different *ideas* expressed in the letter.

Self-check

Now look at your list again and see whether you can classify the ideas so that you end up with a shorter list of bigger groups.

Here is my list:

- complaint (ridiculous price)
- this repair (nature of repair and price)
- television in question (reasons for buying, previous satisfaction)
- reasons for dissatisfaction (previous breakdowns, advice to friends to buy similar sets, similar problems)
- request for advice (keep it, repair it, buy another)

- threat to buy another set
- disappointment
- loyalty to Zanig (other products)

The groups you have listed will differ from mine because there are various ways you could classify this material. The particular way you choose will depend on how you see your purpose and your reader.

The phrases or words used to describe these groups could perhaps, with a little modification, be the headings in the final product. In any case, they will probably be the headings in the skeleton outline or plan which you will need to make (see page 203), in preparation for drafting the final message.

Logical order

Once you have classified your material into logical groups, your next task is to put those groups into a logical order.

Self-check

Look at the following and arrange them in a logical order (not alphabetically).

a Wednesday, Friday, Saturday, Monday, Sunday, Thursday, Tuesday.

b Paragraphs, words, reports, sentences.

c The departments at your college or at your place of work.

d 'The Years of the Depression', 'The Swinging Sixties', 'The Reign of Victoria', 'The Great War'.

e Rent or mortgage, education, clothing, luxuries and recreation, food.

f Rain, snow, sun, flooding, famine, frost, road blockages, drought, dangerous roads.

Why did you put them in that particular order?

Consciously or subconsciously you put them in the order that felt right. Sometimes the order is fairly obvious as perhaps in **a** the days of the week, and in **d** periods of history, which no doubt you put in the order that they come in time. But frequently the order is more difficult to choose, as in **e** and **f**; if you did manage to work out a relationship and therefore a logical order for these two groups, it was probably based on a particular logical connection which you thought of, but which might differ from someone else's. Let's look at the main methods most commonly used for arranging material in a sensible order, when no natural order springs immediately to mind.

Chronological order Useful for describing action or procedures.

A topic which has chronological development is probably the easiest to follow. Each section is arranged in the order it occurred through time – for this reason it is sometimes called 'historical order'. So in **a** above, whichever day you decided to start with, the rest probably followed in chronological order, e.g. Saturday, Sunday, Monday, Tuesday, Wednesday, Thursday, Friday; and similarly in **d**, provided you recognized the description of these historical periods (and your history isn't weak); you will probably have written: The Reign of Victoria, The Great War (1914–18), The Years of the Depression (1930s), The Swinging Sixties.

In giving your message you could reinforce this time order with expressions like 'first', 'second', 'next', 'then', 'after this', 'in the past', 'at present', 'in the future'.

Spatial order (or place order) Effective for describing machinery, buildings, furniture, geographical features. Facts are presented on a geographical basis – from place to place, e.g.

I Music throughout the World
  A Europe
  B The Mediterranean
  C Africa
  D The Middle East
  E The Far East
  F The Americas

Sometimes the topic appears to move from place to place at random but often it is possible to detect a more specific spatial relationship – from north to south, top to bottom, left to right, high to low, in and out, up and down. In the areas listed under 'Music throughout the World', the order starts with the place nearest to Britain and moves further away, although 'The Americas' causes a problem – should it come first or last? Should we move left or right, looking at a map of the world? In putting the departments in **e** in order you may have used spatial order, perhaps starting with your own department and moving out in terms of their geographical proximity; or perhaps moving from left to right as they appear on an organization chart; or you may have started with the biggest and/or most important descending to the smallest and/or least important.

Order of importance *Descending order of importance (or deductive order)*: most commonly used in business writing. The most important point is made first, gaining the reader's attention, and the minor details follow. Another example would be starting with the general and moving to the specific as in **b** perhaps – reports, paragraphs, sentences, words.

Ascending order of importance (or inductive order): not usually advisable in business writing, except in persuasive writing, where it can be very effective. It is, of course, the opposite of the last method, and would mean starting with least important details and ending with the major point. This would tend to be irritating in the normal informational or explanatory writing of business; but if it is used to present, for example, the reasons and justification for an idea before finally presenting the idea, the reader is more likely to accept a proposition or agree with an idea than if he had been presented with it baldly at the start. For examples of the effective use of inductive order in persuasion, turn to page 277.

Ascending order of complexity Useful for presenting technical information with trainees and customers. The simplest ideas are presented first so that the audience is not discouraged. Gradually the information progresses step by step through increasingly difficult and complicated material. This is, of course, typically used in teaching, but is also useful in selling when you do not want to put the customer off with too many technicalities and complexities at the beginning.

Descending order of familiarity Or 'moving from the known to the unknown'. Again this method is very useful in teaching and training but is equally useful in selling since it encourages confidence by starting with what is already familiar and moving on to the less familiar.

Cause and effect Cause and effect relationships give reasons and explain why things happen. Using this relationship helps to organize material which is concerned with explanations of events and processes.

Put simply, cause and effect means 'because of this, then that'. In other words, because this happened, that happened. Let's look at a well-known illustration:

The King died and the Queen died.

Two events, but no cause and effect relationship between them. Reading this, we would not know what was the connection between the King's death and Queen's death. Is the following any better?

The King died, and the Queen died a year later.

There is still no cause and effect relationship. There is now a chronological relationship, since we know the King died first. However, if we say,

The King died, and the Queen died a year later from grief,

the connection between the events is one of cause and effect: the King's death caused the Queen's death.

To check for cause and effect, and to ensure you know which ideas are causes and which effects, ask this question: which event could not have taken place the way it did without the other?

In **f** on page 220 you might have detected a possible cause and effect relationship between weather and natural disasters:

Causes	Effects
rain	flooding
snow	road blockages
sun	famine and drought
frost	dangerous roads

Topical order Frequently used in talks and speeches, the relationship is simply that each item is related to the overall topic.

Without a knowledge of this overall theme we can only guess at the relationship between the items, as in **e** above. At first sight, these items may have appeared totally unrelated, but if the overall theme or topic were, for instance, 'The Effects of the Economic Recession on Family Expenditure', we can see how each item could be related. However, as you will have probably discovered, there is no other relationship between them – no chronological, spatial or cause and effect relationship. Without any other relationship, the items could be logically dealt with in any order. In treating his topic the communicator may choose to give more importance to some than others, in which case rather than being presented in purely random order, he would probably opt for 'order of importance'.

Self check

Which of these various methods of arranging material did/could you use in writing the 'television' letter?

It seems possible to use one of several and perhaps a mixture of several, as long as each paragraph is constructed on the basis of only one method, e.g. cause and effect. Several breakdowns, cost, inconvenience, anxiety that friends' sets will also be troublesome, could all be treated as causes of your disappointment/anger/complaint (effect); or, chronological order could be used for a paragraph describing the series of breakdowns in time order – in fact the whole letter could be arranged on a chronological basis.

Activity

Try rewriting the letter on page 216 experimenting with different relationships and different orders.

Review

Now read the following major divisions of written messages or speeches. Then state what the pattern of development is in each case: chronological, spatial, order of importance, order of familiarity, cause and effect or topical.

a *Social effects of poverty in the nineteenth century*
Inadequate housing
Health
Inadequate education
Little or no vocational training

b *Making a telephone call in a public telephone box*
Have money ready
Lift receiver
Dial number
Wait for someone to answer
Put money in slot

c *Graduate training at Woodwards*
Introduction in 1967
General description of scheme
Recruitment and selection
The training programme
Appraising performance
Evaluation of results

d *Unemployment in Britain*
London and the Home Counties
Wales and the South West
Eastern England
The Midlands
The North
Scotland and Ireland

e *Rising crime rate*
Unemployment
Increasingly materialistic society
More efficient police detection
Falling moral standards
Working mothers

f *The silicon chip and you*
The impact of technology in the 1990s
The businessman and the future
General business training opportunities
A training course for *your* needs

ANSWERS

a Topical.

b Chronological.

c Chronological (think about it!).

d Spatial.

e Cause and effect (some people might argue that each of these *could* be contributory causes of the rise in the crime rate).

f Order of importance. The originator of this message might either want to place the emphasis on 'the impact of technology in the 1990s' and then descend to the more specific in discussing a particular training course (deductive order), or he might want to persuade his audience by leading them through to the only logical conclusion that they must attend his course in order to be prepared for the future (inductive order).

Activity

1 Assess your ability to *extract information* from talks and written material, over the course of the next week:

- Can you work out the central idea and main points in a talk or chapter? Easily? With difficulty?
- Is it still difficult to concentrate?
- Is vocabulary a problem?
- Do you still feel you have to write *everything* down?
- Can you think about what you hear and read?

2 Assess your ability to *arrange material*, over the course of the next week:

- Does your written work indicate that you have planned the arrangement?
- Which 'orders' do you use most? Do you use the appropriate order?
- Could you improve on the order you have used in anything you wrote this week?

Part 5
Say what you mean

In the previous two chapters we looked at the process of preparing and planning to communicate. Although it is very tempting to skip this very vital step in communicating, we have seen that careful preparation and planning not only help us to avoid confusing the receiver and causing misunderstandings, but also help us to work out what we really want to say and how best to say it. Without this preparation, the job of writing and speaking is so much harder; this probably accounts more often than not for complaints like, 'I'm no good at writing (or speaking, or interviewing).'

In order to help ourselves as communicators to get across our message in the way we intend, and fulfil the two overall objectives of business communication –

* transmit a clear message
* promote a harmonious relationship with the receiver

– we must help the receiver in his task of decoding what we mean. The next three chapters look at the way we can use words, sentences and paragraphs in order to make the receiver's job as easy as possible, and the final chapter looks at the all-important subject of non-verbal communication.

12 | Words, words, words

To be effective, communication must be

- clear
- concise
- courteous
- constructive
- correct and
- complete.

But there is no magic formula. The extent to which we can achieve these things depends on our ability to use the code – the English language – selecting and organizing the symbols to convey our meaning as exactly as possible.

In this chapter we shall look at the way different words and different combinations of words can alter the tone and style of what we say.

Although words are our primary symbols, or tools of communication, we should remember that messages can be transmitted without words. Such messages are called non-verbal communication; they are dealt with in greater detail in Chapter 15. But some non-verbal messages are so closely connected to the verbal messages they accompany that we should be aware of their importance as we look at the way we use words and language.

Non-verbal communication is divided into two categories; kinesic communications and metacommunications.

Kinesic communications

'Actions speak louder than words.' A wink, a frown, a smile all convey messages, as do appearance, dress, posture, temper and mood, punctuality, gestures, industry and so on.

Self-check

Look at the following actions and suggest possible messages that might be conveyed.

1 A manager slams down the telephone receiver.
2 An interviewee is kept waiting half an hour for an appointment.
3 Your boss reads through his mail while you explain your problem.
4 A company answers all correspondence within forty-eight hours of its receipt.

Possible messages conveyed by the actions:
1 The telephone call was not a pleasant one.
2 The interviewer has to deal with a crisis, is very busy, is overworked, or wants to show disrespect.
3 Your boss is either not very interested, tired of your always coming to him with what he considers problems you should be able to deal with, or wants to show lack of concern.
4 The company is efficient and considerate, or at least wants to give that impression.

Messages like these are being sent and received continually, and are important because it is often on the basis of these that we come to conclusions about people and organizations. In fact, kinesic messages usually have more impact than verbal ones. If the actions conflict with the words they accompany, we tend to take more notice of the actions than the words.

If the manager says, 'I like to encourage my people to come and talk over their problems with me', while at the same time glancing periodically at his watch or tapping his fingers on the desk, we are more likely to receive the message of impatience conveyed by the action than the message of patient understanding conveyed by his words.

How does a doctor convey that your allotted appointment time is up? By standing up and showing you to the door. You are left in no doubt that he considers your visit is over, even if he keeps talking about your problem right to the door.

We therefore need to be just as concerned about what we do as about what we say.

Metacommunications

'Reading between the lines . . .' we often say. Metacommunications are messages which are not literally expressed in words but accompany messages that are expressed in words:

- 'Thank you for your letter complaining that. . .' ('*I am paid to acknowledge your letter and deal with your complaint.*')
- 'Please make every effort to attend the meeting.' ('*In the past your attendance has usually been very poor.*')
- 'How are you?' ('*I want to be polite, but the last thing I want you to do is to tell me how you are.*')

Sir John Betjeman has compiled an amusing list of this 'double-talk'* which makes us smile all the more because we realize we have probably been guilty of uttering some of the examples ourselves. Here are a few of the more obvious or amusing items.

Can I help you? *(What the hell are you doing here? Go away.)*
. . . carefully considered. *(. . . I've not had time to read it.)*
Correct me if I'm wrong. *(Don't contradict.)*
Everyone's entitled to their own opinion. *(You don't know what you're talking about.)*
I'd be grateful if . . . *(You'd better do it, or else.)*
Far be it from me . . . *(I know better.)*
Fully guaranteed. *(Guaranteed by whom? For what? And for how long?)*
I don't mind constructive criticism but . . . *(Mind your own business.)*
I'll get in touch. *(You won't be hearing from me.)*
I'm sure you're right. *(I'm sure you're wrong.)*
I won't be a minute. *(I could be here indefinitely.)*
In depth. *(Too long.)*
Of course you know best. *(Of course I know best.)*
Off the record. *(I've told twenty-five people.)*
Strictly off the record. *(I've told hundreds of people.)*
We're taking care of it. *(I don't know what you're talking about.)*
With due respect . . . *(Thinking very little of you as I do . . .)*
You and I both know . . . *(You don't know, but I'm telling you . . .)*
You will appreciate that . . . *(You will not like the fact that . . .)*
[The Observer Copyright Ltd.]

* *Observer*, 13.3.77.

Metacommunications and kinesic communication have several characteristics that we should always bear in mind as communicators:

a *They vary in meaning.* Depending on the people involved and the situation or circumstances in which they are uttered, they will convey different meanings. 'I am sorry' can convey real sympathy or mean, 'I heard what you said, but I am not really interested in excuses.' 'Good morning' can convey warm friendship and 'How nice to see you', or it can mean 'I only want to acknowledge your existence.'

b *They are present in all messages.* Every message, be it written or spoken, conveys ideas in addition to the ideas expressed in the words. All actions, or even failure to act at all, have meaning.

c *They may or may not be intended.* Someone who says, 'I've heard that idea before', may intend merely to be stating a fact. On the other hand, he may be saying (using the same words) that your idea is unoriginal and therefore old hat and perhaps not worth discussing.

d *They convey clues about the communicator.* Someone who always uses long complicated words may be transmitting information about his educational background or about his desire to impress.

e *They can make a greater impact than the verbal message.* The expression of happy surprise and the warm smile will make a far greater impression on the receiver than the simple words, 'How nice to see you.'

f *They sometimes contradict the verbal message.* The disapproving frown on the face of a security guard who says, 'Can I help you?' is more likely to convey, 'What are you doing here?' than the apparent desire to help, expressed in the words.

g *They are influenced by circumstances surrounding the message.* Look back at Case 2 at the beginning of the book. The statement. 'Oh! What a relief!' meant one thing in the context of Joan's anxiety about the subject and atmosphere of the forthcoming interview, but had quite a different meaning if heard in the context of the strained relationship which had developed between Joan and Sarah.

h *They may have either positive or negative effects*. Just as any verbal message can be pleasant or unpleasant, so non-verbal messages can be pleasant and unpleasant.

Remember:

- There are no rules on how to interpret kinesic and metacommunications.
- Be aware of their presence and their influence
- Before transmitting a message, check carefully to see whether the words could convey 'between the lines' messages which could be harmful. If so, it may be necessary to do some rewriting.
- While receiving a message, receivers cannot ignore these non-verbal messages. They should be aware of them but not necessarily oversensitive to them. They must be seen against the total message.
- Awareness of the non-verbal messages will increase your likelihood of choosing the right word for your verbal messages.

Choosing the right words

It should be obvious now that to be understood we need to choose our words very carefully. We need to choose words that

- will be understood quickly and easily by the receiver; and
- do not convey overtones which might have an adverse or negative effect on our relationship with the receiver.

Most people would accept in theory that they would probably not use the same language in informal situations – at home, at a party – as they would use in more formal situations – talking to strangers, writing a business letter. And yet in practice many people seem unaware that they do allow inappropriate words to creep into their writing or their conversation. Either they employ, in formal business situations, very casual, colloquial language, or, in attempting to alter their language to suit a business situation, end up using a language which is too formal and pompous. Both these faults can occur particularly when writing.

The different 'languages' that people use are called 'registers'. One way of getting a chance to compare different registers is to listen to all four main radio wavebands in turn. Try it now.

Activity

Ask someone else to tune the radio to any of the four main stations – Radio 1, 2, 3 or 4 – but without telling you which one. Now try to recognize which station you are listening to. Repeat this several times. You may have to wait if there is music playing – and of course this may be a clue in itself.

If you were right each time, try to list those things which gave you clues.

- Subject: this may be the most obvious clue of all. If you are familiar with radio programmes you may be able to recognize the station simply from what is being said. But there are other clues, perhaps more subtle but every bit as powerful in helping you to recognize which station you are listening to.
- Tone of voice: light and bright; serious and thoughtful.
- Accent: the pronunciation of words.
- Dialect: the use of regional language.
- Words.

Activity

Perhaps you did not recognize them all correctly, but whether you did or not now try this exercise.

Tune to Radio 1. Write down the words you hear that are less likely to be heard on Radio 3, or during the reading of the news on any station.

Examples: 'a bit of', 'hi!', 'another great piece of music', 'disco', 'stint', 'fed up with'.)

You will probably have detected less difference between Radio 1 and 2 and between Radio 3 and 4, since Radio 1 and 2 tend to be more modern, relaxed and casual in tone and language than Radio 3 and 4. However, you will probably also have noticed that it depended on the situation – the type of programme (record selection, live broadcast, studio discussion, straight talk or play) – and on the speaker: some people are always more formal than others, some always more casual.

The radio depends on spoken English, which has many characteristics which distinguish it from written English. Spoken English is often very casual and is uttered often in incomplete sentences with odd words and repetition – all of which help to add vitality, but which would be regarded as unacceptable if written down.

However, if you can become sensitive to the subtle differences in register, tone and so on, which are appropriate in different spoken situations, you will become equally sensitive to inappropriate language in different written situations.

> ### Self-check
>
> Compare these two different treatments of the same subject:
>
> **a** Young people tend to get fed up with the life during the early stages of their army training and may give up before they have really got anything out of it.
> **b** There is a very real danger that young people may become disenchanted with the life during the early stages of their army training and so resign before they have derived any real benefit.
>
> In which situation might you use each statement? Why?

In each case the style is consistent. In **a** the style is fairly casual; phrases like 'get fed up with', 'give up' and 'got anything out of it' are all appropriate if the aim is a light, informal style, perhaps for a popular magazine article.

On the other hand **b** is more serious in tone; words like 'disenchanted', 'resign' and 'derived any real benefit' are therefore appropriate in a serious context, perhaps an essay or a report.

Both styles may be appropriate depending on the context, the purpose and the reader.

However, you must take care not to introduce idiomatic or colloquial phrases in the wrong context so that they jar on the reader's ear, as in this example which appeared in a serious factual report:

> The case of being out of stock occurred around twelve times a week which is not too bad considering they have more than 500 orders a week.

Self-check

Which phrase is out of place?

Here the phrase 'not too bad considering' is clearly out of tone with the general style of the report.

To be an effective communicator in business you must therefore learn to recognize the difference in register and to select the appropriate one for the situation and the receiver(s). The following six tips may help you.

Use words that the reader will understand.

Self-check

How many of these words do you understand?

modus operandi	fait accompli	monaxial
a priori	laissez-faire	deflagrate
per se	serum	carbonado
de facto	monition	boot

Now look the words up in a dictionary. Some of the words are Latin, Greek or French, some you will find in the dictionary labelled *obs* – obsolete, *arch* archaic, or *rare*, e.g. boot, which can mean *advantage* or *profit* and can be used in the archaic expression 'to make boot of' meaning 'to take advantage of'. Some are examples of technical words or jargon, e.g. serum, monaxial, which may be a useful shorthand for those familiar with them, but double-dutch to everyone else. Some people use words like these to impress others with their vocabulary, their knowledge or their education.

When receivers come across words which are not in their own vocabularies they may:

- be willing to pass over them without knowing the meaning;
- guess at the meaning and risk misunderstanding;
- stop and find the word in a dictionary; or
- wonder whether the word was used for the deliberate purpose of impressing. The metacommunication 'the writer is trying to impress by using sophisticated vocabulary' may get more attention than does the idea which is conveyed by the chosen words.

After picking up the 'trying to impress me' message between the lines, the receiver could experience a negative feeling that would interfere with comprehension of later sentences that are written in simple language.

Even words which are recognized by the receiver can cause a foggy effect when there are too many together e.g.

There was also support for an affirmative answer to the question of whether a significant difference in retention of benefit knowledge would be found.

You may have been fairly familiar with all these words but still found it necessary to read the passage through several times before you really understood the meaning. Perhaps, like me, you never really did understand what that sentence meant!

Use of complicated words, then, can result in

- no meaning;
- distorted meaning;
- wasted time;
- distraction from the intended message.

Self-check

Write a simpler word which could probably be used as an alternative to each of the following:

approximately	accomplished
commence	demonstrate
modification	purchase

Research studies show that 'social climbers' tend to choose the more complicated words. They have a need to impress. Consequently, someone who has the habit of using the complicated word instead of the simple word may be communicating 'social climber', as a between-the-lines message.

The words above might be more simply expressed as 'about', 'done', 'start' or 'begin', 'show', 'change' and 'buy'. However, as always, you must use your judgement. If a word is commonly used in the receiver's business, its use would be justified even if it is not understood by the general population. For example, one insurance agent writing to another may use the word 'actuary'. Its meaning is clear; and, since the word is common in the insurance business, it will not be identified as a word used purely to impress. But the same agent talking or writing to a client whose knowledge of insurance is limited may (instead of using 'actuary') use 'specialist in determining risks and rates'. Which word (or combination of words) to use will depend on your assessment of the receiver's background. But remember, although lawyers and doctors are usually accused of using jargon, every profession and every job develops its own special words which have a particular meaning for people in that business but which are jargon to everyone else, so don't assume that you are never guilty.

Activity

List some words which you realize are peculiar to your job or your group.

Choosing words which are appropriate to the receiver and the situation not only means avoiding long and complicated words, but also avoiding using *only* short simple words which may create a rather terse, immature style. Use your judgement and aim for variety.

One way to get variety is to use short, simple words for complicated ideas and longer words for ideas which are fairly straightforward.

Avoid the use of unbusinesslike colloquialisms

Informal or colloquial expressions should be used sparingly in business communications. They tend to be undignified and suggest an unbusinesslike manner. If the language you use in informal conversation communicates your ideas effectively, it is not incorrect, but it probably contains some expressions that would be unacceptable in a business situation and is therefore inappropriate, e.g.

to cut a long story short
in dire trouble
to go bust
to bank on ('we cannot bank on getting the parts in time')
not too bad
fed up with

If you frequently use language like this, make sure you can readily convey the ideas in a more acceptable way.

Self-check

Try rewriting the following passage in a rather more appropriate style, avoiding the colloquialisms.

I've no idea whether your order has been sent yet but if not, it's high time it was since everyone's pulling their finger out to get the business finished for the Christmas knees-up, but you know what the Christmas post's like – anything could have happened. Anyway, if it hasn't turned up within a week or so, drop me a line or give me a ring and I'll chivvy them up. If the worst comes to the worst, we'll stick another one in the post.

The following is certainly a more dignified version, but it has gone to the other extreme and sounds unnecessarily longwinded and pompous:

I am instructed to inform you that we are unable to ascertain whether your order has been dispatched to date. However, we are endeavouring to execute all orders extant at time of writing before the Christmas festivities commence. Nevertheless given the opprobrious unreliability of the national postal service, any eventuality may have occurred.

If you are not in receipt of same on the 13th prox. be kind enough to do us the esteemed favour of furnishing us with notification to the effect and we will progress a duplicate order with the utmost haste.

The version that follows is better. The language is straightforward without being too casual, and dignified without being pompous.

I am afraid I am unable to check that your order has been sent but your concern is certainly justified. We are making every effort to ensure that all outstanding orders are dealt with before the Christmas break but it is possible that your order has been delayed in the Christmas post.

If you have not received it by 20 December, please let me know and I will ensure that another order is sent off to you straight away.

Omit unnecessary words

The business writer should always aim for conciseness. No one enjoys reading a long, rambling message that wastes words. As a general rule, it is unbusinesslike for a writer to express in many words a thought that requires only a few. In business, *time is money* and unnecessarily long letters are time-consuming both to their writers and to their readers.

Self-check

Try finding a more concise way to express the following phrases:

a cheque for the sum of £10
for the period of a month
I want to take this opportunity to thank you
in regard to
at the earliest possible date
at a later date
due to the fact that
until such time as
in the event that
in view of the fact that
in relation to

during such time as
arrange for an investigation to be carried out with a view to
   ascertaining
it may be stated with some confidence that
will you be so kind as to
in addition to
basic fundamentals
consensus of opinion
each and every
full and complete
true facts
exact same
personal opinion
refer back to
whether or not

Some expressions can be shortened by changing the word form:

a machinist who takes great care: a careful machinist
in an impatient manner: impatiently
tools for which we have no use: useless tools
person with a lot of energy: energetic person

ANSWERS

a cheque for the sum of £10: a cheque for £10
for the period of a month: for a month
I want to take this opportunity to thank you: thank you
in regard to: about
at the earliest possible date: soon
at a later date: later
due to the fact that: since, because
until such time as: until
in the event that: if
in view of the fact that: because, since
in relation to: for, of, with, about
during such time as: while
arrange for an investigation to be carried out with a view to
   ascertaining: find out
it may be stated with some confidence that: we can say

will you be so kind as to: please
in addition to: besides
basic fundamentals: fundamentals/basics*
consensus of opinion: consensus/opinion*
each and every: each/every*
full and complete: full/complete*
true facts: facts/truth*
exact same: same
personal opinion: opinion
refer back to: refer to
whether or not: whether

Needless to say, this list contains only a few of the many expressions lacking conciseness. Verbiage (the abundance of words without necessity or without much meaning) is one of the worst problems in business writing – wasting the reader's time and confusing him so that he has to search for the message in a maze of words.

Look for opportunities to omit unnecessary words in your own writing. Use your judgement, though: don't eliminate words that are needed to make your meaning clear; don't omit words that are needed for the sake of courtesy. Always ask this question: If I leave this word/phrase out will it affect the meaning?

Be ruthless! Your reader will thank you, and (more important) probably get the message.

Avoid hackneyed expressions (clichés)

Some words and phrases have been used so many times by other writers that they have become worn and stale; some are mechanical and inaccurate. Because hackneyed expressions are common, they suggest a lack of originality (and, therefore, a lack of sincerity) on the writer's part; in fact, they may even suggest laziness. Business writing is particularly liable to these expressions (often known as 'business clichés', 'business jargon', 'businessese', 'commercialese').

The following list contains expressions that have lost their

---

*One or the other, but not both.

effectiveness through overuse. Several are wordy and inaccurate as well.

- 'for your information': sometimes this expression is used specifically to signify 'not for your action' but where it does not, it is being used purely as padding, so omit it. Of course you are writing for the reader's information;
- 'please advise me': don't use 'advise' to mean 'tell' or 'inform';
- 'take the liberty of': unnecessary, trite expression;
- 'your esteemed favour': if your favourite adjective is 'esteemed' you were probably writing letters at the turn of the century;
- 'we await the pleasure of': 'we look forward to';
- 'please oblige': be more specific;
- 'our Miss Peters': use 'our representative, Miss Peters', or simply 'Miss Peters';
- 'please find enclosed': 'I am enclosing';
- 'at your convenience': this phrase is extremely common; try to find an alternative;
- 'thanking you in advance': inappropriate, don't assume a favourable response.

There are of course many more expressions like these. Watch out for them in letters you receive, especially from insurance firms, solicitors, and small building firms, who seem to be particularly keen on this kind of old-fashioned meaningless language, perhaps because they are not used to writing – their skills are different – and when, on occasions, they have to write, they try to use language which seems official.

Some frequently used constructions, of course, are highly acceptable because they are accurate and precise. But you should generally use your own vocabulary to express ideas in your own way.

Avoid needless repetition

A good writer has at his command a variety of ways to express a single idea and this allows him to select the one which is most appropriate for his purpose, his reader and the circumstances. This ability depends on the control of a fairly large vocabulary:

not necessarily complicated words which will challenge the reader's ability to understand, but a stock of common words and expressions in order to avoid annoying repetition. It should not be necessary to use the word 'factory' five times in one paragraph when words such as 'firm', 'plant', 'concern', 'subsidiary' might convey the basic idea just as well.

Self-check

It is difficult to avoid repetition if your vocabulary is limited. The following exercise will test your facility with words. Each of the sentences contains an italicized word. Try to find two words that could be substituted for each word in italics. (Words which have more or less the same meaning are known as synonyms.) Use a dictionary or thesaurus only if you have difficulty in thinking of suitable synonyms.

Example: Do you *see* what I mean? (understand, comprehend)

1 My *job* is to see that everyone finds his allocated seat.
2 Our advertising programme proved to be a *big* success.
3 You will find this is a *hard* assignment.
4 The factory was housed in a *run-down* building.
5 Mr. Probyn is a *nice* man.
6 The purchasing manager was *very* unhappy.
7 The *goods* left our factory on Thursday.
8 The typist who prepared this report is very *good*.

Of course, in searching for synonyms, you must always bear in mind the context. In the last example *good* is a very vague word and it would depend on the meaning of the context whether *efficient* or *accurate* would be an appropriate synonym. *Willing* or *cooperative* might be better if that is what is meant by *good*.

Here are some possible synonyms:

1 responsibility, task
2 great, huge
3 difficult, tough

4 dilapidated, neglected
5 friendly, cooperative
6 extremely, most
7 product, order
8 efficient, accurate

Use sincere words

Reading between the lines, a reader gets messages about a writer's sincerity. Even when a writer is absolutely sincere, poorly chosen words can convey an impression of insincerity. The chances of getting a message across clearly and promoting good human relations are greatly reduced if the metacommunication is that 'the writer is a phoney' or 'the credibility is questionable'. Reactions like these are a strong possibility when writers use:

- words that suggest certain knowledge of future events;
- too many adjectives and adverbs;
- superlatives;
- words that suggest surprise.

Words of certainty Consider this sentence: 'I know you will want to order today.'

Even if the reader does want to order, could the writer really have known beforehand? The reader may even be put off ordering by the apparent cocksureness of the writer. If the reader does not want to order, he is immediately aware that the statement is false. His awareness of (and negative reaction to) artificiality in one sentence may reduce confidence in sentences that follow.

Adjectives and adverbs Adjectives and adverbs often add clarity and variety to a message. They are useful, but they should not be over-used, and they should not be so strong as to seem like exaggerations.

Self check

Rewrite this statement to avoid the exaggeration.

Our exhibition stand was a fantastic success, primarily because of our marvellously arranged displays.

The statement may (because of the words 'fantastic' and 'marvellously') seem like an overstatement. 'Our exhibition stand was successful, primarily because of our unusual displays' is a less forceful statement, but is more believable.

Over-use of strong adjectives and adverbs in one part of a message, which causes a statement to be doubted, can in turn cause the reader to doubt the objectivity of remaining parts.

Self check

What, in this statement, might cause you to doubt the following writer's judgement?

The company has been in existence for twenty-five years and its profits are increasing, but the stock control system is totally unsatisfactory.

If the company is making an increasing profit, then its stock control system cannot be *totally* unsatisfactory.

Superlatives Like adjectives and adverbs, superlatives are useful, but they should be used with caution. Superlatives are seldom unacceptable when they are supported, or at least supportable, by facts. Expressions like 'the youngest member of the staff' and 'the worst attendance record' are acceptable when their accuracy can be verified.

However, superlatives which cannot be supported by evidence can cause the reader to doubt the writer's sincerity. 'This is the best product available' could be true only if its author has knowledge of all products everywhere and if the product is exactly like those with which it is competing. Knowing that these conditions are extremely unlikely, a reader is inclined to doubt the statement, and liable to say to himself, 'Beware of this writer, he stretches the truth.'

Such a reaction can be avoided if a superlative is accompanied by facts or is adequately qualified. At the very least 'our product is the best we can find' is more believable than 'our product is the best available'.

Again a less forceful statement that can be believed is more useful than a strong statement that will be doubted.

Words of surprise Consider how you might react to these statements: 'We are surprised at your complaint.' 'We cannot understand why you have not taken advantage of this offer.'

The metacommunication in these statements is likely to be negative. The message coming through between the lines could be something like, 'Any normal person would not have complained. Your behaviour is abnormal and therefore bad', or 'We regard you as most unreasonable.'

Having received that message, a reader may be so distracted that the worded message fails to register as it should.

Review

Now look at the following statements. If the statement is true, put a T beside it. If it is false, put an F beside it.

1 Metacommunications should be avoided in business writing.

2 A message transmitted through action will have greater impact than a message transmitted through words.

3 If two people read or hear the same worded message, one may pick up an unworded message that is undetected by the other.

4 To gain a reader's respect, a writer should use complicated words instead of simple words.

5 To be readily understood, a message must be clearly expressed in language that is meaningful to the reader, so you should try to use informal, colloquial expressions in business writing.

6 Conciseness is a more desirable quality than clarity.

7 A writer who uses hackneyed expressions risks offending the reader's self-esteem.

8 To be able to choose the right word, a writer must have a large vocabulary.

9 Strong statements containing strong adjectives and adverbs are more likely to be believed by the receiver.

10 Now try to think of six words beginning with C which would describe the qualities of effective communication.

C. . . . .

C. . . . .

C. . . . .

C. . . . .

C. . . . .

C. . . . .

ANSWERS

1 False. Metacommunications accompany every worded message. They cannot be avoided. You should try hard to avoid using words that will cause the metacommunications to be negative or uncomplimentary. Since metacommunications can be positive, they can be helpful. They can help a writer in his attempt to achieve a clear message that also promotes harmony between writer and reader.

2 True. 'Actions speak louder than words.' When a person's actions conflict with his words, the receiver is more likely to believe the message communicated by actions (the kinesic communication).

3 True. Because of varying backgrounds or motives, two people may not get the same message. (See also Chapter 2).

4 False. Use of long words can cause loss of respect, especially if the receiver of the message suspects the long words are being used to impress. Even if the long words cause the receiver to think, 'I wish I had as much education as the writer', the result would be undesirable. The words employed should cause the receiver to think about the message conveyed instead of the sender's educational background.

5 False. Although business communications are better expressed in short, simple, familiar words, informal English contains many expressions which would be considered inappropriate in business, e.g. colloquial, vulgar and slang expressions as well as casual, popular expressions which are often only fashionable for short periods of time and with certain groups of people.

6 False. Both qualities are desirable. An unclear message can cause wasted time, confusion, wrong actions, hurt feelings, additional correspondence and so on. A wordy message requires more time to process, but this is a small problem compared with the consequences of a vague message.

7 True. Someone who reads such a hackneyed business expression as 'I shall appreciate your consideration in this matter' can hardly do so without being aware that the sentence is a standard letter-closing line – one that could be said to almost anyone about almost anything. By using the same combination of words that has been used on many others, a writer risks conveying such a metacommunication as 'You are nothing special to me. For routine people, I use routine words.'

8 True. To be able to choose words which are simple, familiar, concise and appropriate while at the same time avoiding repetition of the same words, you need to have a wide vocabulary from which to select the most appropriate word.

9 False. The metacommunication is more likely to be negative, such as 'subjectivity', 'overstatement', 'exaggeration'.

10 To be effective, communication must be *clear, concise, courteous, constructive, correct* and *complete*, but you may have thought of *comprehensive, comprehensible, coherent*. It is interesting how many words which describe effective *communication* begin with the letter C.

Now try putting those principles into practice.

Self-check

Rewrite the following sentences. Eliminate or change any expressions that would not be completely acceptable in business writing. Most of the sentences contain more than one such expression.

Example: 'I shall appreciate it if you will ensure that a catalogue is issued to each and every customer' – rewritten as: 'Please ensure that a catalogue is issued to every customer'; or if you wish to express your gratitude, rather than merely issuing an instruction under the guise of a request: 'I should appreciate it if you would ensure that a catalogue is issued to every customer.'

1 We should be grateful if you would telephone us in the event that you are unable to deliver the goods.
2 There are at the time of writing two vacancies in the accounts department.
3 Enclosed herewith please find the price list you requested.
4 Consequent on our discussions of the above mentioned matter. . .
5 In compliance with your request, we have dispatched a credit note to the value of £20 for the attention of your accountant.
6 I was quite put out to read your complaint.
7 Please oblige by sending information in reference to the new policy.
8 Would you be so kind as to comment upon the accuracy of the above statement.
9 I am taking the liberty of asking for your assistance in the formation of a local branch of the Institute of Personnel Management.
10 Our Mr Sharpe will be happy to call on you at your convenience.

Here follow my suggestions for each of those sentences; yours will probably be slightly different. However, make sure that you have not just written equally unacceptable expressions in your alternatives.

1 Please telephone us if you are unable to deliver the goods.
2 There are at present two vacancies in the accounts department.
3 I am enclosing the price list you requested.
4 Following our discussions of this matter. . .
5 As you requested, we have sent a credit note for £20 to your accountant.
6 I was very concerned by your complaint.
7 Please give us the following details about the new policy.

8 Please let us (me) know if the preceding statement is true.
9 Would you be interested in helping us to form a local branch of the Institute of Personnel Management.
10 Mr Sharpe, our representative, will be happy to call on you whenever it is convenient.

13 | Constructing effective sentences

The ability of men and women to construct strong sentences – sentences that communicate ideas clearly and forcefully – can undoubtedly enhance their chances of promotion in business. In this chapter we look at the variety of ways in which sentences can be constructed in order to create different effects, and at the pitfalls which await the careless writer. Although I use some grammatical terms, don't be put off by this; the terms don't matter as long as you can avoid the errors! So concentrate on doing the activities in each section; if you do these correctly you'll be all right. There are thousands of good writers who have no idea of the names for the principles they follow naturally.

This chapter assumes that you know the basic structure of an English sentence – subject–verb–complement – and that sentences can be simple, complex or compound. If you have forgotten or are unfamiliar with either of these notions then you should read the relevant chapter ('What is a verb, then?') in the companion volume to this book, *The Business of Communicating*.

I am also assuming in this chapter that you recognize the importance of variety in all mature writing. Good writers use simple, complex and compound sentences of varying lengths to hold the interest of their readers. A series of short, choppy simple sentences can be just as dull and uninspiring as a series of long, involved compound sentences. In professional writing, variety really is the spice of life.

Unity

A sentence should have only *one main idea*. In building a sentence, you should therefore include only very closely related ideas. A sentence is said to lack 'unity' if it includes ideas that are not closely related. A lack of unity, or oneness of aim, can unduly challenge the reader who has to struggle to work out what is the main idea. Consider this sentence:

> The panel will be composed of Edward Simmonds, a banker; Glyn Edwards, an industrialist; and Oliver Lynch, whose eldest son shot down seven enemy planes during the last war.

This sentence is concerned with the composition of a panel. Two members have been identified logically by name and occupation. The mention of Mr Lynch's son and his heroic exploits would distract the average reader. Because the idea of the panel and the idea of the son's wartime experience are not closely related, the sentence lacks unity. Here are two more examples of what to avoid:

> Mr Jones is our oldest employee, and the firm lost money last year.
> Roger has three children, and life insurance is a good investment.

This last sentence would not have broken the rule of unity if it had been expressed in this way: 'Because Roger has three children, he should invest in a life insurance policy.'

Simple, complex and compound

The following *simple* sentence contains one idea:

> The secretary typed the minutes.
>   (subject) (verb)   (object)

Because only one idea is included, clarity is easy to achieve. Within the sentence, the idea of who typed the minutes has no other idea with which to compete. Therefore, the thought stands out vividly in the reader's mind. When an idea is especially important, when it deserves emphasis, try placing it in a simple sentence.

The following *complex* sentence contains two ideas – a primary idea and a secondary idea:

> (secondary idea)   (primary idea)
> According to the witness, the secretary typed the minutes.
>   (dependent thought)   (independent thought)

Because a reader encounters more than one thought in a complex sentence, each thought is less vivid than it would be in a simple sentence. Each shares part of the limelight with the other. However, the independent idea (the idea that would make sense if it stood alone in the sentence) gets the stronger light; it gets more attention. When an idea is not particularly important, or when it is unfavourable and should not be stressed, place it in the dependent part of the sentence. In the example above, the dependent thought happens to be first; but it can come after the independent thought:

The secretary typed the minutes, according to the witness.

Or it can split the independent thought (parenthetical):

The secretary, according to the witness, typed the minutes.

The following *compound* sentence contains two complete thoughts:

The secretary typed the minutes, but the chairman dictated them.

Whereas in the complex sentence one thought has more weight than the other, in a compound sentence the two parts have about equal weight. The relationship of the two parts is indicated by the conjunction (linking word) that comes between. 'But' indicates that the second idea is in contrast with the first.

Note: 'and' would have indicated that the second idea is in addition to the first. Coming between two thoughts, 'therefore' or 'consequently' would suggest that the second resulted from the first. 'Nevertheless' would suggest that the second resulted in spite of the first. Take care to use the conjunction which best suits the relationship you want to convey. Don't use 'and' where you mean 'but', for example.

When two ideas are of about the same importance (deserve about the same emphasis), this equality can be conveyed through use of a compound sentence:

Joan has a poor attendance record, and her performance is deteriorating.

But supposing you had a favourable idea and an unfavourable idea to convey:

Joan has a poor attendance record. Her performance is improving.

For human relations reasons you wish to de-emphasize the

unfavourable idea. How could you put both ideas into one sentence?

Answer: one way to keep the thought from standing out so vividly in the reader's mind is to place the unfavourable thought in one part of a compound sentence and the positive thought in the other:

Joan has a poor attendance record, but her performance is improving.

In this way the unfavourable idea is counter-balanced by the favourable idea. However, a *complex* sentence could further de-emphasize the unfavourable:

Although Joan's attendance record is poor, her performance is improving.

The improvement in performance (appearing in the independent part of the sentence) gets more attention than the attendance record (appearing in the dependent part).

Excessive detail

Although compound and complex sentences can be very useful when used in this way to balance ideas, and increase or reduce emphasis, you should avoid including too many ideas or details in one sentence. Even ideas that are closely related should not be included in a single sentence if they are likely to confuse the reader. The following sentence would prove troublesome to any reader, not because it seriously lacks unity but because it contains excessive detail:

Miss Dixon, who answered the flashing light, the usual signal that her boss wanted her to take dictation, took the notes he dictated on the arsonist's conviction for setting fire to four houses in which ten people were injured (most of the residents got out safely) and typed out four letters.

Self-check

Several lines of thought are expressed in this long, loosely connected sentence. Try writing it as a paragraph instead, to make it more forceful and easier to understand:

Because her boss had signalled that he wanted her to take dictation, Miss Dixon went into his office. His dictation concerned the conviction of the arsonist who had set fire to four houses and, in the process, injured ten people. Miss Dixon typed four letters from her notes.

Loose and periodic sentences

A *loose* sentence has the main clause representing the main idea at the beginning and the subordinate details at the end. As its name suggests, the danger is that the author is tempted to add fact after fact as they occur to him until the sentence has lost its unity.

a The new product appears to be selling well, which is encouraging, since profits have been falling during the last year, although the appointment of our new sales manager has meant that the morale of the sales team has improved and this has been reflected in the sales figures recently.

However, used with control and judgement, the loose sentence has the advantage of placing the main idea first in the reader's mind and then adding the supporting detail.

By contrast, a *periodic* sentence postpones the main clause, representing the main idea, until the end. It therefore stimulates the reader's curiosity; only when he has read your whole sentence does he know your meaning.

b After months of hard work and long hours, and a setback, which at one time appeared to threaten the whole venture, the factory finally opened in June.

The danger with the periodic sentence is that the author gets so carried away with details and subordinate clauses that the poor reader is left desperately trying to remember all the detail so that he can link it to the main idea when he finally gets to it.

c Owing to the poor weather conditions, which as you know have been particularly severe this year and which we hope will improve before long, as the forecasts promise, and since we have had to contend with several industrial disputes causing additional delays, the building is not yet ready.

Of course, in many sentences, the main idea comes not at the beginning, not at the end, but in the middle. These sentences are also classed as loose, since strictly speaking only those sentences that have their main idea at the end are called periodic sentences.

> ## Self-check
>
> Try writing each of the example sentences above **a**, **b** and **c** with the opposite structure, i.e. write **a** as a periodic sentence and **b** and **c** as loose sentences.

Using all loose sentences will make your style rather plodding and immature; using all periodic sentences can make your style distractingly artificial.

> ## Self-check
>
> However, which of the two – loose or periodic – would be better when speaking?

Loose sentences are probably preferable when speaking, since if the listener knows what the sentence is about, he can then consider the detail which follows, in relation to the main idea. Periodic sentences, by their nature, may require a second consideration. This is possible when reading, but not when listening. No writer should subject his reader to the task of having to read every sentence twice in order to grasp the meaning. As is always the case with effective communication, the choice between loose and periodic construction will depend on the circumstances and the context, and the best advice is probably to aim for variety.

Positive and negative

A *positive* sentence is one that places emphasis on the pleasant instead of the unpleasant, on the good instead of the bad, on what *can* be done instead of what cannot be done, on the favourable instead of the unfavourable. A *negative* sentence is the opposite.

Typically, positive sentences have two advantages over negative sentences. They give

• more complete information; and

- seem more pleasing, thus promoting business harmony.

Compare the pairs of sentences below:

> The work is not finished.
> The work will be finished tomorrow.
>
> The files are not stored alphabetically.
> The files are stored numerically.

The second sentence in each pair gives more complete information.

Now compare the following pairs of sentences:

> You have not provided sufficient information.
> May we have the following information.
>
> Your order will not be ready until Friday.
> Your order will be ready on Friday.

The second sentence in each pair seems more pleasing and less likely to annoy.

Remember that normally a communicator is trying to achieve both clarity and harmony. Sometimes circumstances require that clarity be given preference. For example, assume a supervisor has watched an operator working incorrectly and says: 'Let me show you how to get that machine to work perfectly.' This statement seems more pleasant than 'You don't seem to know how to operate the machine.' However, if that and subsequent efforts result in no improvement, a negative statement might shock the operator into a realization of the need to improve: 'You are still making mistakes.' But *normally* it is best to try to use positive statements. Even when an idea is unpleasant, positive words can keep the negative impact from seeming too severe.

Self-check

Make the following sentences positive:

    a We do not stock red wellingtons in adult sizes.
    b We cannot promise to send you your first colour choice.
    c You have not signed the cheque.

Sentence **a** could be less negatively expressed as 'We stock red wellingtons only in children's sizes'; and **b** as 'We will send your second colour choice, if your first colour choice is unavailable.' Notice that I have avoided using the word 'promise' in the positive sentence, since I think it might result in legal difficulties, if for any reason it was impossible to send the second colour choice as well. In sentence **c** the tone might sound less critical if it were expressed as 'You have forgotten to sign the cheque' or 'You have omitted to sign the cheque.' Strictly speaking, words like 'forgotten' and 'omitted' also convey a negative meaning but they are not quite so definitely negative as phrases that contain the word 'not'.

Indicative, imperative or subjunctive

A writer's attitude towards ideas being expressed is referred to as 'mood'.

The *indicative* mood makes a statement of fact or asks a question:

The window needs opening.
Will you open the window?

The *imperative* mood states a request or command:

Open the window, please.

The *subjunctive* mood mentions conditions that do not necessarily exist. It suggests doubt, supposition, probability, wishfulness, or sorrow:

If it were raining (but it is not) we would have to shut the window.

When a writer is in a position where he can issue commands (and most of us are at some time or another) harmony between sender and reader may seem less important than clarity. Nevertheless, commands sometimes sound more brutal and tactless than necessary:

Check column five, Mr Jones.

In a brief memo, this may express very clearly exactly what the writer wants done, but Mr Jones may feel rather resentful because of the abrupt tone conveyed by the imperative mood.

Even the addition of 'please' does not soften the tone very much. The same command could be expressed just as clearly if stated in question form –

> Will you check column five, Mr Jones.

– and is likely to cause less resentment than would a direct command.

> May I have the information on my desk by tomorrow

seems more considerate than

> Get the information on my desk by tomorrow.

Note: a full stop – instead of a question mark – is placed after a command which is stated in question form.

The subjunctive mood can also be used to soften the tone of a command, without really affecting the clarity of the sender's intention:

> Could you turn off the lights.
> Would you like to see to that.

As well as helping to soften the tone of a command, the subjunctive mood can also be used to keep a negative thought from sounding too unpleasant. In response to the question 'Do you deliver?' a writer could say, 'No, we do not.' But the negative statement could be expressed in the subjunctive mood: 'We wish we could' or 'We would if we could get the drivers.' The subjunctive sentences go rather further than simply saying, 'No, we do not.' They employ positive terms, which sound more pleasant, and they reveal a more considerate attitude.

Self-check

Imagine that the following are spoken. Rewrite them making them more acceptable.

a Will you go to the meeting tomorrow?
b Give me a hand, please.
c Take them to Personnel and bring the new cards back.
d Can you drive?

In both b and c the tone of command could be softened without losing clarity, by using the subjunctive mood: 'Could you give me a hand, please' and 'Could/Would you take these to Personnel and bring the cards back.' The use of 'please' never goes amiss, and the tone of voice that is used is often even more significant, in indicating politeness and consideration, than any words could be. But in written requests and instructions the words you choose must make up for the missing tone of voice.

In both sentence **a** and **d**, since they are written here and therefore show the question mark, they must be taken as simple questions meaning, 'Are you going to the meeting tomorrow?' and 'Have you learnt to drive?' But, when spoken, these sentences might be ambiguous, since they could be interpreted either as simple questions or as commands in the question form. If they are commands then they would be more clearly expressed in the subjunctive mood: 'Would *you* go to the meeting' and 'Could *you* drive.' Of course all ambiguity could be removed if 'instead of me' were added.

Active or passive

'Voice' is the term used to indicate whether a sentence subject *acts* or *is acted upon*. If the subject *does* something, the sentence is in the active voice; if the subject has something *done to it*, the sentence is in the passive voice.

Self-check

Look at these sentences:

Active	Passive
Mr Wells signed the contract.	The contract was signed.
	The contract was signed by Mr Wells.
The foreman stopped the machine.	The machine was stopped.
	The machine was stopped by the foreman.
The inspector examined all the goods.	All the goods were examined.
	All the goods were examined by the inspector.

|| Which sentences do you prefer? Which are easier to read? Why?

Most people prefer active sentences because they are more vivid. It is easier to visualize events in active sentences. You can picture Mr Wells signing the contract, the foreman stopping the machine and the inspector examining the goods. But in the passive sentences, your attention was probably first directed to the contract, the machine and the goods, and you may or may not have discovered the doer. Since passive sentences do not provide a reader with the vivid pictures that active sentences provide, active sentences are usually preferred.

Passive sentences seem to have the following disadvantages:

- They contain less information (if they do not contain the name of the doer – see the first sentence in each pair).
- They are longer than the corresponding active sentence (if they do contain the name of the doer – see second sentence).
- They are less vivid.

For these reasons they are best avoided whenever possible. However, in certain circumstances, passive sentences can be more effective in promoting good relations between the sender and the receiver.

Since passive sentences do not emphasize the doer, they can be used to de-emphasize the person responsible for the action:

The report has not been corrected yet.
The error was not detected in time.

The equivalent active statements, 'Geoff has not corrected the report yet' and 'You did not detect the error in time', in being more vivid, tend to emphasize the unpleasant idea and the people responsible, more than perhaps they deserve. To those involved, the passive sentences would seem more tactful.

Conversely, when you want to emphasize the person involved in a pleasant idea, active sentences are more effective:

You completed the job in record time.
The girls solved the problem.

'The job was completed in record time' and 'The problem was solved (by the girls)' – both passive statements would be less vivid and would not provide the emphasis these pleasant ideas (and the people concerned) deserve.

Sometimes the doer of action is not particularly important. Sometimes you may not want to reveal who the doer is. In such cases, the passive can be very useful:

> The factory was closed. (*Who* exactly closed it is not important.)
> We were given a clue to his identity. (The source of the clue is not to be revealed.)

Summary

Active voice	Passive voice
More vivid	Less vivid
Reveals more information	Can conceal the doer – when doer is not important or best concealed
Emphasizes the positve	De-emphasizes the negative

Rely mainly on the active voice but remember these suggestions. You are always justified in deviating from them if doing so best serves your purpose of clarity and harmony.

Self-check

Change the following sentences from the passive voice into the active voice:

a A survey was conducted to discover the attitudes of the employees.

b The report was produced by the Finance and General Purposes Committee.

c After investigation, the machine was found to have a broken pinion.

You will have probably had to invent some details, but the following are active versions of the sentences above:

a The company commissioned a survey to discover the attitudes of the employees.

b The Finance and General Purposes Committee produced the report.

c The investigating team found that the machine had a broken pinion.

Abstract or concrete

In order to write clearly you should always try to avoid using abstract words as the subject of sentences. People and things are much easier for readers to imagine or visualize.

> ### Self-check
>
> Which of the following words are easier to visualize?
>
> | | |
> |---|---|
> | indication | project |
> | people | concealment |
> | you | admiration |
> | analysis | completion |

Since abstract nouns like 'indication', 'analysis', 'concealment', 'admiration' and 'completion' are hard to visualize, reading is made much more difficult when they are used as the subject of a sentence.

> ### Self-check
>
> Rewrite the following sentences so as to avoid having an abstraction as the subject of the sentence.
>
> Example: 'Indications were that sales were rising' – rewritten as: 'The figures indicated that sales were rising.'
>
> 1 Analysis of the situation would suggest that our products could be exported.
> 2 Concealment of the facts led to delay in reaching a solution.
> 3 His admiration for the new design was offset by his criticism of the packaging.
> 4 Completion of the project was held up by the strike.

The following alternative versions would be much easier to take in and understand than the original sentences:

1 The results of the survey suggest that our products could be exported.

We conclude that our products could be exported.

2 Certain facts were concealed and this led to a delay in reaching a solution.

They concealed the facts, which led to a delay in reaching a solution.

3 He criticized the packaging, although he admired the new design.

4 The strike held up completion of the project.

The project was not completed on time because of the strike.

As you can see, there are sometimes several ways in which you can express the original sentence. Which is the most appropriate will depend on the context and indeed, in some circumstances, the original sentence might be the most appropriate. Using an abstraction as the subject of the sentence is not an error; but, particularly when vivid writing is essential, it is wiser to use abstractions as little as possible.

Specific or general

Just as the active voice and concrete words create a more vivid picture for the receiver, so does language which is specific rather than general. Compare these pairs of sentences:

The manager showed his disapproval of their behaviour.
The manager frowned at their late arrival.

In view of the management's lack of cooperation, industrial action is a definite possibility.
Since management has refused to agree to our pay demands, we are considering an overtime ban.

The sentences in italics are more specific and therefore communicate more vividly.

However, in some situations, general language may be preferable:

- when specific details are not necessary;
- when the details are already known to the receiver;
- when expression of specific details would place too much emphasis on a negative idea.

Specific words, like the active voice, tend to emphasize. General words, like the passive voice, tend to reduce the emphasis.

Unequivocal or weasel

A weasel sentence is one in which the writer tries to escape responsibility for the idea being expressed:

> It could be said that the experiment was a success.
> Many people might feel that this is unsatisfactory.

These weasel expressions tend to be uttered by people who are reluctant to commit themselves and are trying to avoid saying, 'I think the experiment was a success' or 'I feel this is unsatisfactory'. Generally readers have more confidence in writers who are prepared to commit themselves and use unequivocal statements.

Subject–verb–object word order

Normally the order of words in the English language is subject, verb, object. When a writer deviates from this order, sentences become more difficult to assimilate quickly:

> *There are* two possible explanation for this trend.
> *It is* likely that sales will start to rise.

In these two sentences the words in italics add nothing to the sense of the sentence and only delay the subject of the sentence. Recast, they are more conventional, easier to understand and a little shorter:

> Two possible explanation for this trend are . . . (or) This trend has two possible explanations.
> Sales will probably start to rise.

Always check your sentence to make sure that the subject–verb–object order is present wherever possible and that there are no unnecessary words.

Emphasis

If a speaker wants to emphasize a particular word or idea, he can use vocal stress, and the listener will *hear* the emphasis. But in writing, emphasis must be *seen* or *felt*.

We have already looked at several ways in which ideas can be emphasized.

║ *Self-check*

║ List three or four that we have come across so far.

1 An idea placed in a simple sentence attracts all the reader's attention. An idea placed in the independent part of a complex sentence will attract more attention than the idea in the dependent part of the sentence.
2 An active sentence emphasizes the doer of an action and can also be used to emphasize a favourable idea.
3 Concrete nouns – people and things, which are easier to visualize – can be used to make ideas stand out more vividly in the reader's mind.
4 Specific words tend to emphasize ideas.

Visual emphasis Perhaps the simplest way to emphasize a particular word or phrase in a sentence is to use underlining or italics, but these are considered rather crude methods and should be used only as a last resort.

Effective word order Your experience of listening to and reading messages will tell you that the human mind remembers best what it perceives at the beginning and the end – rather than the middle – of an experience. Remember this when you are constructing sentences. Whenever possible, state your *key* ideas at the beginning or the end – rather than in the middle – of a sentence.

║ *Self-check*

║ Look at the first two sentences at the start of this section
║ under the heading 'Emphasis'. These sentences are de-
║ signed to contrast and therefore emphasize 'hear' and 'seen
║ or felt'. Try rewriting them so that the italics are unnecess-
║ ary, but these three words are still emphasized.

By changing the sentence, in order to place the words to be emphasized at the end of the sentence in both cases, the two ideas are emphasized and contrasted without the need for italics:

> If a speaker wants to emphasize a particular word or idea, he can use vocal stress, and the emphasis will be heard. But in writing, emphasis must be seen or felt.

Notice also that in that sentence emphasis is achieved not only by placing the key words at the end of the sentences, but also by balancing the construction of the two contrasting ideas in form. 'Will be heard' and 'must be seen or felt' are both in the passive voice allowing the words to be emphasized to come at the end of the sentences. Compare these constructions with those in the original sentences.

To begin or end a sentence with words that require emphasis, you should usually place 'therefore', 'however', 'nevertheless', 'moreover', 'also' and so on *within* the sentence. Such words, however, should appear early in the sentence in order to create their qualifying effect. However, a sentence in which you want especially to emphasize the link or contrast with preceding statements may well begin with 'therefore', 'however', or similar terms. (Look at the last two sentences and compare the effect produced by placing 'however' in different positions.)

Note: 'also' should never be used to start a sentence. It is an adverb, not a conjunction, and cannot be used to join words, phrases or clauses unless preceded by a conjunction.

Self-check

Turn the following *weak* word order sentences into *strong* word order sentences:

Weak word order

a Generally speaking, you will improve your messages by deliberate emphasis, if circumstances permit.

b Your work has been excellent. You are being promoted therefore.

c This machine is more efficient than the old one, I think.

d We shall start work on the order on 1 January and by the end of June the order will be completed.

‖ **e** In business as in personal life, perfection is what we strive to achieve, although we do not always attain it.

The sentences below have a much stronger and more emphatic word order:

Emphatic word order

a Deliberate emphasis will usually improve your message. (idea at beginning) Your message will usually be improved by deliberate emphasis. (idea at end)

b Your work has been excellent. You are therefore being promoted.

c This machine is, I think, more efficient than the old one.

d Work on the order will start on 1 January and be completed by 1 July. (emphasis by balance)

e In business as in personal life, perfection is what we strive to achieve, not what we always attain. (emphasis by contrast)

Short or long

For clear, fast reading, short sentences are preferable. They are easier to understand and as we have seen usually more vivid. For business writing, the average sentence length should be between sixteen and twenty-two words. But variety is important. Two- or three-word sentences are acceptable; so are forty-word sentences, as long as they are clear. If the ideas you are trying to express are complex, aim for short sentences. They will help you to sort out what you want to say and prevent grammatical tangles which get out of control. If the ideas you are expressing are fairly simple you can afford to increase your sentence length. But if in doubt keep your sentences on the shorter side.

Parallel construction

We have noted that using corresponding constructions in a sentence, or in two contrasting sentences, can be a useful technique of emphasis. But it is always advisable to aim for parallel constructions. A sentence in which the structures are consistent is easier to read than one in which sudden and unnecessary 'shifts' occur. Avoid the confusion that results from switches of *voice*, *tense*, *mood* and *person* within a sentence.

Here are some examples of the fault:

> *Faulty:* First ease the wheel nuts with a well-fitting spanner – you should take care not to remove them – then knocking-out of the spindle may be performed.
> *Improved:* First ease the wheel nuts with a well-fitting spanner, taking care not to remove them. Then knock out the spindle.
> *Faulty:* Customers soon reported a weakness in the new model: you found difficulty in changing from second to first.
> *Improved:* Customers soon reported a weakness in the new model: they found difficulty in changing from second to first.

Self-check

Try to improve this sentence:

> *Faulty*: If you are planning to expand a small business thought must be given to ways of raising the necessary capital.

There are two possible ways of improving that sentence:

> If you are planning to expand a small business you must give (some) thought to ways of raising the necessary capital.

> Or: When expansion of a small business is being planned, thought must be given to ways of raising the necessary capital.

Although strictly speaking correct, since both parts of the sentence now employ the passive, this last version has the disadvantages we have learned to associate with the passive.

Inconsistent construction is particularly serious when a sentence contains a list or series of related units.

Self-check

> The company has three primary objectives for the coming year: increasing production, to raise wages and the training of office employees.

Try rewriting it.

A sentence like this could make the reader think, 'Because the ideas are stated differently, they don't belong together', or 'The writer is unorganized, careless or uneducated.' To make the construction parallel, two versions are possible:

> The company has three primary objectives: to increase production, to raise wages, to train office employees.

> The company has three primary objectives: increasing production, raising wages and training office employees.

This neglect of parallelism often extends beyond the bounds of a single sentence. In a closely connected sequence of sentences (or clauses) the first sentence establishes a pattern that remains in the reader's mind as he reads the next. Consequently, an abrupt and unnecessary change in the pattern checks understanding. When parallel constructions are not used, the reader finds it difficult to follow the development of the thought and, even when he can grasp the thread, he is irritated at being put to needless trouble.

Self-check

How would you improve the following paragraph?

> The committee decided to conduct a survey to establish the number of school-age children in the district. They designed and produced a questionnaire to be used to interview every householder. They divided the district into areas and allocated one area to each member. The results were collated and analysed by the committee at the end of July. They produced their report in September.

In this paragraph the construction pattern (active sentences) established in the first three sentences, and continued in the last sentence, is suddenly interrupted by a sentence in the passive voice (fourth sentence). No doubt the paragraph could be improved in other ways, but it does serve to demonstrate the disconcerting effect of unexpected changes of construction.

This paragraph also serves to remind us that just as a word can often only be judged as appropriate in relation to its context, so a sentence can really only be judged as effective in relation to the paragraph of which it is a part. Let's move on in the next chapter to look at the principles that govern the building of effective, easily understood paragraphs.

14 | What is a paragraph?

You may find it difficult to answer this question and may be forgiven for thinking that paragraphs are just chunks of prose which are used purely to break up a page of solid print by indenting every so often in a fairly arbitrary way. But paragraphs, like sentences, form the building blocks by which we construct a well-organized piece of writing out of a jumbled assortment of ideas. The construction process is at three levels: the sentence, the paragraph and the composition as a whole. Any writer in setting out to write a letter, a report, an essay or even a book must have an overall purpose – a main idea. (In a longer piece of work he may divide his material into sections or chapters, each of which should also have a main idea.) This main idea is then divided into sub-ideas. It is these sub-ideas which form the basis of each paragraph.

In this chapter we examine the characteristics of well-structured paragraphs, and the devices you can use to help your reader follow your train of thought.

Unity

Just as we have seen that a sentence, properly constructed, has only one main idea, so the essential feature of a paragraph is unity. It is the thoughtful, planned and rounded-off expression of one idea or topic. Everything in the paragraph must have a direct bearing on that idea, and the whole should be capable of being expressed or summed up in a single sentence.

A good way of achieving paragraph unity is to announce the idea or topic in a *topic sentence*. All the other sentences should develop that topic sentence. There must be no unrelated ideas, or blind alleys which do not bear on the main idea.

Self-check

Look at the first paragraph under the heading 'unity'. Which is the topic sentence?

Yes, the first one. The main idea of the whole paragraph is, in fact, summed up in that first sentence. The remaining sentences develop that main idea.

Activity

Check some paragraphs you have written to see whether a reader could sum up the paragraph thought or topic in one sentence.

The purpose of paragraph division is to help the reader in grasping the sequence of thought. He should be carried by means of successive paragraphs step by step along the writer's train of thought from the beginning to the end of the whole composition. It is obvious, then, that unless the paragraph divisions do reflect the train of thought, rather than just breaking up a forbidding mass of writing or print, they will only confuse rather than clarify the reader's understanding.

Just as the main idea of a sentence may be at the beginning or the end, and sometimes the middle, so the main idea of a paragraph – the topic sentence – may be at the beginning or the end of a paragraph, and sometimes in the middle.

Naturally, the major idea deserves more emphasis than do the supporting details; and just as the first and last words in a sentence are in emphatic positions, so are the first and last sentences in a paragraph.

Coherence

A good paragraph is marked by coherence as well as unity. In a coherent paragraph, the sentences follow each other in a logical order, leading the reader sensibly from one thought to the next You can achieve paragraph coherence by three chief methods:

● logical relationships;

- logical order;
- continuity.

Logical relationships

When the writer has decided what the topic of a paragraph is to be, he must next consider how the topic is to be developed. Insufficient shaping and development of the leading idea is the most common fault in paragraph construction: a thought abandoned as soon as it has been expressed and left standing in isolation, unsupported by other material and incapable of leading the reader forward to further development; or a thought which is followed by a confusing mixture of unrelated ideas which leaves the reader floundering to make sense of the writer's thought process.

An initial statement may be explanation or justification; it may pose a question to be answered or a problem to be solved; it may require amplification or support by means of further details or examples. These supporting details can be related to the main idea in varying ways; a knowledge of the different types of paragraphs can help you to give your paragraphs the form and structure they need if they are not to be merely blocks of ill-assorted sentences. Here are examples of each of the six main types of paragraph with topic sentences in italics:

Illustrations and examples
1 *Directors of a public company do not enjoy an easy life if they make relatively low profits*. They are subject to criticism from financial commentators; they may also have difficulty in raising capital; additionally they run the risk of a take-over and finding themselves jobless.

Enumeration
2 *There were three chief reasons for the emergence of the Social Democrat Party*. First, the Militant Tendency in the Labour Party had been gaining strength. Second, a number of politicians who were more liberal than socialist had joined the Labour Party in recent years; and third, the party was being controlled by the trade union block vote.

Cause and effect

3 *When paragraphing is done carelessly, readers may have difficulty in understanding the material.* They may also draw uncomplimentary conclusions about the author's ability to organize and express himself clearly; and they may become so irritated by the effort required to follow the author's train of thought that they may give up altogether.

Comparison and contrast

4 *Arbitration, in my view, has both advantages and disadvantages.* Its advantage is that in some circumstances it . . . and . . . Finally, arbitration is particularly suitable for. . . . On the other hand, the disadvantage of arbitration is that. . . . and. . .

Definition

5 *By industrial relations is meant the employment relationship.* Good industrial relations exist when the employment relationship, i.e. between employer and employee, contributes to the achievement by all concerned of their respective objectives. Thus. . .

Question and answer

6 *The most crucial question for organizations in respect of performance appraisal schemes is simply – are they worth it?* Clearly, the personnel function would have to make out a persuasive case for any revolution in performance assessment practices, because of the political implications and the increase in costs of the new approach. Managers' time is taken up, training is required and a team may need to monitor the process.

Logical order

In each of the six examples above, the topic sentence is placed at the beginning of the paragraph.

Self-check

Try rewriting each paragraph with the topic sentence at the end. Notice the changes you have to make – however slight – to make the paragraph make sense.

Examples **1**, **2**, **4** and **6** can be reversed fairly easily with only minor changes – omission, addition or replacement of odd words. However, in number **5**, placing the topic sentence at the end would make it sound like an afterthought, and in number **3** the topic sentence would need to be split to ensure that the cause/effect relationship is maintained. 'When paragraphing is done carelessly' is the cause. The rest of the paragraph lists the effects of this cause; so reversed, the paragraph would have to look like this:

> Readers may have difficulty in understanding the material; they may also draw uncomplimentary conclusions about the author's ability to organize and express himself clearly, and they may become so irritated by the effort required to follow the author's train of thought that they may give up entirely – all because the paragraphing is done carelessly.

But it is still not entirely successful, is it? Why?

What was the effect of reversing the order of the sentences in this and each of the other paragraphs?

When the major idea appears in the first sentence of a paragraph, a reader gets a preliminary idea of what to expect in the remaining sentences – support for the point just made. Since this pattern lets the reader know what to expect, the reading is fast and easy.

When the major idea appears in the last sentence of a paragraph, it should not come as a surprise to the reader, because he has been introduced to the idea by the details which precede. The major idea therefore is accepted as a logical result.

But just as periodic sentences can be difficult to grasp, so paragraphs with the main idea at the end, as in the paragraph given above, can be difficult to follow.

You should choose the pattern that best serves the purpose of the message:

Deductive pattern (topic sentence first)
- Quickly reveals the subject of the paragraph.
- Makes reading easy.

Inductive pattern (topic sentence last)
- Can provide a build-up effect which increases emphasis.
- More useful when persuasion is necessary or when, without some preliminary justification, the major idea might be rejected by the reader.

For example, let us assume that on reading the first sentence of a paragraph, the reader's reaction is, 'I disagree', or 'The author is illogical', or 'I don't see why'. From that point on, the reader may (instead of trying to understand the supporting details) try to think of arguments against the idea, to find support for his initial negative reaction. If the same major idea had been written *after* the details, his negative reaction might have been avoided.

In the following example, the author gets across his main idea far more persuasively, by building up to it, than he might have done had he presented his readers with such a controversial point of view right at the start:

> So long as NHS hospitals have massive waiting lists, so long as parents worry because their children are not prepared adequately to compete for scarce jobs, and so long as the fear prevails that inflation will beggar coming generations of the elderly on state pensions, the private market will present itself as an alternative.

(Inductive.)

As usual, the purpose of the writer and the nature of the audience will determine whether the deductive or the inductive method is the most appropriate and effective.

Self-check

Each of the following groups of sentences contains the material to make a unified, coherent and well ordered paragraph. Arrange the sentences in each group to make a clearly sequenced paragraph and then underline the topic sentence.

A 1 Two thirds were equally ignorant regarding the concern of the European Community.

2 To coincide with today's debate the report is published in English and limited numbers are available free from the European Communities Commission.

3 The committee's report, *European Women in Employment: Their perception of discrimination at Work*, has confirmed suspicions that very many women are ignorant of their entitlement.

4 Whether the EEC will establish a Community Equal Opportunities Commission depends on the results of today's debate in the European Parliament on the work of the ad-hoc Committee on Women's Rights.

5 An astonishing forty-two per cent of the British sample questioned for the study either gave a 'don't know' or expressed the belief that there were no laws regarding equality of treatment at work.

B 1 There is only one valid definition of business purpose: *to create a customer*.

2 If we want to know what a business is we have to start with its *purpose*.

3 In fact, it must lie in society since a business enterprise is an organ of society.

4 And its purpose must lie outside of the business itself.

C 1 The Department of Employment in January of this year was able to report that the number of stoppages commencing in 1979 was the third lowest over the last twenty years.

2 And in the light of answers to these questions, what kind of strike record can we look forward to in the 1980s?

3 Judging from recent figures of strike activity it might seem that Britain's long standing strike problem is diminishing.

4 Is this the start of a real downward trend or are we just going through an exceptional phase?

5 And the figure for the first six months of this year is down by more than a quarter on the same period last year.

ANSWERS

A. 4, 3, 5, 1, 2. (Topic sentence is first.)
B. 2, 4, 3, 1. (Topic sentence is first.)
C. 3, 1, 5, 4, 2. (Topic sentence is last.)

Continuity

You should have noticed that when you reversed the order of the paragraphs on page 274 and unscrambled those on page 278 it was necessary to change some words in order to ensure the paragraph still made sense. You will probably have had to change nouns to pronouns and vice versa, (e.g. 'Directors'/'they' in **1** on page 274), remove some link words ('first', 'second', 'third' in **2**), introduce relative pronouns ('there were three chief reasons' becomes '*These* were the three chief reasons') and perhaps add 'therefore' into the topic sentence of **4**.

These link words are essential in achieving coherence in a paragraph. They help to show how the train of thought progresses and how the various elements in the paragraph are linked together.

The main link words, are:

- conjunctions ('and', 'but', 'therefore', etc.)
- relative and other pronouns ('their', 'his', 'whose', 'which', etc.)
- adverbs ('first', 'second', 'finally')
- phrases and clauses used as 'bridge words' ('as we have already noticed', 'on the other hand')

These link words must be handled sensibly. It is important that they are chosen to be clear and suitable. For example, it is surprising how often writers use 'and' carelessly when they mean 'but', e.g.

It is possible that the machine operator was not bored with his job *and* just gave the impression that he was.

Conjunctions especially serve as signposts to the reader, telling him what to expect: more of the same argument, an opposing view, a conclusion. Turn back to Chapter 9, page 161, for a list of verbal signals or signpost words, and remember to use them to help the reader follow your thoughts.

. Now look at the three-paragraph article which follows and notice how link words help to guide the reader along the writer's train of thought, not only *within* a single paragraph but *between* paragraphs. Notice also how use of repetition and parallel constructions can help to achieve continuity and coherence.

At 52, Harold Evans is probably Britain's best-known editor. *He* is *a keen evangelist* on press freedom and *a leading spokesman* for the profession. *He* wrote the standard textbooks on journalism and has recently been seen in a TV series aimed at showing the public how newspapers are made. *His* well-publicized battles to publish the Crossman memoirs and the story behind the thalidomide tragedy have changed the law and brought him an international reputation.

Even so, his appointment has raised a few eyebrows. *This* is mainly because of the contrast between the racy personality of *Evans, son of a Manchester engine-driver*, and the man he succeeds, *William Rees-Mogg, a donnish West Country squire*. It is *also* because he is the first editorial appointment made by Rupert Murdoch.

His relationship with *the new proprietor* will be the key to his performance at *The Times*; *both* are fast-moving, fast-thinking men who prefer action to analysis.
[The Observer Copyright Ltd.]

Activity

Now underline the words and phrases in this paragraph which help to guide the reader along the writer's train of thought:

The job of developing tomorrow's managers is both too big and too important to be considered a special activity. Its performance depends on all factors in the managing of managers: the organization of a man's job and his relationship to his superior and his subordinates; the spirit of the organization and its organization structure. No amount of special manager-development activities will, for instance, develop tomorrow's managers in an organization that focuses on weakness and fears strength, or in one that scorns integrity and character in selecting men for managerial appointments. No amount of activity will develop tomorrow's managers in a functionally centralized organization; all that it is likely to produce are tomorrow's specialists. Conversely, genuine federal decentralization will develop, train and test a fair number of managers for tomorrow without any additional manager-development activity as such. [Peter Drucker, *The Practice of Management.*]

Length

Just as with sentences, there are no rigid rules on paragraph length. Length will depend on the scale of the whole composition; longer paragraphs being suitable for a full report, for example, where shorter ones would be preferred in a business letter. Length will also vary within the composition, according to the subject matter of the paragraph. It is unwise to make paragraphs too long (they are daunting to read) or too short (if they leave unsaid the supporting detail the reader needs). However, a single-sentence paragraph which requires no development can stand out vividly among longer paragraphs. Variety in length is therefore natural and welcomed.

Review

Which of the following statements are true and which are false?

1 A topic sentence (major idea of a paragraph) is preferably placed about the middle of a paragraph.
2 When a paragraph is written to persuade, the arrangement should be deductive.
3 In reports, the paragraphs should contain no more than ten lines and no fewer than eight.
4 In letters, paragraphs are normally shorter than in reports.
5 A good writer tries to avoid abrupt changes in thought.

ANSWERS

1 False. Major ideas deserve emphasis, and greater emphasis rests in the first or last positions in the paragraph.
2 False. If the deductive arrangement is used to persuade, a receiver is told what to do (or invited to agree) before seeing any justification for doing so. Having rejected the idea contained in the first sentence, the receiver may stubbornly hold

on to his initial reaction while being exposed to the supporting detail.

3 False. Paragraphs should be as long as is necessary to express sufficient detail to complete the discussion of the general idea. But remember, shorter paragraphs are more inviting to read.

4 True. Typical reports are longer, more complicated and need more supporting material than do letters. In letters, short paragraphs look better on the page and are less off-putting for the reader.

5 True. If the techniques for achieving coherence and continuity are used, the reader will have no trouble following the writer's thoughts. Abrupt changes in thought can cause a reader to miss the point, to be distracted by being confronted with a new topic without warning, or by thinking uncomplimentary thoughts about the writer's techniques and abilities.

Activity

1 Read through a newspaper article, underlining the topic sentence and the link words. (Note that paragraphs in newspapers are often very short to make reading easy, and could be joined together at times, without sacrificing unity.)

2 Write paragraphs developing these topic sentences (remember the topic sentence need not necessarily appear at the beginning:

a People who concentrate on what another person is saying pay the speaker a compliment.

b There are two good rules to follow in communicating with people higher (or lower) in status than you.

c Your whole life will therefore be more rewarding and fulfilling if you have good communication skills.

d Is the British system of minimal interference in collective bargaining and the internal affairs of unions still viable?

e The history of trade unionism is the story of struggle.

Activity

A case of petty theft has been detected in your office/at your college. Write an account of the incident:

a in a friendly letter to a colleague who is away on holiday;
b in a personal report to your departmental chief/principal of your college, who is away for a week at an annual conference;
c in a formal report for submission to the directors of the company/governors of the college.

Now look at each piece of writing in the light of these questions:

1 Does the communication indicate that you knew:
   ● your purpose?
   ● your reader?
   ● the context?
   ● your subject?
2 How does each communication differ from the others in terms of: ·
   ● sentence structure?
   ● length of sentences and paragraphs?
   ● language?
   ● tone and style?
   ● amount and kind of information provided?

15 | The silent languages

Fred Baker had just had a flaming row with his wife and walked out of the house with the sound of his wife's angry words echoing in his ears. While he sat impatiently in traffic jam after traffic jam, he went over in his mind what he would really like to have said to his wife (and to his mother-in-law, for that matter!) and arrived at work late, frustrated and angry. As he pushed open the swing doors he was met by the cheery smile and bright 'good morning' of Mrs Pembroke, one of his most loyal and hard-working employees. Without an ounce of courtesy, he pushed past her, as if he hadn't even seen her.

Mr Baker had never cut her dead before! What had she done? She began to wonder...

It is impossible *not* to communicate – that is, the absence of words does not mean that there is an absence of communication.

We have seen that even when we are not making any conscious effort we are constantly receiving messages from the world outside us; in the same way, we are always communicating something to other people, whether we mean to or not. Everything we do is a form of communication, even when we are not saying a word.

What is non-verbal communication?

Non-verbal communication is anything other than words that communicate a message. The way we stand, walk, shrug our shoulders; the clothes we wear, the car we drive, or the office we occupy all communicate ideas to others.

You may say of someone: 'He *said* he thought it was a good idea, but I got the feeling that he wasn't very happy with it.' How did you get this feeling, this message? It may have come from a particular expression on his face, which seemed to imply that despite what he said, he did not like the idea. It may have been something in his tone of voice which did not sound very enthusiastic: something which, in effect, did not fit with what he was saying.

All these things which we take into account in interpreting what someone is saying, over and above the actual words, are referred to as 'metacommunication'. 'Meta' is from the Greek and means 'beyond' or 'in addition to'; hence, metacommunication is something 'in addition to communication'.

In the example above, if you got the impression that the speaker was unhappy with the idea because of the expression on his face, or because something in the movement of his body told you he was not enthusiastic, he communicated this by means of metacommunication.

However, if you got the impression from the inflection of his voice, then he communicated this by means of what we call 'paralanguage'. Frequently paralanguage conveys the opposite of the words themselves. When this happens, we usually pick up the meaning of paralanguage rather than the meaning of the language being used. In other words we often say, 'It's not what he says, but the way he says it.'

For example, a sarcastic parent may comment on something very *un*helpful that a child has done by saying, 'Thank you very much', in such a tone of voice, and with a particular emphasis on the 'you' perhaps, that leaves the child in no doubt at all that the parent is *not* thanking him at all, just the opposite!

Of course, we often communicate in a completely non-verbal way by means of gestures, facial expressions and other body movements. A shrug of the shoulders (indicating, 'Don't ask me. I don't know'), or a hand-clap (expressing appreciation), or someone storming out of the room and slamming the door (indicating anger) communicates every bit as effectively as words might have done.

Although you cannot help but be affected by this non-verbal communication, it is often interpreted subconsciously. Similarly, you may be unconscious of the ways in which *you* may be inadvertently communicating.

Non-verbal channels are the ones of which we seem to be *least* aware in ourselves, but *most* aware in others.

Since non-verbal communication is such an important part of the process of communication, you should know what is involved, so that you can become more consciously aware of non-verbal messages and make them work for you, rather than against you.

In this chapter we shall look at the non-verbal language of silence and time, as well as what is commonly called body language.

The language of silence

Activity

Have you ever been 'cut dead' by someone? How did you feel? The speech or lecture is finished, the chairman asks for questions – how do you feel about the silence?

'Silence is golden', so the saying goes, but is it? Fred Baker in the story above was silent, but he communicated very 'loudly', and Mrs Pembroke did not find the silence very golden. A long period of silence may be golden for some people in certain circumstances, but most of us find that it can be embarrassing and sometimes even threatening.

When someone asks us a question and we fail to answer, we communicate something. When a speaker reaches the end of his talk, invites questions and there is total silence, the audience is also communicating. It may be difficult for the speaker to interpret the silence correctly – boredom? disagreement? total rejection? total satisfaction? Without any clearer feedback, the silence is ambiguous and the speaker is left to guess the meaning – perhaps wrongly.

We are social creatures and our society is made up of responses to each other. We need reassurance from those around us: not just that we exist, but that those around us are friendly and not hostile. One of the cruellest social punishments is to 'send someone to Coventry'; one of the cruellest official punishments, and the most damaging, if it lasts for a long time, is solitary confinement. So although holding one's tongue can sometimes be wise, it can also be an act of rejection; silence builds walls – and walls are barriers to communication.

On the other hand, by using silence carefully at strategic times – by being prepared to listen, in other words – we may encourage someone to carry on talking or reveal certain feelings and attitudes which they might not otherwise have done. Silence can be an effective technique in encouraging feedback, or real two-way communication.

Silence, then, is a powerful tool of communication, but it must be used skilfully.

Activity

When you next watch television or overhear a conversation in a bus or train, be aware of silence. How and why are people using it, and what effect is it having?

The language of time

Activity

1 *Think about your attitude to time.* Does punctuality matter to you? always? or only on some occasions? If so, which ones?
2 Can you recall an incident lately when you noticed that someone else's attitude to time was different from yours? What effect did it have on you?
3 Can you recall turning up for a meeting at work, or with a friend, early? late? You may have had good reasons but how might the other person have interpreted it?

It is easy to assume we all experience time in much the same way. After all an hour is an hour, isn't it? And yet time is experienced differently by different nationalities, societies and cultures.

In our culture, we have divided time into years, each of which consists of 365 days (365¼ to be exact), whereas the Muslim year is ten or eleven days shorter. Our years are numbered from the year of the birth of Jesus Christ, whereas the Muslims start in 622 AD, the year in which Mohammed fled from Mecca to

Medina. So in our year 1979 the Muslims started their fourteenth century.

Even within a particular culture, different communities will divide time into different periods. The business community will concentrate on the commercial week from Monday to Friday, while the shop-owners' week will be Monday to Saturday; the retail trade will see their year divided into the periods of Christmas, the January sales, the summer sales and perhaps the summer months if they are in a tourist area, whereas a farming community may well not be so conscious of weeks and weekends and will track the course of time according to farming activities and the seasons – the ploughing season, the sowing season and the haymaking season, or the lambing season and the sheep-shearing season.

What is perhaps more important because it is not always so obvious is that individuals have different time scales too. In the context of their own position and circumstances, people will value time differently. The time of a nation's president will differ from that of a retired couple whose 'time is their own'.

Activity

Would you describe yourself as a person for whom time is very important? Are you a fast-moving, energetic person? Or a slow, cautious person? Do you expect other people to be like you? Does it irritate you when they're not? For example, do you get irritated by people who are always rushing about at work? Or by people who seem to do everything at an infuriating snail's pace?

Have you ever thought that your attitude to time may annoy other people?

The different values we attach to time are reflected in the words we use. The busy executive may impatiently describe a thirty-minute chat with someone he did not want to see as having 'wasted hours'. Most children will know only too well how ambiguous the phrase 'just a minute' can be when uttered by a harassed parent. It could mean literally 'one minute'; it could mean 'when I've finished this'; it could (and frequently does) mean 'never', unless the child keeps pestering. One person may say they will do a job 'as soon as possible' and mean that they will do it immediately after finishing a couple of more important or urgent jobs; someone else may say the same thing but mean that they will not get round to it until you have reminded them two or three times.

Perhaps even more significant in its effect on communication is the way we use time. If you arrange to meet someone at 10.00 a.m. and turn up at 10.30 a.m. you would be communicating something – about your attitude to the meeting, or to the other person, or about your attitude to yourself and the importance of time to you. If you turn up early to a lecture it may say something about your interest and enthusiasm. You would be using time to communicate your eagerness.

Again there are cultural differences in the use of time, which the business executive would do well to be aware of. In Western society, business people tend to move pretty much by the clock, with clocks and watches, diaries and calendars almost governing our lives – a two o'clock appointment usually means two o'clock or something within five or ten minutes of it. But in some other cultures, a two o'clock appointment may mean three o'clock; and if you arrive to transact business at the appointed two o'clock, you may actually offend the other person.

Similarly, if you are invited to a meal in the West it is usually considered impolite to leave immediately it is over, whereas in Saudi Arabia, for example, the socializing and chatter usually take place before the meal, and guests commonly leave as soon as the meal is finished. At a business meeting in Britain, it is customary to exchange a few short pleasantries and then get quickly down to business, but in Saudi Arabia, because the Saudis set more value than us on the exchange of small favours in their everyday affairs, no business is discussed at all until coffee or tea has been served and time has been spent on elaborate personal exchanges. Undue haste to get down to business is taken to be a sign of bad manners and possibly even lack of business expertise. However, at the end of the meeting your host, no matter how busy he is, will press you to stay; but you should still leave politely.

Before you travel and/or do business abroad you should check carefully on local customs, cultures and communication and remember that people do things differently just as people within your own culture have different values, attitudes and customs.

Body language

> *Activity*
>
> Do you think a person's appearance matters? What factors make up 'appearance'?

A favourite sport of many people is 'people watching' or, as Desmond Morris has called his very popular book, *Manwatching*. While waiting on a railway station or even in a doctor's waiting room, have you ever watched the crowd and tried to imagine the occupation, the problems and the thoughts of various people? Have you ever tried to work out what sort of person someone is from the way they are dressed? Have you watched two people talking out of earshot and tried to guess from their gestures, facial expressions and manner of walking and standing what they might be talking about?

Whether we are aware of it or not, each of us spends a lot of time decoding body language, or as it is also known, 'kinesics'. These body movements should be considered in relation to the message itself; however, many times the non-verbal communications come through louder than the words that are actually being spoken and are frequently the means by which we reveal the emotional side of our communications.

In recent years, more and more interest has been taken in body language and researchers have tried to establish the exact nature of the relationships between this kind of non-verbal communication and the effect it has on the receiver. Although this research is still in its infancy, there are already several books which cover the subject of body language in far more detail than is possible in this book. However, no book on communication would be complete without at least an introduction to the subject, since it is essential that anyone trying to improve his communication techniques should be sensitive to the human relations aspects in the communication process – and these human elements are often vividly revealed in body language.

Activity

How do you know that someone agrees with you, when you are speaking to them? Can you tell whether someone has understood you, from the way they look?

The non-verbal messages of a speaker tend to reveal the degree of presence of sincerity, conviction, honesty, ability and knowledge; they reveal, too, a lot about the speaker and his attitude and feelings about the message he is transmitting. Body language of the receiver also reveals a lot about him and his feelings. But, more important, it frequently tells the speaker the extent to which his audience is accepting or not accepting the message. In other words, body language provides instant feedback to the speaker and tells him how he is doing. If this feedback is available but the speaker is insensitive to it, not aware of its significance, or unable to interpret or read the language, a valuable contribution to his own communication effectiveness is being wasted.

It follows that to be a good reader of body language you need to sharpen your powers of observation and your ability to decode the messages: you need to be more aware of the presence of these messages and their possible meanings; to be constantly alert to the effect of your body language on other people and constantly alert to the feedback available so that you can immediately use your other communication techniques if the feedback tells you it is necessary.

Space

Before we look at the way we move the various parts of our body, we should first examine our attitude to the space in which that movement takes place. Just as silence and time speak, so does space. Not only does space affect the way we communicate, but we also *use* space to communicate.

First of all, each of us has spaces that we feel are our own. The Three Bears' complaint that 'someone's been sitting in my chair' may seem petty, but reflects a very real sense of possession of space and invasion of privacy. Many families have a particular chair which is 'Dad's chair' and woe betide anyone else who dares to sit in it.

Similarly it would be unthinkable for a subordinate to walk into a boss's office and sit down in the boss's chair, unless specifically invited to do so; and 'Old Tom' may become quite upset if an unsuspecting stranger should inadvertently sit on 'his' stool at the bar.

Activity

Do you have a particular space at work which you feel is your own? If you are a student, do you always tend to sit in the same place in the lecture room? Do other people seem to have this attitude to 'their space'? What effect does it have on other people's behaviour?

Space and status

In business offices, space is usually directly related to status, in that the higher up the organizational ladder people go, the more square feet of floor space they have in their offices. Some large companies even have rules which lay down the amount of room, and possibly even the size of the desk top, to which a particular level manager is entitled. At lower levels in the organization, too, acquisition of private space is reflected in the fact that it is better to be given an office on your own, even though it may have a smaller floor area than one which you have to share with others.

There are cultural differences in the way in which we use space to say something about status, particularly in formal situations like offices. Europeans, for instance, are most likely to put their desks in the centre of the room, as authority is seen to flow outwards from the centre. Proximity to the centre is one way of saying, 'That person is important'. Americans, on the other hand, tend to distribute their working space around the edges of a room, leaving the centre open for traffic and casual conversation.

Territory

Our apparent need to stake a claim on a particular area of space has been examined in a fascinating book by Robert Ardrey called *The Territorial Imperative* in which he argues that the instinctive need, or 'imperative' of animals to guard their territory may be shared by humans. Whether it is inherited or not, observations of our fellow men indicate that there is little doubt that man has a sense of territory, which prompts him to erect fences around his garden and protect his home against the uninvited stranger. Even in public spaces – in a classroom, in the underground or in a lecture hall – as long as there is freedom to choose, most people will tend to sit as far as possible from strangers.

Next time you go to the seaside, watch the way a beach fills up. First thing in the morning, when there are few families on the beach, each new arrival will find its own territory, virtually equidistant from its nearest neighbours. The territory will then be staked out by means of towels, windbreaks and so on. As the beach fills up, each new arrival fills in the available spaces, until by the peak period you may find yourself practically sitting on the towel of a complete stranger; but had you sat that close to a total stranger first thing in the morning when the other person was the only one on the beach, your behaviour would have been regarded as extraordinary and the stranger would have made it very obvious that you had invaded his territory.

Activity

How do people at work stake their claim on a particular territory? How do you stake your claim? How do you indicate to the rest of the world that this is your patch, whether it is your office space or your work station or your room at home? How do you feel when people invade your territory?

PERSONAL SPACE

This idea of territory is taken one step further by Edward T. Hall in his book *The Hidden Dimension*, in which he discusses the idea that each of us, possibly in an attempt to carry our territory around with us, is surrounded by a 'space bubble' or sense of personal space; that is, a distance at which we are prepared to interact with others. We are prepared to vary this distance according to how well we know someone and the activity or type of communication taking place. For example, while you may be quite happy for a close friend or relative to carry on a fairly intimate conversation at very close quarters, you are likely to become very uneasy if a total stranger speaking on a very formal matter were to stand only one foot away from you.

Hall classifies these 'space bubbles' or distances in four types (each of which has a close phase and a far phase):

Intimate distance

Close phase (actual contact or touching): this is reserved for making love, for very close friendships and for children clinging to a parent or to each other, but it would also include wrestling or fighting. In our culture it is acceptable between women, and between men and women on intimate terms, but it can be embarrassing between men, or between men and women not on intimate terms. However, in Arab culture it is perfectly normal to see men walking in the street with their arms round one another.

Far phase (up to 1½ feet): still close enough to clasp hands but not acceptable for people not on intimate terms, unless circumstances, like a crowded lift or underground train force it. In this case, other behaviour – drawing away, tensing muscles, not looking – sends the message: 'I am sorry to intrude on your private space. I don't mean anything intimate by it.' If the rules of acceptable behaviour are broken, then trouble can ensue.

Personal distance:

Close phase (1½–2½ feet): this distance is reserved for more than just a casual friend or fleeting encounter. Contact is possible but more difficult. Hall points out that: 'Where people stand in relation to each other signals their relationship, or how they feel toward each other, or both. A wife can stay inside the circle of her husband's close personal zone with impunity. For another woman to do so is an entirely different story.'

Far phase (2½–4 feet): the limit of physical domination. It provides a degree of personal privacy to any encounter but close enough for personal discussion. Two people who meet in the street may stop to chat at this distance, but at a party they tend to close in to the close phase of personal distance. This distance can communicate various messages, from 'I'm keeping you at arm's length', to 'I have singled you out to be a little closer than the other guests.' Moving too far in when you have a far distant relationship could be interpreted as 'I'm available'.

Social distance

Close phase (4–7 feet): used for impersonal business and casual conversations – the businessman meeting a new client, a prospective employee or perhaps an unknown colleague; the housewife talking to tradesmen at the door or in a shop. This distance can be manipulated to indicate domination, superiority or power without having to speak any words.

Far phase (7–12 feet): used for more formal social and business relationships. The chief executive may actually have a large enough desk to ensure that this kind of distance is maintained but if he comes out from behind the desk and reduces the distance, he is signalling a willingness to be more personal, less superior. This distance allows greater freedom of behaviour: you can keep working at this distance without being rude, or you can stop working and talk. Similarly people on very intimate terms may assume this far social distance to relax. A husband and wife, for example, can talk to each other if they want to or simply read instead of talking.

Public distance

Close phase (12–25 feet): suitable for informal gatherings such as a manager talking to a meeting of workers or a lecturer talking to a room full of students.

Far phase (25 feet or more): usually reserved for politicians and public figures, since it provides the necessary security and emphasizes domination particularly where a platform must be provided to ensure that all can see and hear.

You may feel that these rather exact distances are a little farfetched or arbitrary. They are only an attempt to standardize what observation seems to indicate and are based on the way in which people do tend to interact, rather than on strict measurement.

Activity

Think of examples from your own experience of the way in which space speaks.

Do these classifications agree with your own experience of the way in which people use their personal space?

How do you feel when someone gets 'too close?

If someone moves closer than is appropriate for the activity and relationship, we may become tense or even hostile, and this will affect the nature of the communication that is possible.

However, here again there are cultural differences. Most Americans and Englishmen prefer a certain distance for normal conversation. They feel more comfortable if that space between themselves and the other person is maintained. This can often cause problems for the American or British businessman visiting Latin countries, for example, where a smaller distance is preferred, or Japan where crowding together is often welcomed and not seen as an invasion of personal space.

When there is an invasion of territory or personal space, the person who feels invaded will often retreat to maintain the distance. But when he can retreat no further he may, if he is aware of what is going on, start to advance in turn in order to threaten the invader, so forcing him to retreat. While this return invasion might work in America or Britain, it would probably fail in Latin countries where the new proximity would be welcomed.

Since space and its use make such a contribution to your total communication effort, you should know how to encode and decode these 'space messages' in order to avoid unconsciously offending others or being offended.

Touch

Touching is obviously closely related to the idea of personal space. Although it was probably among the earliest forms of communication and is still used by small children when they are unable to communicate verbally, we tend to be very cautious in our use of touch as a means of communication. In times of trouble or sorrow it can be one of the most effective methods of communicating sympathy or protection, but generally America and Britain would not be described as tactile societies, and touch is usually reserved for the intimate distance mentioned above, and for communication between close friends or relatives. While it is acceptable for women to touch in public, it is not usually considered appropriate for men to do so. Quite small boys soon learn to shake off physical signs of affection from even their mothers and fathers in embarrassment.

Activity

If touching can be so effective in times of trouble and to show affection, do you think communication could be improved if we were less inhibited in our use of touch?

Orientation and posture

We can influence communication and signal our attitudes not just by our proximity to others but by the position and posture we adopt. Experiments have shown that people who want to cooperate will tend to sit or stand side by side whereas if they feel in opposition they will tend to position themselves head-on or opposite the other person. Watch the behaviour of people at meetings and you will often see that people tend to argue far more with people across the table than with those alongside them. A wise chairman may, in fact, contrive to seat potential opponents along the same side of the table if he particularly wants to avoid conflict at a meeting. Similarly, a good interviewer will recognize that seating a candidate directly opposite him and with a desk between them will not be conducive to the kind of easy cooperative conversation which he wants to create. For this reason you may frequently find that you are shown to an easy chair near a low table and the interviewer will sit at roughly a ninety-degree angle in relation to you in a chair the same height, as this kind of arrangement has been shown to encourage easy non-threatening discussion.

In the same way bodily posture can communicate, often involuntarily, social status or the desire to be dominant or submissive. Hunched shoulders and a lowered head may signal shyness and inferiority; standing erect, with head tilted back and hands on hips, may indicate superiority and self-satisfaction.

People all have different styles of walking, standing, sitting and so on, which may reflect past and present roles – as in the case of a policeman; or they may reflect a person's self-image, self-confidence or emotional state.

Self-check

Look at these drawings of body postures. Which of the following adjectives describes which posture?

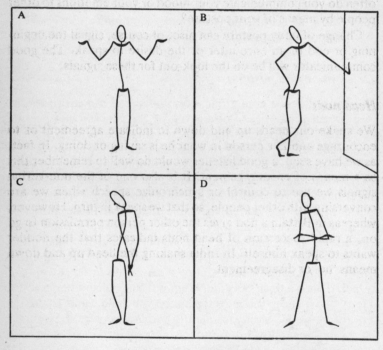

surprised	disinterested	doubtful	aloof
shy	self-satisfied	casual	sad
ashamed	dominating	suspicious	describing
impatient	modest	self-conscious	questioning
resigned	angry	undecided	

Two social psychologists* found in experiments that these four postures tended to be associated with certain emotions and activities in the following way:

Posture A	Posture B	Posture C	Posture D
disinterested	self-satisfied	shy	surprised
describing	impatient	self-conscious	dominating
resigned	describing	ashamed	suspicious
doubtful	casual	modest	undecided
questioning	angry	sad	aloof

How well did you read these examples of body language? How often do you communicate your mood or your emotions to other people by means of your posture?

Change of body posture can also, of course, signal the beginning or end of an encounter or the desire to speak. The good communicator will be on the look-out for these signals.

Head nods

We shake our heads up and down to indicate agreement or to encourage another person in what he is saying or doing. In fact, as we have seen, a good listener would do well to remember this as a means of encouragement. It is also one of the non-verbal signals we use to control or synchronize speech when we are conversing with other people, so that we speak in turn. However, whereas in Britain a nod gives the other person permission to go on, a rapid succession of head nods indicates that the nodder wants to speak himself. In India shaking the head up and down means 'no' or disagreement.

*T. R. Sarbin and C. D. Hardyk, 'Contributions to Role-taking Theory: Role-perception on the Basis of Postural Cues', unpublished (1953), cited by T. R. Sarbin, 'Role Theory', in G. Lindzey (ed.), *Handbook of Social Psychology*, Cambridge, Mass.: Addison-Wesley, 1954.

Facial expressions

Of all body movements, facial expressions are the ones we are most able to control. Although a person's face may provide a continuous commentary on their reaction to what you are saying – surprise, disbelief, agreement, disappointment, anger and so on – and you can learn much about a person's true feelings from studying their facial expressions, they should be read in relation both to the words being uttered and to other body movements which are more reliable as communicators of real feelings because they are so much more difficult to control.

Eye movements

In contrast to other body signals, movements of the eyes have an effect quite out of proportion to the physical effort exerted; some eye movements are quite uncontrollable but nevertheless send out very strong messages which we receive almost without being aware.

The movements of the eyes perform a number of important functions in social interaction. When two people are engaged in conversation they look each other in the eye intermittently. Usually each looks for between twenty-five and seventy-five per cent of the time. The glances vary in length but we tend to look twice as much while listening as while talking. The amount of look is related to the amount and kind of interest: if we are interested in someone or what they are saying we will look at them, whereas we will tend to direct our eye gaze away if we are uninterested. Long periods of looking indicate a desire for intimacy, so in our culture there tend to be unwritten rules about the length of time we may look at a person in certain circumstances. In a crowded lift or train we may glance but not stare. For an unwary male to stare at a woman longer than is proper in a public place is to court all sorts of unpleasant consequences. However, there are obviously moments when longer periods of looking are expected, even desired. When people are interacting but are far apart, they will tend to look more, as if to compensate for the distance.

People look primarily to obtain information: people look

while listening to get visual messages to supplement the words, to help them understand what they are hearing. They look while they are talking to get feedback on the person's reactions. If a speaker looks while he is talking, then not only will the other person feel that the speaker is really interested in him rather than just the subject of conversation, but he will also feel that the speaker is more confident, more believable. These impressions seem to be justified since people look more when they like the person they are talking to and when they are telling the truth.

Eye movements, like head nods and grunts, are also used to synchronize speech. The speaker will tend to look away from the other person just as he starts talking. This seems to be because he wants to avoid distraction from too much incoming information, just at the moment he is planning and organizing what he is going to say. Similarly he may look away when he is speaking hesitantly, but when he is speaking faster and more fluently he will look at the other person; and more important, at the end of what he is saying he will give his listener a prolonged gaze. This is because he needs to see how the other person is reacting; although, unconsciously perhaps, he also signals to the other person that he has finished what he wants to say. At pauses in the middle of long speeches, he will look for permission to carry on; the other person will usually nod or grunt if he is agreeable to this.

For many people one of the most fascinating discoveries that have been made about eye movements is that the pupils of the eye dilate or grow bigger when we look at something which arouses or excites us. Although the pupils normally dilate in darkness and in response to certain drugs, experiments have shown that women's pupils dilate especially when they are shown pictures of babies, and men's in response to pictures of naked women. This rather special movement of the eyes, which is beyond our control, also communicates the other way. Not only does pupil dilation reveal arousal and interest, but it also tends to make a person look more attractive, so it is likely that the attraction can become mutual without either person being precisely sure why they are attracted.

The eyes do not communicate in isolation. There is an endless number of messages which can be sent when one thinks of eyes combined with different movements and positions of eyelids and eyebrows and other parts of the body. As with all forms of non-verbal communication, messages sent by the eyes should be decoded in terms of the words accompanying them.

Gestures

Other movements of parts of the body – hands, arms, even legs and feet – grouped under the heading of gestures are perhaps the most commonly thought of method of non-verbal communication. We probably all know someone who 'talks with their hands'; some people punctuate their communication with such extravagant gestures that it is almost dangerous to stand too close when they are talking.

The kinds of meaning conveyed by gestures are certainly too numerous to mention here, but generally speaking gestures serve the following purposes:

Communicating information A hand raised in greeting, the 'V' sign of Winston Churchill, a clenched fist, the pointed finger are all examples of the ways in which non-verbal communication can be used either to supplement the meaning of words or, in some cases, even replace speech altogether, where normal speech is either difficult or impossible. Examples of hand movements and gestures becoming highly developed and systematized into a language which can replace speech completely are the sign languages used in television broadcasting studios, by ground crews on aerodromes, by the deaf and dumb and by some Australian aboriginals.

Although the meaning of gestures will often vary between cultures, there appear to be certain basic gestures that have the same meaning in many cultures.

Communicating emotion As with gestures used to communicate information, there appear to be a few specific gestures like hands raised to the mouth in surprise or fist-shaking which have been found to accompany particular emotions in widely varied cultures. This suggests that such expression may be innate and universal.

General emotional arousal tends to produce diffuse, apparently pointless, bodily movements: a nervous lecturer may appear to be constantly on the move. On the other hand, more specific emotions tend to produce particular gestures – hand-clapping (appreciation), fist-clenching (aggression), face-touching (anxiety) and so on.

Supporting speech While a person is speaking he moves his hands, body and head continuously. These movements are closely coordinated with speech and form a part of the total communication.

Head and body movements are often used to give emphasis and meaning to words, to point to people and objects and to give illustrations of shapes and sizes or movements; but they are also closely related to the pattern of speech, so that gestures often reflect the structure, i.e. large movements correspond to large verbal units like the paragraph, and smaller, finer movements which may be barely visible are related to sentences, phrases or even individual words.

An obvious example might be a speaker raising his arm in a wide gesture with three fingers raised as he says: 'There are three main reasons. . .' Then as he deals with each reason in turn he raises one finger, then two and finally three to reflect non-verbally that he has got to the third reason.

These kinds of gestures are often the equivalent in speech of the signposts used in writing which we looked at in the chapter on effective reading, and again in the last chapter.

Gestures also contribute to the synchronization of speech between two or more people. A raised hand may indicate that the listener wants to interrupt the speaker to say something himself or to ask for clarification. A gesture extending an up-turned palm may indicate an invitation to the other person to speak.

Expressing self-image You may convey the image you have of yourself by body movements and gestures. If you have an extrovert personality, you may subconsciously communicate this to the world by means of wide, energetic gestures; whereas, if you are rather a shy, retiring personality your gestures may be less frequent, smaller and restricted to the area close to your body.

Activity

Next time you are in conversation, try clasping your hands together so that you can't move them. Does it feel awkward, as if your hands are fighting to get away? Do you find it difficult to talk naturally?

Some speakers who may nervously grasp the edges of the lectern, or plunge their hands deep into their pockets, reveal that they are restricting their natural gestures, as their hands still try to move either in rather a tied-down way on the lectern, or causing the sides of their jacket to flap rather like bird wings!

Expressing relationships Kinecists, or those who study the way in which body language can reflect attitudes and emotions, have discovered that we often tend to adopt or 'mirror' the gestures and body movements of other people with whom we are talking. These shared postures and movements often reflect mutual interest or shared points of view. For example, if two people are chatting and are either attracted to one another or are in agreement, when one crosses his legs, the other person is very likely to do the same. This kind of mirroring of gestures and postures is usually completely subconscious and goes unnoticed by the participants, but it can be fascinating to watch this behaviour as an onlooker from a distance. Desmond Morris in his very comprehensive book *Manwatching* includes some convincing photographs of 'postural echo'.

Activity

Next time you are in a group conversation, look at the posture and gestures of those in the group and see if there is a link between shared gestures and posture and shared opinions and attitudes.

Not all body language is easily read, but we ignore it at our peril. Concentrating only on what we say and what we hear, rather than how it is communicated, can lead to bad feelings, misunderstandings and missed opportunities for really effective communication.

Body language is a fascinating area of study. Many people are devoting their lives to a study of this subject, and much remains to be learned about it. By becoming a better observer, by sharpening your powers of perception and by knowing as much as possible about your audience, you should be able to translate more accurately the non-verbal and verbal messages, as well as understand what you are really communicating to others and how they 'read' you.

Conflict between verbal and non-verbal communication

Finally, then, everything you do is a communication; actions speak louder than words. Quite often a verbal message is sent with a non-verbal one; you may be greeted at a friend's door by a welcoming 'Hello! Come in! Would you like a cup of tea?' But the non-verbal communication, consisting of frequent but surreptitious glances at the clock, may indicate that you are not so welcome after all. Then there is the employee who tries to sound relaxed and comfortable when talking to the boss, but his toe tapping on the floor or his fidgetting hands tell another story.

Interestingly enough, whenever the meaning of the non-verbal message conflicts with the meaning of the verbal message, we are more likely to believe the non-verbal message. If we are alert, we will detect the anxious person who really exists behind the good-humoured, back-slapping 'hail fellow well met' façade; we will recognize the rocky relationship of a married couple, despite their protestations of undying love; we will discern the worried, unhappy employee fighting to get out from behind the apparently carefree mask. . .*if* we are alert!

Review

1 What is 'metacommunication'?
2 How can silence serve as an effective method of encouraging communication?

3 If you arrive half an hour late for an interview, without apologizing, how might the interviewer interpret your late arrival?

4 What is the term given to the science or study of body language?

5 Dr Hall in *The Hidden Dimension* has noted that human beings have a sense of 'personal space' which is divided into four types of distance each appropriate for different kinds of interaction and relationships. What are the names of the four types of distance?

6 Other things being equal, what is the impression you are likely to convey if you look at someone while you are talking?

7 When two or more people are conversing they must take it in turns to speak, and usually achieve a fairly smooth pattern of synchronizing. Which non-verbal signals in particular are used in controlling the synchronization of speech?

8 If the verbal message and the non-verbal message conflict, which are we likely to believe?

ANSWERS

1 'Metacommunication' literally means 'in addition to communication', so the term is used to refer to all those things which we take into account in interpreting what someone is saying, over and above the actual words.

2 By remaining silent at strategic moments we may encourage someone to carry on talking and in doing so we are providing them with the opportunity to communicate feelings and attitudes which they might not otherwise have done. It can therefore encourage feedback and real two-way communication.

3 He may think:

a You are not a very punctual person.

b You are not very interested in getting the job.

c You are not very concerned with other people, since it apparently doesn't bother you that you may have caused someone inconvenience.

d You are rude and discourteous because you did not apologize.

4 'Kinesics' is the study of body movements which convey information in the absence of, or in addition to, speech.

5 The four types of distance are: intimate, personal, social and public.

6 You are likely to be perceived as more confident, more believable and more interested in your audience than the content of your speech.

7 Shifts of gaze and head nods, as well as grunts, gestures and changes of body orientation, help to synchronize speech in conversations.

8 We are more likely to believe the non-verbal message.

Additional reading

Michael Argyle, *The Psychology of Interpersonal Behaviour*, Penguin Books, 1972.

R. Ardrey, *The Territorial Imperative*, New York: Atheneum Publishers, 1966.

Julius Fast, *Body Language*, Pan Books, 1978.

Edward T. Hall, *The Hidden Dimension*, Garden City, New York: Doubleday, 1966.

Desmond Morris, *Manwatching*, Triad/Panther Books, 1978.

A final word

Throughout this book we have concentrated on the basic principles that lie behind the skills of listening, reading, writing and speaking in business. You will have discovered that there is no magic lamp that you or I can rub to make you an effective communicator. It is a question of being aware of the nature of communication and the principles which govern the process, and then being prepared to make the effort to put those principles into practice.

If you are willing to think sensitively when you communicate and always keep the other person – the receiver – constantly in mind both before you communicate and while you are communicating, you will automatically discover the answer to those familiar questions: What shall I say? How shall I say it? and What does he mean?

In other words, communication is a selfless process in which, to stand any chance of success, we have to fight constantly our natural instinct to be self-centred. We have to guard against our very natural inclination to concentrate on ourselves, on what we *want* to say, and try instead to consider the other person and focus on what we *need* to say and do, both to help him understand what we mean and to help him tell us what he means.

Real communication, then, is a two-way process. We must be prepared to listen as much as speak and we must listen effectively to what is really being said – and to what is not being said. We must be conscious of what may be being communicated between the lines when we listen and read and when we speak and write – in other words we must be aware of the total message. Above all, we need to be constantly aware of the potential difficulties that beset communication, and alert to the ways in which we can strive to overcome them, or at least reduce their effect.

We will not always succeed. Communication is by nature a

human and therefore an imperfect process, but our efforts to improve will be rewarded in countless ways. In any case, just trying to understand how communication works and how we can try to perfect our ability to communicate effectively can in itself be a rewarding task.

If your appetite has been whetted, you will find that the companion volume to this book, *The Business of Communicating*, takes these basic principles further. It provides you with more specific help with the business of writing letters and reports, using the telephone, interviewing and being interviewed, speaking in public and communicating in small groups and meetings, as well as making use of visual communication and visual aids to help you get your message across. *The Business of Communicating* is structured in the same way as this book, allowing you to practise the techniques as you go along and assess your own progress, and involving you actively in the process of learning even though you may be studying alone.

Index

Nicki Stanton
The Business of Communicating
improving communication skills

Advice on the key elements of communication: writing letters, using the phone, interviewing, speaking in public. This book develops the principles explained in *What Do You Mean, 'Communication'?*. Coverage is geared to communication courses at BEC National and Higher levels whilst serving various other syllabus requirements: RSA Stage II, LCCI Intermediate, City & Guilds Communication Skills, foundation courses for professional examinations.

A Pan Breakthrough book, published in collaboration with the National Extension College.

David Floyd
Making Numbers Work
an introduction to business numeracy

A book to introduce the basic skills of business numeracy and explain how to apply them. An ideal text for the BEC General Module on Business Calculations, it also meets requirements of BEC National Module on Numeracy and Accounting, RSA Arithmetic Stages I, II and III and relevant parts of RSA Stage I Mathematics.

A Pan Breakthrough book, published in collaboration with the National Extension College.

Roger Oldcorn
Management
a fresh approach

A fresh introduction to the role of the modern manager. Coverage is geared to various syllabus requirements including the CNAA Diploma in Management Studies and those of the Institute of Industrial Management, Institute of Personnel Management, Institute of Purchasing and Supply and BEC Certificate in Management Studies courses.

A Pan Breakthrough book, published in collaboration with the National Extension College.

Terry Price
Practical Business Law

Pinpoints and explains the key areas of law which govern commercial life.
The book is designed for use over a wide range of syllabuses: BEC General
level Law and the Individual, BEC National level Organization in its
Environment, RSA Stages II and III Commercial Law, LCCI Commercial Law
syllabus higher stage, AEB O and A level Law, Oxford Local Examinations
Board O and A level Law.

A Pan Breakthrough book, published in collaboration with the National
Extension College.

John Etor and Mike Muspratt
Keep Account
a guide to profitable bookkeeping

Introduces and explains the basic principles of profitable bookkeeping. An
ideal text for BEC General level Accounting, GCE O level Accounts and RSA
Stage I bookkeeping syllabuses, it will also serve students on foundation
courses for professional accounting qualifications.

A Pan Breakthrough book, published in collaboration with the National
Extension College.

Peter Clark
Using Statistics in Business 1

Volume *1* shows how to acquire, judge and apply statistical information. Especially suitable for statistics courses at BEC National level in Numeracy and Accounting, RSA Stage II and LCCI Intermediate, it will also serve students of professional syllabuses: Institute of Chartered Accountants, Institute of Cost and Management Accountants, Institute of Chartered Secretaries, and Association of Certified Accountants.

A Pan Breakthrough book, published in collaboration with the National Extension College.

Using Statistics in Business 2

Volume *2* shows how to present and draw conclusions from statistical information. It develops the ideas explained in volume 1, and is especially suitable for statistics courses at BEC National level in Numeracy and Accounting, RSA Stage II and LCCI Intermediate. It will also serve students of professional syllabuses: Institute of Marketing, Institute of Personnel Management, Institute of Chartered Accountants, Institute of Cost and Management Accountants, Institute of Chartered Secretaries and Association of Certified Accountants.

A Pan Breakthrough book, published in collaboration with the National Extension College.

Reference, language and information

☐	**A Guide to Insurance**	Margaret Allen	£1.95p
☐	**The Story of Language**	C. L. Barber	£1.95p
☐	**North-South**	Brandt Commission	£1.95p
☐	**Manifesto**	Francis Cripps et al	£1.95p
☐	**Save It! The Energy Consumer's Handbook**	Gary Hammond, Kevin Newport and Carol Russell	£1.25p
☐	**Mathematics for the Million**	L. Hogben	£1.95p
☐	**Militant Islam**	Godfrey Jansen	£1.50p
☐	**The State of the World Atlas**	Michael Kidron and Ronald Segal	£5.95p
☐	**Practical Statistics**	R. Langley	£1.95p
☐	**A Guide to Speaking in Public**	Robert Seton Lawrence	£1.25p
☐	**How to Study**	H. Maddox	£1.50p
☐	**Dictionary of Life Sciences**	E. A. Martin	£1.95p
☐	**Your Guide to the Law**	ed. Michael Molyneux	£3.50p
☐	**Breakthroughs**	Charles Panati	£1.95p
☐	**The Modern Crossword Dictionary**	Norman Pulsford	£1.95p
☐	**English Proverbs Explained**	James Reeves	£1.75p
☐	**Pan Spelling Dictionary**	Ronald Ridout	£1.50p
☐	**A Guide to Saving and Investment**	James Rowlatt	£2.50p
☐	**Career Choice**	Audrey Segal	£2.95p
☐	**Logic and its Limits**	Patrick Shaw	£2.50p
☐	**Names for Boys and Girls**	L. Sleigh and C. Johnson	£1.50p
☐	**Straight and Crooked Thinking**	R. H. Thouless	£1.50p
☐	**The Best English**	G. H. Vallins	80p
☐	**Money Matters**	Harriet Wilson	£1.25p
☐	**Dictionary of Earth Sciences**		£1.95p
☐	**Dictionary of Economics and Commerce**		£1.50p
☐	**Dictionary of Philosophy**		£2.50p
☐	**Dictionary of Physical Sciences**		£1.05p
☐	**Harrap's New Pocket French and English Dictionary**		£1.95p
☐	**The Limits to Growth**		£1.50p
☐	**Multilingual Commercial Dictionary**		£1.95p
☐	**Pan Dictionary of Synonyms and Antonyms**		£1.95p

All these books are available at your local bookshop or newsagent, or can be ordered direct from the publisher. Indicate the number of copies required and fill in the form below   5

Name_____
(Block letters please)

Address_____

_____

Send to Pan Books (CS Department), Cavaye Place, London SW10 9PG
Please enclose remittance to the value of the cover price plus:
35p for the first book plus 15p per copy for each additional book ordered to a maximum charge of £1.25 to cover postage and packing
Applicable only in the UK

While every effort is made to keep prices low, it is sometimes necessary to increase prices at short notice. Pan Books reserve the right to show on covers and charge new retail prices which may differ from those advertised in the text or elsewhere